NOT YET DEMOCRACY

NOT YET DEMOCRACY

West Africa's Slow Farewell to Authoritarianism

Boubacar N'Diaye

Abdoulaye Saine

Mathurin Houngnikpo

CAROLINA ACADEMIC PRESS

Durham, North Carolina

Library of Congress Cataloging-in-Publication Data

N'Diaye, Boubacar, 1956-
    Not yet democracy : West Africa's slow farewell to authoritarianism /
by Boubacar N'Diaye, Abdoulaye S. Saine, Mathurin C. Houngnikpo.
        p. cm.
    Includes bibliographical references and index.
    ISBN 0-89089-533-3
        1. Civil-military relations--Africa, West. 2. Democratization--Africa,
West. 3. Authoritarianism--Africa, West. 4. Africa, West--Politics and
government--1960- I. Saine, Abdoulaye S., 1951- II. Houngnikpo,
Mathurin C. III. Title.

JQ2998.A38C585 2003
322'.5'0966--dc22

                                                                          2003065295

CAROLINA ACADEMIC PRESS
700 Kent Street
Durham, North Carolina 27701
Telephone (919) 489-7486
Fax (919) 493-5668
E-mail: cap@cap-press.com
www.cap-press.com

Printed in the United States of America

DEDICATION

We dedicate this book to all Africans anywhere
who died fighting
who went to prison
who keep on fighting

for the advent of genuine democracy and respect for Human Rights
and dignity

CONTENTS

PREFACE

Not Yet Democracy: West Africa's Slow Farewell to Authoritarianism is the product of the collaborative work of three eyewitnesses to and stakeholders in West Africa's checkered democratization experiments. It crystallizes the authors' shared, deep commitment to a symbiosis between, on the one hand, the inquisitive and evaluative look of scholars and, on the other, the earnestness of believers in genuine democracy in seeing the total eradication of authoritarian practices in Africa. That others before us have attempted to provide similar interim assessments of the democratization process does not make the task of writing this book any easier. It still entails risks and is bound, as such studies usually are, to raise criticisms. On the one hand, it is often argued that, in light of the situation in the sub-region even in the most touted cases, the term 'democratization process' is a singularly generous characterization of the developments of the last decade or so. On the other hand, some charge that many analysts easily succumb to a resurgent Afro-pessimism. In doing so, they miss the immense progress recorded in this area in a short period compared to the three decades that preceded Africa's rendition of Samuel Huntington's so-called "third wave." In addition to these ready no-win criticisms, the most significant challenge, from where we stand, has been the dizzying pace of developments in West Africa. The most inspired analysis seems to be constantly trying to catch up to these events. Even our sober findings and predictions about the evolution seem to be overtaken by the rapidity with which change (for better or worse) is occurring.

These common criticisms and frustrating odds notwithstanding, it is crucial that a progress report be done, particularly about small (and mostly *Francophone*) states that tend to be left out of most analyses, which often focus on more prominent countries such as Nigeria or Ghana. The experiences of smaller African countries hold a wealth of lessons for others in the sub-region and Africa more generally. Moreover, the central role of the military in charting this historic phase of the evolution of West Africa's political systems deserves special attention. It highlights the critical balancing of the civil-military relations equation that West Africans must consider as they think through and contrive new political dispensations. The ambition of *Not Yet Democracy* is to do all the above.

We have tapped our collective, intimate understanding of the general political dynamics, particularly the civil-military relations of the states studied, to present an accurate, theoretically and empirically insightful accounts of the fits and starts of democratization, the hopes it aroused, its challenges, slow progress, and disconcerting setbacks. When feasible, we have made predictions or proffered recommendations to speed up this historic process of turning the page on a debilitating and onerous era of West African history. Even before the publication of the book, some of our predictions, such as the likely retrogression of Togo toward a "presidential monarchy" of sorts and the ineluctability of an attempt by Arab Nationalist groups within the Mauritanian military to overthrow Ould Taya's regime, came to pass. Many other notable developments have occurred in West Africa since the manuscript's completion. An epilogue was added to the conclusion to update West Africa's *Slow Farewell to Authoritarianism* generally, and in the states studied more specifically.

ACKNOWLEDGMENTS

As for any worthy endeavor, *Not Yet Democracy* would not be possible without the morale-boosting, graciousness, encouragement, support and help, individual or collective, direct and indirect, of many people and institutions. Though we can specifically name only a few of the dozens who helped along the way, we owe to all a debt of gratitude. Our grateful thanks go first to our families for their loving support and forbearance: Haje, Mamoudou, and Aiche Vall; Paula, Marget, Roy, and Taj. Professor Abdoulaye Saine expresses his appreciation for the financial support offered by the College of Arts and Sciences, Department of Political Science, the Hampton Fund, and the Office for the Advancement of Scholarship and Teaching of Miami University. Similarly, Professor Boubacar N'Diaye is grateful for the institutional support provided by The College of Wooster through the offices of the President for Academic Affairs, and the Dean of the Faculty. His special thanks go to countless colleagues and friends for their encouragement and insights and specifically to Mueni Muiu of Winston-Salem State University for her enthusiastic support for the project. Finally, we sincerely thank Carolina Academic Press and its able staff for their patience, courtesy, and solicitude throughout the process. Of course, the usual disclaimers apply and the responsibility for shortcomings in the study rests entirely with the authors.

NOT YET DEMOCRACY

INTRODUCTION

... Transitions are delimited, on the one side, by the launching of the process of dissolution of an authoritarian regime and, on the other, by the installation of some form of democracy, the return to some form of authoritarian rule, or the emergence of a revolutionary alternative.[1]

With the end of the Cold War in 1989, and the incipience, at least conceptually, of a "New World Order," it became possible, indeed imperative, for African states to move away from the authoritarian modes of government that have held sway for most of the independence era. Throughout the 1990s, a succession of events around the world, particularly the waning of ideological and military rivalries and developments in Africa's own political economy, combined to profoundly alter the African landscape. All across the continent and in rapid succession, authoritarian regimes, both military and civilian, were forced to carry out urgent political and economic liberalization, when they were not swept out of power altogether. Not unlike the euphoria and high hopes that accompanied Africa's breaking free from direct colonial rule, in many respects, the onset of the era of democratization occasioned tremendous anticipation that, at long last, a new, qualitatively better era is about to dawn upon Africans. All of a sudden, a "rebirth," a "new start," a "second liberation," were declared to be under way on the continent and, indeed, as Leonardo Villalon

---

1. Guillermo O'Donnell and Philippe Schmitter, "Introduction to the Latin American Cases," in Guillermo O'Donnell, Philippe Schmitter and Laurence Whitehead, eds., *Transitions from Authoritarian Rule: Prospects for Democracy*, Baltimore, Johns Hopkins University Press, 6.

observes, "an explicit, and at times gushing, optimism"[2] seemed to get hold of even the most placid Africanists. Even the most skeptical observers were willing to concede that Africa may well have been given a second chance to get things right. This new era, rightly likened to a second breath of freedom for Africans, was launched by the first wave of national conferences in Francophone Africa, and the continent-wide rejection of antiquated politically and economically bankrupt regimes. A veritable democratization *tsunami* swept from power the most entrenched authoritarian regimes and forced others to abandon overtly repressive practices of the past.

To put this mindset and these events in context, one must recall that a generation ago another era full of optimism and the sense of possibility had started. It was in the middle of the first decade of African independence that one of Kenya's founding fathers published a political autobiography he entitled "*Not Yet Uhuru.*"[3] In light of the evolution in Kenya under Jomo Kenyatta and Daniel Arap Moi, this book turned out to possess remarkable foresight. Ojinga Odinga pulled the alarm on the unmistakable drift of the post-colonial regime toward the betrayal of the hopes and expectations staked on *Uhuru* (freedom) that the Kenyan people had paid so dearly to achieve. The book chronicles the author's disillusionment with the orientation and policy choices of leaders in the crucial early years of independence and statehood in Kenya. For example, Odinga wondered whether his country was condemned to witness "government and high office riddled with corruption and men in power using force and maneuver to block the expression of popular will."[4] It is remarkable how valid Odinga's analysis was, both of Kenya specifically and Africa as a whole. In this regard, his analysis echoes French agronomist René Dumont's *False Start in Africa*.[5] The behavior and attitudes

---

2. Leonardo A. Villalon, "The African State at the End of the Twentieth Century: Parameters of the Critical Juncture," in Leonardo A. Villalon and Philip A. Huxtable, eds., *The African State at a Critical Juncture: Between Disintegration and Reconfiguration*, Boulder, Colo., Lynne Rienner Publishers, 2000, 3.

3. Ojinga Odinga, *Not Yet Uhuru*, New York, Hill and Wang, 1967.

4. Odinga, 314.

5. René Dumont, *False Start in Africa*, New York: Praeger, 1969.

of leaders and their responsibility to involve the people in the benefits of freedom from colonial rule was one of his central themes. While times have changed, it is evident that the crucial challenge of the relationship between the elite and their people seems to have remained constant.

More than a decade into what was dubbed the African rendition of Samuel P. Huntington's 'third wave' of democratization,[6] the distinct euphoria that accompanied the sudden liberalization of entrenched authoritarian (civil as well as military) regimes has given way in most cases to bitter disenchantment. In West-Africa, with the notable exception of Mali, Benin, and Senegal, and with the jury still out on key states, the high expectations for an unabashed embrace of democratic values and practices were dashed as the emphasis on "democracy" and "democratization" noticeably started to make room for what Fareed Zakaria called, in another context, "illiberalism."[7]

How should students and practitioners of democratization approach the role of military establishments in the delicate phase of the transition (both its design and its conduct) to a new political order, one of the hallmarks of which will necessarily be, of necessity, the democratic civilian control of the military? What lessons can be learned from the paths followed by individual states of West Africa? How did the civilian opposition fare in these transition processes and what lessons do these experiments hold? What to make of constrained multiparty elections within a politically proscribed system? In other words, should Africans accept as fate and accommodate the notion that genuine democracy will continue to be an elusive pursuit? These are pertinent questions to ponder for West Africa, and, indeed, the entire continent. To be sure, many scholars have scrutinized the era of democratization in Africa as a whole, and analyzed its limits, im-

---

6. See Larry Diamond and Mark F. Plattner, eds., *Democratization in Africa*, Baltimore, The Johns Hopkins University Press, 1999.

7. Fareed Zakaria, "The Rise of Illiberal Democracy," *Foreign Affairs* 76, 1997, 22–43.

8. See Richard Joseph, "Africa, 1990–1997: From Abertura to Democracy," *Journal of Democracy* 9 (2), 1998, 3–17; Crawford Young, "The Third Wave of Democratization in Africa: Ambiguities and Contradictions," in Richard Joseph, ed.,

plications, and prospects.[8] Studies of the convulsions of this 'democratization' era have generally exposed the complexities and contradictions, and identified the limited nature of the strides toward the fulfillment of the hopes it raised. In general, all have traced the onset of the democratization era back to an array of factors. These range from the longstanding struggles of African masses for democracy to the end of the Cold War and the pressures by Western states to insure a political environment conducive to a liberal Brave New World.[9]

The Democratization Nexus

The various analyses in this book readily identify with the allegory implied in Odinga's admonition that ominous indications in the policies, behavior, and attitudes suggested that freedom was not, as yet, achieved in Kenya, even as direct colonialism was coming to an end. In actuality, a more tangible link exists between the gist and objective of *Not Yet Uhuru* and, a generation later, the excruciatingly slow embrace of what Africans of Odinga's generation fought for. Political independence was pursued, after all, only so that the long muzzled voice of Africans can be heard, their choices respected, their aspirations for decent and fulfilling lives realized. Therefore, one of the objectives of the book is to call attention to and facilitate the understanding of the historical continuity involved in the dynamics of the ongoing painful transformation of the political landscape in West Africa. Viewed from this perspective, the study is also an inquiry into the manner in which the current crop of political elite have handled the second chance afforded them to grant Africa long

---

State, Conflict, and Democracy in Africa, 15–38, Boulder, Colo., Lynne Rienner Publishers, 1999.

9. See Young, "The Third Wave of Democratization in Africa," 21–22; also Mohameden Ould Mey, "Structural Adjustment Programs and Democratization in Africa: The Case of Mauritania, in John M. Mbaku and Julius O. Ivhonbere, eds., *Multiparty Democracy and Political Change: Constraints to Democratization in Africa*, Brookfield, Ashgate, 1996, 33–46.

denied basic human rights, the main promise of political independence.

Through a close analysis of an edifying sample of states, the book documents and illustrates how the experiment of abandoning authoritarianism has unfolded in West Africa. It singularly contributes to the ongoing debate on the pace, prospects, and dynamics of democratization in West Africa, arguably the most volatile region of the continent. With a larger number of countries than the other geographic regions of the continent, West Africa has displayed the most stubbornness in turning its back on the ways of the past. It was in this subregion, for example, that the overwhelming majority of (successful or failed) coups have occurred since 1990. The successful coups in Nigeria (1993), The Gambia (1994), Niger (1996, 1999), and Ivory Coast (1999), and the numerous attempts in others are cases in point. Even considering the situation in the Great Lakes region, West Africa is the region where the most destructive wars are taking place. The recent developments in Côte d'Ivoire, in the wake of similar events in Sierra Leone, Liberia, Guinea-Bissau and Guinea, are eloquent testimony to the volatility of this sub-region, the intractability of its political phenomena, and the difficulty in predicting what the future holds.

The conceptual starting point of the book is that there is a discernable connection between the singular itineraries West African states have followed in their ongoing efforts to extricate themselves from their long history of authoritarianism. To be effective, a study of the dynamic of this checkered democratization process must focus on these links and the underlying understandings they offer. Therefore, the five chapters of the book variously and complementarily shed light on three critical and interconnected dimensions of the civil-military relations framework: the role the military, the security apparatus, can generally play in facilitating or hindering democratization and, finally, democratization and democratic sustainability in the sub-region. The first dimension pertains to the conditions or factors that led to the unexpected and dramatic breakdown of some of the longest running civilian regimes in Africa. Even after the 1990 political change Côte d'Ivoire was not a democracy. However, the case of The Gambia, a long reputed pluralist democracy until the 1994 military coup, adds interest to the dimension of civil-military relations and their place in the democratization question. What lessons can be gleaned by looking beyond the precipitants of the Christmas Eve 1999 coup (in Ivory Coast) and 1994 coup (in The Gambia) and the factors that shaped their aftermath? Beyond the insights they offer analysts, it is evident that the cases of Côte d'Ivoire and The Gambia have implications for the civil-military relations of states that are emerging slowly from authoritarian (civilian or military) rule. These two cases substantiate the now accepted lesson in civil-military relations that, as Diamond and Plattner emphasize, "military role and expansion of military coups are *politically* driven processes" (emphasis in the original); in other words, the military takes power as a result of "manifest failures of governance."[10] The recent developments in Ivory Coast vindicate the analysis in chapter 1, which was completed long before the situation worsened considerably. The turn for the worst in this country seems also to point to the necessity to heed Diamond's and Plattner's advice that democratically elected leaders following autocratic regimes should combine "gradualism," tactfulness, diligence, and strict adherence to democratic values in their dealings with the military.[11] The current situation in Côte d'Ivoire suggests that the Gbagbo government did not adhere to these recommendations.

The second dimension of the nexus identified above flows from the first dimension: analyzing the ways in which the independent role of the military as a corporate institution matters in deciding the outcome of a democratization process once the fateful step of running the country has been taken. Did scholars and practitioners of democratization in Africa pay sufficient attention to the potential the military has in being a "friend" of democracy? Can a second, more perspicacious look at the contrasting roles of the militaries in Benin and Togo, two strikingly similar states, teach any lessons in this re-

---

10. Larry Diamond and Mark F. Plattner, "Introduction," in Larry Diamond and Mark F. Plattner, eds., *Civil-Military Relations and democracy*, Baltimore, The Johns Hopkins University Press, 1996, xxix. See also, Boubacar N'Diaye, *The Challenge of Institutionalizing Civilian Control*, Lanham, MD, Lexington Books, 2001.

11. Diamond and Plattner, 1996, xxix.

gard? These questions are at the heart of the second issue the book seeks to explicate by taking a fresh evaluative look at the role the authoritarian regime's security apparatus (by no means a monolith) plays in the initial stages and throughout the move away from authoritarianism. This role seems crucial for the survival and consolidation of democracy, as the evolution of Benin and Togo singularly illustrates. While Benin is celebrated as a very encouraging instance of democratization, Togo remains mired in an unending political crisis. The military's role has a lot to do with these strikingly different outcomes.

Finally, the third component of the nexus is related to and flows from the two first dimensions, encompassing them both. It pertains to the consequences of ending a civilian regime and the emergence of a military 'strong man' whose rule comes with the imperative of externally driven or exacted democratization. This component of the nexus is addressed by scrutinizing the dynamics of a singularly West African phenomenon, which Abdoulaye Saine has labeled 'Soldier-Turned-Civilian' President.[12] The late General Robert Guei, the coup leader in Côte d'Ivoire, failed in his attempt to emulate his predecessors in this category. However, an analysis of the respective itineraries of Gambia's Lieutenant Yahya Jammeh and Mauritania's Colonel Maaouya Ould Sid'Ahmed Taya, Togo's General Gnassingbe Eyadéma, and their success in outmaneuvering their domestic opposition and pacifying their international critics, can enrich the theoretical debate on aborted or sluggish democratization. This is true also to a lesser degree of General Mathieu Kérékou's failure to retain power in 1990. The discussions deepen insights into this phenomenon, which severely limited the ability of the movement toward democratization in the sub-region to reach its potential. An extension of this phenomenon, the concept of "negative consolidation" discussed in chapter 4, certainly challenges the traditional conception of 'consolidation' so

---

12. See Abdoulaye Saine, "The Soldier-Turned Presidential Candidate: A Comparison of Flawed Democratic Transitions in Ghana and Gambia," *Journal of Political and Military Sociology*, 28 (2), (winter 2000), 191–209; see also Julius Nyang'Oro, Critical Notes on Political Liberalization in Africa," *Journal of Asian and African Studies* 31 (1–2), 1996, 117–18.

prominent in the transition literature. Juan J. Linz and Alfred Stepan and others theorists have posited that "only democracies can become consolidated democracies."[13] This is obvious enough. However, even if the literal etiology of the concept of consolidation is accepted, this does not say much about the case of Mauritania. Here, a non-democratic regime seems to have used to its advantage all the trappings of *democracy* and the interested beneficence of Western countries and financial institutions to solidify its grip on power. In the process, it seems to have been granted the blessings and certification of Western referees of democracy. There certainly seems to have occurred a 'consolidation' of sorts of 'something,' not a democracy to be sure, but the phenomenon deserves more scrutiny in the quest for a better understanding of the processes that have been taking place in Africa generally during this era of 'democratization'. That only democracies are capable of being consolidated is not enough. The analyses of this peculiarity of 'democratization' in West Africa, the third dimension of the nexus (the nature of civil-military relations, their role in facilitating or subverting democratization, and finally the features of democratization and its sustainability in West Africa), can be instructive for theorists as well as democratic activists.

The Cases

"Côte d'Ivoire's Civil-Military Relations: The 'Miracle' that Wasn't," examines the evolution of civil-military relations in Côte d'Ivoire over the last forty years and the prospects for a stable, democratic, civilian-controlled political system in the future. These relations, long assumed to be exemplary, took a dramatic turn when, on Christmas Eve, 1999, a coup removed Côte d'Ivoire from the short list of African states never to have been ruled by the military. The coup itself and the ease with which the forty-year old civilian regime unraveled surprised most observers. It ushered in a critical era in Côte d'Ivoire's civil-military relations and politics, with six military interventions in

---

13. Juan J. Linz and Alfred Stepan, "Toward Consolidated Democracies," *Journal of Democracy* 7 (2), 1996, 16.

just thirteen months and widespread violence, which degenerated in September 2002 into a full fledged armed insurrection or civil war. The chapter argues that the coup and its aftermath introduced profound divisions in the military and threatened peace and stability not only in Côte d'Ivoire but also throughout the West African subregion. The central thesis of the chapter is that Côte d'Ivoire's current situation must be traced to dynamics in the Ivorian body politic, particularly the deeply flawed civil-military relationship that had developed since the country's independence in 1960. The unimaginative policies and practices, and the crass conduct of former President Henri Konan Bedié during the last months of his tenure served to precipitate the coup, which had already been in the making. Additionally, the chapter analyzes the deep divisions the coup caused in the military and the body politic, the consequent collapse of the transitory military regime, General Guei's miscalculations, and external involvement. Finally, the implications of these variables for Côte d'Ivoire are examined with an eye toward bringing about viable civil-military relations (broadly construed), and a reconstituted, democratic, civilian-controlled and people-centered political system. The chapter also examines the volatile ongoing crisis that threatens the very existence of Ivory Coast and the entire subregion with widespread instability and humanitarian catastrophe. Against the expectations of most observers, the worst case scenario of a complete breakdown of civil order and an abrupt halt to any progress toward democracy has come to pass. This has made many Ivoirians long for the days of the benign autocracy of the Houphouet-Boigny era, an illustration of what Huntington identified as the "authoritarian nostalgia"[14] that accompanies similar situations. This syndrome must have also arisen in the case of The Gambia, when on a fateful day in July 1994, the military rose and put an end to the only truly multiparty democratic experiment in West Africa and ushered in a period of trials and turbulence.

This experiment and its aftermath is examined in "The Military and 'Democratization' in The Gambia: 1994–2002." When junior of-

---

14. Samuel Huntington, *The Third Wave: Democratization in the Late Twentieth Century*, Norman, University of Oklahoma Press, 262.

ficers of the Gambia National Army (GNA) overthrew the democratically elected government of Sir Dawda Kairaba Jawara on July 22, 1994, they ended the longest surviving democracy and the tenure of the longest serving head of state in Africa. Under the leadership of Lt. Yahya Jammeh, they created the Armed Forces Provisional Ruling Council (AFPRC). However, international economic sanctions combined with domestic pressure cut a four-year transition timetable to civilian rule to two. This culminated in presidential and national assembly elections, neither of which were deemed free and fair by leaders of the opposition and the international community. Consequently, since 1996, The Gambia's political landscape has been mired in controversy over regime legitimacy, rules of the game and endemic corruption.

This chapter, similar to chapter 4 on Mauritania's experiment, analyzes primarily the process of limited "democratization" under a quasi-military regime. Additionally, it provides policy recommendations, the primary objective of which is to help unhinge the current political impasse between the regime and opposition parties and their leaders. This impasse was particularly important as Gambians were preparing for the October 2001 presidential elections. The chapter is sub-divided into four sections. Section one provides an overview of the Jawara years (1965–1994). In section two, emphasis is placed on the transition program to "civilian" rule. In section three, Human Rights protection under the "new" and "civilianized" regime is evaluated on the presumption that Human Rights protection is a good litmus test of democracy and democratization. An optimist might interpret the improvement in political rights noted by Freedom House to suggest that, in the wake of Decree 89's repeal, The Gambia's political parties and civil society may now enjoy opportunities to constrain President Jammeh's authoritarian impulses. Perhaps political parties and the democratically inclined portions of civil society will even be able to nudge the political system in a democratic direction. Moreover, the unconditional amnesty that ex-president Jawara received, and his subsequent return to The Gambia in June 2002, may indicate that President Jammeh hopes to promote national healing and reconciliation. This bodes well for democracy, especially if amnesty is extended to those former officials of Jawara's government who remain in exile. The final section provides a conclusion and relevant policy recommendations to accelerate the democratization process in The Gambia.

The next chapter, a logical follow up to the preceding one, offers a critical analysis of the October 2001 elections, which confirmed President Jammeh's grip on power. "The October 2001 Presidential Elections in The Gambia" scrutinizes the various maneuvers, calculations and events that led up to these high stake elections, as well as the role of the former regime of Dawda Jawara. The dynamics and outlook of this second election under Jammeh's rule eloquently captures the flaws and chilling effects of post-1990s regimes in most states of the region. Various scholars have already identified and decried the systematic rigging of election.[15] The nature and significance of the electoral results in selected electoral circumscriptions are also explained, in light of the advantages incumbency affords. Could Jammeh have won without these advantages? It seems unlikely, all things being equal. But all things are seldom equal in elections, especially in Africa. Incumbents the world over have added advantages and resources at their disposal. In addition, Jammeh launched an effective campaign centered on both contrasting Jawara's failed policies with development successes under his own rule, and promises of a better future, despite increasing poverty in The Gambia. However, in light of official figures from the 2001 presidential poll, if opposition leader, Darboe's allegations of non-Gambian participation and 'extra-registration' are accepted, there would have been a run-off between Jammeh and Darboe. If this had obtained, the figures strongly suggest that Darboe may well have defeated Jammeh in a run-off. The chapter then untangles the complex and baffling relationship between Jammeh and his opposition as well as the intra-opposition maneuvers. It focuses on their respective attempts to woo Gambian voters who, weary of harsh economic circumstances and endless, often murderous political bickering throughout Jammeh's tenure, have become dis-

---

15. See Michael Bratton, "Second Elections in Africa," in Larry Diamond and Mark F. Plattner, eds., *Democratization in Africa*, 18–33, Baltimore, The Johns Hopkins University Press, 1999; and Celestin Monga, "Eight Problems with African Politics," in Larry Diamond and Mark F. Plattner, 1999.

trustful of most of the political class. Finally, the chapter offers recommendations aimed at fostering genuine progress toward democracy, the rule of law and respect for human rights in The Gambia
from the perspective of a participant and stakeholder in the efforts to
democratize political life there. The Islamic Republic of Mauritania
is another example of "electoral democracy" that is characteristic of
most of the post-1990s regimes in West Africa.

Chapter four presents the relevant political background to Mauritania, a little known country, which straddles North and West Africa.
"Mauritania's 'Democratization Process' 1991–2001: A Case of 'Negative Consolidation'" presents evidence that Mauritania's 1991 "democratic" reforms were imposed by strong Western pressure after the
Gulf War, not by a mobilized political opposition. However, three domestic factors help explain why, despite its democratic trappings,
Mauritania's — 'civilianized' — regime remains an authoritarian military backed regime, a "paper democracy." These factors are the dramatic awakening of President Maaouya Ould Sid'Ahmed Taya's tribal
instincts in an ethnically divided country, the reverberations of the
massive repression of non-Arab Mauritanians, and the transfer of the
national economy to a Smassid (Ould Taya's tribe) business class.
These explain why a transition process, much less a genuine democracy, remains elusive. To legitimize his regime, consolidate his power
and carry favor with the West, Ould Taya undertook canny military-
like maneuvers domestically, and shrewd diplomatic moves internationally. A consummate dosage of intimidation, co-optation, 'divide
and rule' tactics and outright crackdowns succeeded in frustrating
and estranging the opposition but did nothing to resolve Mauritania's
daunting problems. Prominent among these are the heavy human
rights 'deficit,' and dangerous ethnic and racial tensions, exacerbated
by the widening gap between the social classes. While the regime
seems firm, it is only a perverse "consolidation," not the kind envisioned by theorists of democratization and transition. The resulting
political impasse seems only to increase the likelihood of violent al-
ternatives to change the regime, as the way of the ballot appears
tightly shut by frequent bans of major political parties and an active,
repressive security apparatus. Mauritania shares these features with
Togo, another *Francophone* state of the sub-region in which the re-

cent modification of article 59 of the Constitution has made President Eyadema a de facto President for life. The role of the army in backing the deliberate non-transition to democracy in these two countries is another commonality they share, in sharp contrast to Benin.

First viewed as a symbol of national sovereignty in the early years of de-colonization, the African military increasingly became a part of the ruling elite's repressive arm. Although the actual size of the military and its relationship to the rulers varied, the armed forces in most countries became powerful political actors. With veritable "governments in waiting"[16] for decades, the military's perpetual involvement in African politics makes it understandably difficult for scholars to praise the contribution of military establishments to the democratization project. However, scholars have long demonstrated that military establishments, when engaging in politics as well as when withdrawing from politics are not the indistinguishable mass of one mindset they are presumed to be. On the contrary, when examined closely, they display a complex and dynamic array of political orientations, aspirations and objectives, the interaction and outcome of which defy explanations of the military as a unified and consistent actor[17] bent on subverting democracy. The divergent attitudes and behavior of the militaries during the political changes in Benin and Togo respectively provide another opportunity to reevaluate more discerningly the military's role, impact and the dynamics behind both. Additionally, as Houngnikpo has argued, the successful democratic transition in Benin, compared to Togo's ongoing travails, illustrates that democracy's "birth" does not depend solely on civil society's dynamism and endurance.[18] It depends also, perhaps more importantly,

---

16. Boubacar N'Diaye, "Introduction," *Journal of Political and Military Sociology* 28 (2), 2000, 187.

17. See, for example, Robin Lukham, "Taming the Monster: Democratization and Demilitarization," in Eboe Hutchful and Abdoulaye Bathily, eds., *The Military and Militarism in Africa*, 589–98, Dakar, CODESRIA, 1998.

18. See Mathurin Houngnikpo, "Democratization in Africa: A comparative Study of Benin and Togo," *Journal of Political and Military Sociology* 28 (2), 2000, 210–29.

on the military's collaboration. Through a comparative analysis, "Friend or Foe?: The Military in the Transition Processes in Benin and Togo" examines the political role of the military in Benin and Togo respectively, and explains why the armed forces cooperated with civilians in Benin, while they vetoed the democratic process in Togo. Finally, the chapter draws out lessons for democratic transitions, especially the military's role in helping or hindering the process. The concluding chapter takes stock of the critical role the military has played, and is likely to continue to play as West Africa sorts out its checkered civil-military relations.

Indeed "Not Yet Democracy"

Since the 1990s, African leaders have missed no opportunity, in regional clusters or as an entire continent, to reiterate their conversion and commitment to democratic precepts, conduct, and practices. The Kampala document on the Conference on Security, Stability, Development and Cooperation (CSSDCA), the Cairo Agenda for Action, the African Union charter, and, of course, the New Partnership for Africa's Development (NEPAD), to name a few, illustrate this flurry of pledges to tenets of liberal democracy and responsiveness to their peoples. Of all African regions, West Africa and its regional organization, the Economic Community of West African States (ECOWAS), has arguably done most—at least on paper—toward bringing stability, good governance, and democratization. The protocols and agreements signed by the states in the sub-region, notably the protocol on the Mechanism for Conflict Prevention, Resolution and Management, Peacekeeping and Security, and the Protocol relating to the Community Parliament are examples of these efforts. In spite of these efforts, instability, itself traceable to non-democratic governance, has not been eliminated, the progress accomplished in Sierra Leone, for example, notwithstanding. The complete abandonment of the ways of the past and the embracing of democratic forms of governance envisioned when the dismantling of authoritarian systems started does not seem to have taken root despite noteworthy instances of thriving plural and open societies in Mali, Senegal, Ghana, and Benin. This suggests that the region's slow farewell to authoritarianism will continue for a while longer. It certainly confirms the analyses and predictions made by most observers at the beginning of the era of 'democratic transitions' as well as in the decade since, that changes seemed "cosmetic and/or temporary"[19] and the "balance sheet on democratization is...mixed...[and] mildly positive."[20] The states reviewed in this book tend to confirm this rather sobering assessment of what was, the latest hope of Africans for a long-awaited, genuine democracy and people-friendly practices.

When Odinga warned that *Uhuru* had not yet come, in addition to corruption, the subversion of the will of the people by the post colonial regime in Kenya, he also called attention to the issues of landlessness, unemployment, education, health, and living standards, that were generally not addressed.[21] On this account also, his admonition also retained its relevance. These are indeed central dimensions of democratization, and the inability or unwillingness of many states in the sub-region to address them only further slow the attainment of genuine democracy. The perverse effect of this state of affairs is that when people do not see a substantial difference in the attitudes and practices of their (former or reformed) authoritarian and 'democratic' leaders they are not likely to support, accelerate or deepen the democratization movement. For even in states such as Mali where a faster pace toward democracy was achieved in spite of widespread poverty, one might emphasize, as a keen observer of the process put it, that "people do not eat democracy."[22] This is critical to the future of democracy in the context of deepening poverty and recurring weather related (or policy induced) famine in the sub-region. While economic performance and its slowdown effect on democratization

---

19. Samuel Decalo, "The Process, Prospect and Constraints of Democratization in Africa," *African Affairs* 91, 1992, 8.

20. Young, "The Third Wave of Democratization" 35.

21. Odinga, 314.

22. See Thandika Mkandawire, "Economic Policy-making and the Consolidation of Democratic Institution in Africa," in Havenic K. and B. Vanarkadi, eds., *Domination or Dialogue? Experiences and Prospects for African Development Cooperation*, Uppsala, Scandinavian Institute of African Studies, 1996, 43.

were not the focus of the studies in this book, they were an important part of the analyses. Beyond the various maneuvers of leaders and the mechanisms used to frustrate hopes for political transparency and fairness, these social and economic necessities are definitely part of the democratic equation in West Africa and, indeed, the entire continent.

CHAPTER I

CÔTE D'IVOIRE

The Miracle that Wasn't,
Flawed Civil-Military Relations,
and Missed Opportunity

Introduction

Long touted as an island of political stability and (relative) economic prosperity in West Africa, Côte d'Ivoire* seems to have become, since December 1999, and more so since September 2002, a praetorian state mired in political uncertainty, unending turbulence, and a full-blown civil war. Though the military regime of General Robert Guei lasted less than ten months, many observers would trace this stunning deterioration to the military takeover of Christmas Eve 1999. Nordlinger's definition of Praetorianism[1] fitted Ivory Coast perfectly until it descended, seemingly inexorably, into chaos and civil

---

* By decree dated October 14, 1985, the Ivoirian government decided to name the country "Côte d'Ivoire" and to no longer accept translations of this French name. However, the English translation is still widely used by American writers. "Ivoirian" is the English translation of the French adjective "*Ivoirien.*" This decision revealed the "special" relationship between the country's elites and the French language. We fail to see the point of accepting only one foreign language version of a concept when the overwhelming majority of the country's population does not speak that foreign language. Therefore, we have decided to use both versions.

1. Eric Nordlinger has defined praetorianism as "a situation in which military officers [non-officers as well it turns out] are major or predominant political actors by virtue of their actual or threatened use of force," *Soldiers in Politics: Military Coups and Governments*, Englewood, N.J., Prentice Hall, 1976, 2.

war on September 19, 2002. Between December 1999 and 2001 alone, Ivory Coast experienced six instances of military interventions in the political process, even as its neighbor, Ghana, for decades a praetorian state, prepared an orderly transfer of power to a new democratically elected leader. Political violence has already claimed hundred of victims and the situation has considerably worsened since 2002. The threat to the country and to the entire sub-region of a devastating disturbance of unpredictable consequences has now materialized. One of the difficulties of analyzing the recent evolution of Côte d'Ivoire is that the situation is fluid and quickly evolving. Nevertheless, the evolution of Côte d'Ivoire can shed a bright light on the root causes of the praetorianism that has gripped the country and ground to a halt its farewell to authoritarianism which started, as elsewhere in West Africa, in the early nineties.

On December 24, 1999, Côte d'Ivoire certainly entered a critical era in its civil-military relations and general evolution toward an open and democratic political system. The decaying condition of civil-military relations and, indeed, the unraveling of the State itself, make it imperative to attempt to understand what went wrong and start redesigning sound civil-military relations. To rebuild these civil-military relations, indeed the whole political system, on sound foundations and to turn the page on authoritarianism will necessitate major efforts. As Claude Welch rightly pointed out, "[t]he first overt seizure of power by the armed forces constitutes the most important shift in civil-military relations... It is a step not readily reversed."[2] As too many African states illustrate, once that fateful step is taken, a pernicious "military-as-a-justifiable-player" mentality seems to permeate the polity, increasing the likelihood of the military becoming a fixture of national political life. Since September 19, 2002, the worse case scenario of a total collapse of the post 1999 political order and the onset of rampant violence has unfortunately come to pass. In spite of the current situation, the good news is still that, to many experts' surprise, General Guei failed miserably to install the "civilianized" military

---

2. Claude Welch, Jr., ed., *Civilian Control of the Military: Theory and Cases from Developing Countries*, Albany, State University of New York Press, 1976, 324.

regime that he strenuously worked to usher in. The remarkable role civilians played in toppling the military regime, another astonishing development, may have an impact on civil-military relations in a democratic setting in Ivory Coast and West Africa generally.

To the casual observer, it all seems to have started on Christmas Eve 1999, when a mutiny of gun-toting petty officers and soldiers formed into the full-blown coup d'état that toppled President Henry Konan Bedié. The coup, which took most observers by surprise, was remarkable in how easily it unraveled the forty-year old civilian regime. However, as Boubacar N'Diaye has argued, the current situation is the outcome of dynamics in the Ivorian body politic and a derivative of singular civil-military relations concocted since the country's independence in 1960.[3] To understand the intervention of the military and the subsequent degradation of the country's situation, it is critical to look beyond the unimaginative policies and even the crass conduct and practices of President Bedié during the last months of his tenure. While these may have precipitated the coup, the roots of the "praetorianization" of Ivorian politics are deeper and more ancient.

Only an analytical, retrospective look can provide insight into the setback of Côte d'Ivoire's abandonment of authoritarian rule launched by President Felix Houphouet-Boigny in 1990, three years before his death. This analysis will also contribute to efforts to devise viable civil-military relations in the framework of an institutionalized, democratic and civilian-controlled political system throughout West Africa. To this end, it is first necessary to critically analyze the evolution of the political situation in Ivory Coast since independence, particularly the civil-military relationship that developed between 1961 and 1999. It will be argued that the roots of the successful Christmas 1999 coup and its catastrophic consequences must be traced to the distinctive and singular civil-military relations characterized by obsessive efforts to prevent coups. Secondly, the reasons for the collapse of the military regime are analyzed. The analy-

---

3. See Boubacar N'Diaye, "Ivory Coast's Civilian Control Strategies 1961–1998: A Critical Assessment," *Journal of Political and Military Sociology* 28 (2), 2001, 246–70.

sis focuses on the coup, its aftermath, the divisions it injected in the military, General Guei's and Laurent Gbagbo's maneuvers and miscalculations, as well as other relevant political considerations. Finally, the slow and much compromised farewell to a long legacy of authoritarianism, and the nefarious throes of ethnic politics are also examined.

Brief Historical Background

A former French colony in West Africa, Côte d'Ivoire became an independent state on August 7, 1960 after centuries of French colonial presence. Unlike most other colonies, independence was not the objective of Ivory Coast's main political leaders in the late 1950s. Independence came only after the failure of the *"Communauté Franco-Africaine,"* set up in the late 1950s, to salvage France's crumbling colonial empire in Africa.[4] Even after independence, Ivory Coast kept unique relations with France, thanks to the imposing personality of Felix Houphouet-Boigny, who, at the time of his death on December 7, 1993, had served as Ivory Coast's president for almost 34 years. As Aristide Zolberg documents, Houphouet-Boigny, along with the party he created (*Parti Démocratique de Côte D'Ivoire*, PDCI), was the principal architect of every major policy orientation and decision of the Ivory Coast over the last half century.[5] Under his leadership Ivory Coast pursued a resolutely pro-Western, capitalist economic strategy and foreign policy. The country experienced extraordinarily rapid economic growth during the 1960s and 1970s. It also stood out in the West African sub-region for its political stability. Houphouet-Boigny enjoyed the reputation of a man of wisdom and peace,[6] an image created and skillfully perpetuated by the French press.

---

4. Yves Faure, and J.F. Medard, *Etat et Bourgeoisie en Côte d'Ivoire*, Paris, Khartala 1982, 22–23.

5. See Aristide Zolberg, *One Party Government in the Ivory Coast*, Princeton, Princeton University Press.

6. See Jeanne M. Toungara, *Generational Tensions in the Parti Democratique de Côte d'Ivoire*, African Studies Review, 38 (2), 1995, 32.

The much-lauded "Ivorian economic miracle" experienced a severe crisis in the 1980s with profound political as well as social consequences. Politically, Ivory Coast's image, along with its reputation for stability, was all but destroyed by the time Houphouet-Boigny died. The deepening economic crisis gave rise to ever more pressing demands for radical changes in the country's macroeconomic orientation and distributive policies. As in other states of the region, an emboldened political opposition vociferously demanded the end of the PDCI's monopoly on power.[7] After much resistance and violence, multiparty elections and other reforms were introduced in 1990, not coincidentally after the La Baule France-Africa Summit during which French President François Mitterrand launched a new policy tying French aid to political liberalization. By December 9, 1993, when National Assembly President Henri Konan Bedié was sworn in as the head of state in accordance with article 11 of the Constitution, the face of Ivory Coast had changed beyond recognition. However, the only seemingly immutable variable was the unique relationship, often characterized as neocolonial, that Ivory Coast had developed and maintained with France. Nowhere has that relationship been more consequential than in the area of regime maintenance (in the African context, this meant mainly preventing a military coup, in addition to internal and external security). Consequently, a meaningful analysis of the successful overthrow of the Bedié government on Christmas Eve 1999, manifestly against the tide of a worldwide democratization and demilitarization of African politics, must start with the long running, entangled Franco-Ivoirian efforts to prevent precisely that outcome. While Bebié's political recklessness ultimately precipitated his overthrow by the soldiers, flawed civilian control strategies, broadly construed, and a legacy of authoritarianism, are the root-causes of the military intervention in the political process in Côte d'Ivoire and its catastrophic aftermath. As these events have amply illustrated, yet again, a direct and tangible correlation exists between how the security apparatus of the state

---

7. Richard C. Crook, *Côte d'Ivoire: Multi-party Democracy and Political Change*, in John Wiseman ed., *Democracy and Political Change in Sub-Saharan Africa*, New York, Routledge, 13–17.

and the civil-military relations are managed and the evolution of the political system. Before examining this correlation and the deeply flawed coup prevention strategies implemented by the post-colonial regime in Côte d'Ivoire, it is useful to take a quick look at the Ivoirian military.

The *Forces Armées Nationales de Côte d'Ivoire* (FANCI), the Ivoirian national armed forces, was created in 1961 by the 61-209 Law which organized national defense following the French government's 1960 *plan raisonnable* establishing armies in its former colonies.[8] According to the International Institute for Strategic Studies,[9] the armed forces of Côte d'Ivoire stood at a total of nearly fourteen thousand prior to the current civil war situation. The largest service was the army (6,800), followed by paramilitary bodies, the *gendarmerie* (4,400), and the presidential guard (1,100). The Navy (900) and Air Force (700) were the smallest services. In addition, there were 12,000 reservists, and 1,500 militia members. As will be discussed later, France, the former colonial power and Côte d'Ivoire's closest ally, played a major role in the set-up and training of these forces. In a West-African Sub-region infamous for its countless coups, military regimes, and turmoil, Côte d'Ivoire enjoyed exceptional stability until the 1990s. Beyond the personal leadership qualities often attributed to Houphouet-Boigny and the remarkable economic growth the country experienced in the 1960s, 1970s, and early 1980s, the exceptionality of Côte d'Ivoire in this regard is better analyzed in light of policies to consolidate and perpetuate the post-colonial regime. As David Goldsworthy has noted, "the dominant long-lived civilian leaders of Africa do not leave their relations with the soldiers either to chance, or to the growth rates, or to the broader working of [socioeconomic structural variables]."[10]

---

8. Moshe Ammi-Oz, "La formation des Cadres Militaires Africains Lors de la Mise sur Pied des Armées Africaines," *Revue Francaise d'Etudes Politiques Africaines*, 133, 1977, 84–99.

9. International Institute for Strategic Studies, *The Military Balance* 1999/2000, London, International Institute for Strategic Studies, 2000, 259.

10. David Goldsworthy, "Armies and Politics in Civilian Regimes" in Simon Baynham ed. *Military Power and Politics in Black Africa*, London, Croom Helm, 1986, 182.

France and West Africa: A Background[11]

After the failure of the joint defense structure France had envisioned as a part of a scheme to retain close ties with its soon to be former colonies in Africa, the overwhelming majority of newly independent states entered into a series of defense agreements with France. Generally, the defense agreements provided for the establishment, training and equipping of African militaries and the presence of French (military and civilian) technical advisers. They also enable African states to call on France to ensure their external and internal security (reestablishing law and order),[12] including the prevention of "putsches, and other coups d'état."[13] For its part, Côte d'Ivoire, signed a defense agreement on April 24, 1961. This agreement provides for the permanent basing of French troops, contains ultra-secret clauses, and has not been renegotiated for nearly thirty years.[14] The importance of Côte d'Ivoire to France was unmistakable. Along with Senegal, it was singled out by General De Gaulle as a country in which France would intervene if necessary.[15] Danielle Domergue-Cloarec, has argued that some of the defense agreements signed between France and its former colonies, contain secret clauses to guarantee the personal safety of heads of states and their families.[16] Given Houphouet-Boigny's central role in the post-colonial political and security arrangements, it is reasonable to assume that such a secret

---

11. For an informative discussion of the past and present military relations between France and Africa, though without reference to coup prevention nor to the coup in Ivory Coast, see Shaun Gregory, "The French Military in Africa: Past and Present," *African Affairs* 99, 2000, 435–48.

12. Dominique Bangoura, *Les Armées Africaines 1960–1990*, Paris, Centre des Hautes Etudes sur L'Afrique et L'Asie Modernes, 1992, 25.

13. Pascal Chaigneau, *La Politique Militaire de la France en Afrique*, Paris, Centre Des Hautes Etudes sur L'Afrique et L'Asie Modernes, 1984, 27.

14. John Chipman, *French Power in Africa*, Cambridge, Basil Blackwell Ltd., 1989, 119, 129.

15. Phillipe Gaillard, *Foccart Parle: Entretiens avec Phillipe Gaillard*, Vol. 1 Paris, Fayard/Jeune Afrique, 1995, 228.

16. Danielle Domergue-Cloarec, *La France et l'Afrique Après les Independances*, Paris, SEDES, 1994, 72.

clause existed with Ivory Coast. Thus, a noticeable characteristic of these accords is that, as Chester Crocker noted, they "imply a commitment to regimes, as opposed to states."[17] What precedes constituted the setting for the civil-military relations that developed over the forty years of post-colonial regime in Côte d'Ivoire.

Coup Prevention Strategies: The Seeds of Military Intervention

In the context of rampant praetorianism in West Africa, and ideological rivalries with its neighbors (mostly Guinea under Sékou Touré and Ghana under Kwame Nkrumah), the regime of Houphout-Boigny could not feel too secure. In such conditions, the preservation of the regime assumed paramount importance. Observers of civil-military relations in Africa have noted that the cornerstone of the strategies of the Ivoirian regime to retain power has been the continued presence of French troops and military advisors.[18] While this was indeed the primary strategy, the measures taken to insure that Côte d'Ivoire remained coup-free also included shrewd secondary strategies to prevent the military from taking power. Finally, while these flawed civil-military relations sowed the seeds of the December 1999 coup in the narrowest sense, other policies, particularly the total disregard of the most basic norms of democracy and the corrupt management of the economy must also be examined.

---

17. Chester Crocker, *The Military Transfer of Power in Africa: A Comparative Study of Change in the British and French System of Order*, Baltimore, A Ph.D. Dissertation, The Johns Hopkins University Department of Political Science, 1969, 497–98.

18. Samuel Decalo, "Modalities of Civil-Military Stability in Africa," *Journal of Modern African Studies* 27(4), 1989, 547–78; Chipman, 1989; Goldsworthy, 1986; Claude Welch, "Côte D'Ivoire: Personal Rule and Civilian Control," in Claude E. Welch ed., *No Farewell to Arms?* (172–94), Boulder, Westview, 1987; Pascal Koffi Teya, *Le roi Est Nu*, Paris, L'Harmattan, 1985.

The French Military Presence

Decades ago, Ruth First observed that Houphouet-Boigny's close relationship with France was "the soundest insurance against a successful coup."[19] There is no doubt that the PDCI regime owes most of its longevity to the presence of French troops and French military assistants at all levels in the ranks of the Ivorian military. This "external guarantee strategy"[20] consisted of stationing hundreds of French Marines near Abidjan as a deterrent, the presence of French military advisors, a sustained program of training for the Ivorian military, and a significant reduction of defense expenditure. However, it also has had fatal flaws. Along with the other equally flawed (but somehow secondary) regime maintenance schemes, the strategies undermined the professionalization, autonomy or political insulation of the military. Combined, these strategies further heightened the military's awareness of the low legitimacy of the political system and the regime. The evidence suggests that it is the alienation of the Ivorian military, its politicization and (the resulting) long history of restiveness that culminated in the Christmas Eve coup. The corporate and political demands of mutinous soldiers on September and thereafter only substantiates this conclusion.

Since the independence of Côte d'Ivoire, France has constantly maintained hundreds of marines on its military base of Port-Bouet near Abidjan. The number of these troops steadily increased over the years, no doubt signaling a strengthening of the French commitment to the survival of the Ivorian regime. In 1999, even as the coup unfolded, French troops numbered nearly 600.[21] In addition to these readily available troops, France could airlift its domestically based *Force d'Action Rapide* (FAR) to any trouble spot in Africa within hours.[22] While in power, Houphouet-Boigny left no doubt that he would not hesitate to call on France to help him retain power. In 1971

---

19. Ruth First, *The Barrel of a Gun: Political Power and the Coup D'État*, London, Allen Lane, 1970, 424.
20. Decalo, 1989, 575.
21. Institute for Strategic Studies, 2000, 259.
22. Domergue-Cloarec, 1994 74–76.

French troops intervened to put down a rebellion by the *Bete*, an ethnic group traditionally opposed to the Baoule (Houphouet-Boigny's ethnic group).[23] In 1990, in the face of a combined civilian and military threat, Houphouet-Boigny once again solicited French intervention (though to no avail this time, see below). Indeed, until 1999 (for reasons to be discussed later), France's military was ready to see to it that, should the need arise, any coup attempts (at least ones it did not approve of) failed. Pascal K. Teya has argued that French troops used demonstrative maneuvers to deter and dissuade potential opponents from even attempting a coup, often injuring the patriotic sentiments of the Ivoirian military.[24]

The presence of French military advisors was another dimension of the strategies the Ivoirian regime used to prevent coups. For years, until it was surpassed recently by Madagascar, Côte d'Ivoire constantly had the highest concentration of French nationals in Africa. Up until the 1970s, various high-level civil servants, often in sensitive positions, including the president's chief of staff, were French citizens. Nowhere has the presence of French nationals been as consequential as in the military. In the efforts of the Ivorian and French governments to prevent coups, these military assistants were an "even more important army" than the regular French troops.[25] Data compiled from various sources indicate that the number of these military advisors drastically dropped to 111 in 1980 from its 1965 peak (248), and remained roughly constant since the mid-1980s (about 70).[26] The decline is more noticeable after 1980 when anti-French sentiments ran high and the close ties with France were increasingly criticized as neo-colonial. More than a change in strategy, this decline most likely reflected the necessity for the Ivoirian government to decrease the visibility of French military advisors. Evidently, because of their access to intelligence, these advisors' main role was to ensure that nothing France did not like happened in Côte d'Ivoire.

---

23. Welch, 1987, 180–81.

24. Teya, 1985, 86–87.

25. Howard French, "The End of an Era," *Africa Report*, 39 (2), 1994, 21.

26. Robin Luckham, "French Militarism in Africa," *Review of African Political Economy* 24, 1982, 55–84; Domergue-Cloarec, 1994; Chipman, 1989.

Co-optation, Manipulation, and Politicization of the Military

While Houphouet-Boigny, and later his successor Henri Konan-Bedié, relied heavily on the close political and military ties with France to ward-off military intervention, they also pursued other strategies to further reduce the likelihood of a military takeover. These flawed schemes consisted, among other measures, in the ethnic and political manipulation of the military, the co-optation of officers in the political and administrative ruling circles, the spoil system, and the exploitation of inter-service rivalries. All of these also contributed to the ultimate overthrow of the PDCI/Bedié regime.

Houphouet-Boigny was keen to integrate military officers into the machinery of the PDCI regime. For instance, more than 30% of the prefects "who exercise[d] significant powers" in their administrative districts were members of the military; the objective, more or less explicit, was to lessen the risk of military intervention.[27] The 1999 coup, which originated among petty officers, (and the September 2002 mutiny) seems to give credence to Teya's analysis. He argues that the top brass of the Ivoirian military was cleverly compromised by the regime in the mismanagement of the national economy and in politics in order to neutralize it.[28] To give the military a stake in the regime, high-ranking officers were even brought into government in 1974. According to Claude Welch, Jr., Houphouet-Boigny made "political reliability...the dominant criterion for promotion" in the military.[29] Other co-optation and manipulation measures were evident. Shielded from the harsh, belt-tightening measures of the 1980s, the military was indeed "well treated" economically.[30] Additionally, military officers were put in charge of parastatals and given the opportunity, indeed encouraged, to enrich themselves illegally. When, for some reason, top officers became unreliable, they were given positions in state-owned companies or in diplomatic missions to distance them from active service.

---

27. Welch, 1987, 182.
28. Teya, 1984, 85
29. Welch, 1987, 182.
30. Welch, 1987, 181, 184.

The ethnic manipulation of the military was yet another alarming scheme the civilian regime employed to prevent coups. In the early years of independence, Houphouet-Boigny took advantage of a (never proven) "conspiracy" to overthrow his regime to shrewdly disarm the army, fragment and entirely reconfigure the ethnic make-up of the Ivorian military.[31] A critical element of this re-structuring was the creation of a 3,000 person strong PDCI-controlled militia (the presidential guard) made-up exclusively of *Baoule*, the President's ethnic group.[32] Another indication of this approach was Houphouet-Boigny's heavy use of what Howard William has called "a system of ethnic quotas" as an instrument of governance,[33] which he extended to high-ranking officers as well. In 1982, he had a group of high-ranking *Bete* officers publicly express their support for him (to dissociate themselves from a growing opposition with ethnic overtones).[34] The military was manipulated in other ways as well. In 1990, with his power weakened by pro-democracy movements and political parties, Houphouet-Boigny called on the army to brutally repress his opposition. None other than Robert Guei, the future junta leader (who was then a colonel) was charged to carry out that mission. Houphouet-Boigny is said to have promised to "fill up [Guei's] pockets with money."[35] For selfish reasons, on the eve of the 1995 presidential election, President Bedié continued to follow essentially the same approach. He manipulated inter-service rivalries by playing the army off against the *gendarmerie* and dismissed General Robert Guei, then the joint chief of staff, for apparently requesting written orders to prepare to use the army against Bedié's opponents in the 1995 elections.[36]

---

31. Welch, 1987, 180.

32. Aristide Zolberg, *One Party Government in the Ivory Coast*, Princeton, Princeton University Press, 1969, 350.

33. Howard William, "The Crisis of Succession," *Africa Report* 33 (3), 1988, 54.

34. Welch, 1987 183. The *Bete* are the second largest ethnic group in Côte d'Ivoire. They have a long history of opposition to the regime perceived as dominated by the Baoule (the ethnic group to which Houphouet-Boigny and Konan Bedié belong). Laurent Gbagbo, the current President is a *Bete*.

35. Florentin Kassy, *"L'Adieu aux Armes,"* *Jeune Afrique*, 1885, 19–25 February, 1997, 32.

36. Geraldine Faes and Elimane Fall, "Le Vrai-Faux Coup d'État du Général Guei," *Jeune-Afrique*, 1817, 2–8 November, 1995, 16–19.

Effects of the Coup Prevention Strategies

Obviously, the primary effect of the combined strategies implemented by the PDCI regime has been to keep Côte d'Ivoire coup-free for nearly forty years. As the Christmas Eve coup would stunningly demonstrate, however, these same strategies contained the seeds of the undoing of the civilian regime. These strategies had grave implications and consequences for the political system as a whole and on civil-military relations specifically. First, the survival of the regime rested not on healthy, sound foundations such as legitimacy and the will of the people, but on the will of the French government to save it. Second, the various manipulations and machinations sapped the military's professional, corporate self-image, and heightened its political and social awareness of the flaws in the system. They made elements within the military realize that, not only was the regime's claim to legitimacy tenuous, but that, just as force helped it to survive, force could undo it. Third, the frequent use of the army against the opposition politicized the military even more dramatically. The military came to see itself as a bona fide political player, as evidenced by General Guei's refusal, in 1995, to carry out Bedié's orders to crackdown on the opposition during a tense pre-electoral period.[37] This increased the likelihood of military intervention in the political arena. However, these interventions were on the military's behalf, for its own corporate interests, not to save the regime from its opponents one more time. Finally, the disastrous management of the affairs of the country, the neglect of the needs of the Ivoirian people and the working and living conditions of the soldiers, all of which are important dimensions of civil-military relations broadly construed, did nothing to legitimize or consolidate the post-colonial regime.

A closer look at the implication of these overall strategies will help explain this outcome. The web of economic, political, military and cultural relations between France and the Ivory Coast has been described as an example of French neo-colonialism.[38] Edouard Bustin has force-

37. Faes and Fall, 1995, 17.

38. Edouard Bustin, *The limits of French Intervention in Africa: A Study in Applied Neo-Colonialism*, Boston, African Studies Center, 1982; Samir Amin, *Neo-Colonialism in West Africa*, New York, Monthly Review Press, 1973; Teya, 1984.

fully argued that, in the domain of civil-military relations in particular, African states are ultimately the losers in neo-colonial arrangements. First, the defense agreements typically give the French president the ultimate decision to intervene, undermining national sovereignty,[39] and giving the protégé regime much to worry about. For example, in a blatant effort to pressure Houphouet-Boigny into abiding by the La Baule summit dictate (that African states should accept multiparty politics), France ignored his request and refused to intervene to put down a military mutiny in June 1990. This uncertainty does not promote civil-military stability. It is indeed dangerous to protégé regimes, for France has been known to ease out presidents it can no longer depend on as in Cameroon and Niger.[40] As will be discussed below, this scenario is precisely what appears to have happened in December 1999.

Second, the dependency on an external guarantor inherent in neo-colonial arrangements can have perverse effects. In Côte d'Ivoire, military officers frantically cultivated self-serving relations with French military authorities. Many were willing to carry out various activities, even coups, on their behalf. Such a situation confuses the military elite by giving them mixed loyalties. The officers know that any move against the regime is likely to be detected in time or crushed by the French military. At the same time, they must remain distant enough from the same regime should it become doomed. They will therefore display insincere loyalty to the regime. The French led the ouster of "emperor" Jean Bedel Bokassa in the Central African Republic and of Hissen Habre in Chad, both of whom were installed by France but later embarrassed or defied their protector. The cozy relations between general Guei and the French military establishment were made evident when the former French army chief of staff, retired general Jeannou Lacaze, tried to help him retain power. In addition, as Chipman has stressed, the presence of French military advisors perversely entrusts French nationals with sensitive positions in African militaries and gives them access to information they can use to directly and decisively influence the course of do-

39. Bustin, 1982, 13.
40. *Ibid.*

mestic events.[41] This cannot but negatively affect the morale and sense of institutional pride of African militaries.

The implications and effects of the coup prevention schemes concocted by presidents Houphouet-Boigny and Bedié also lead to the inescapable conclusion that they contributed to the demise of the civilian regime. One of the first effects of their policies has been that, instead of eliminating military restiveness and instilling civilian supremacy in the military, they produced the opposite. While the Ivoirian military only succeeded in displacing the civilian regime in the 1999 coup, it has had a long history of various forms of intervention in the political process. These include other coup attempts and conspiracies. Already in 1962, 1963, 1973, and 1980, groups in the Ivoirian military conspired, and in some instances attempted, to overthrow the government.[42] As recently as in the 1990s, conspiracies fomented by officers of the Ivoirian military were uncovered.[43] Other forms of military interference in the political process include mutinies and various types of overt political insubordination. In 1991, members of the military went on strike demanding higher wages and some soldiers even briefly occupied a radio station. One year earlier, soldiers occupied the Abidjan airport, while others roamed the streets at night and engaged in acts of banditry.[44] In April 1990, in conditions very similar to those that eventually led to the successful coup, president Houphouet-Boigny was forced to meet with mutineers complaining about their living and service conditions.[45] A third form of military interference in the political arena, though not initiated by the military, has been its zealous repression of political opponents. In

41. Chipman, 1985, 24–25.

42. "Ten Years in French Speaking Africa," *Africa Digest* 27 (5), 1970, 85–89; *Africa Research Bulletin* (Political and social series) June, 1973; Efrem Sigel, "Ivory Coast: Booming Economy, Political Calm.," *Africa Report* 15, 1970, 18–21; Welch, 1987, 180.

43. Fall, 1991, 10–11; *Africa Research Bulletin* August 1991 and November 1996.

44. *Africa Research Bulletin*, June 1990; Kaye Whiteman, "The Gallic Paradox," *Africa Report* 36(1), 1990, 17–19.

45. Kassy, 1997, 31.

1969, in the late 1980s and again in the 1990s, Houphouet-Boigny and Bedié used the military to suppress their political opposition.[46] In 1971 for example, the army, along with French troops, participated in the massacre of members of the *Bete* ethnic group accused of separatism and opposition to the Houphouet-Boigny regime.[47] In 1991, during sustained pro-democracy demonstrations, the military brutally repressed university students. The repression was so vicious that even the Prime Minister considered it "revolting." As recently as 1995, the military was used against the political opposition on the eve of the succession struggle. In the city of Gagnoa, several opponents were killed. The politicization of the Ivoirian military was already deepened by charging it with the "civic and moral education" of union members and students who were leading the opposition in the late 1980s. Incidentally, it was during that period that current president, Laurent Gbagbo, then an ardent opponent, was sent to undergo "reeducation" in a military barrack commanded by a certain Captain Robert Guei.

Given this thorough politicization, it was hardly surprising that during the succession struggle between Bedié and Alassane Dramane Ouattara (Houphouet-Bogny's prime minister), the army, a supposedly neutral institution, seemed to have sided against president Henri Konan Bedié who, in the end, prevailed in the contest.[48] While this version is not unanimously agreed to, it is certain that the military through none other than Robert Guei did get involved in the succession dispute. Finally, it is evident that no analysis of the Christmas Eve 1999 coup can be complete without a discussion of the policies Houphouet-Boigny and indeed Bedié have pursued in the overall management of the country. These are germane to any analysis of civil-military relations, as they invariably constitute the backdrop of the military intervention and are used to justify it. As will be examined later, the Ivoirian coup was no exception. Indeed, these policies and attitudes also further contributed

---

46. *Africa Research Bulletin*, May 1991, February 1992; Mark Huband, "Silencing the Opposition," *Africa Report* 37 (3), 1992, 55–57.

47. Welch, 1987, 180; William, 1988, 54.

48. "Power Struggle Is Simmering in Ivory Coast," *New York Times*, December 9, 1993, A3, 3.

to digging the grave of the PDCI regime and to slowing down Ivory coast's transmutation into a democracy.

The evidence overwhelmingly indicates that the affairs of the state were conducted with a high degree of mismanagement and corruption. Many authors attribute the economic crisis that befell Ivory Coast to the wasteful and corrupt neopatrimonial practices associated with Houphouet-Boigny.[49] He once publicly urged his ministers to enrich themselves, and most of his ministers were found to be "self-serving and corrupt."[50] This partially explains why as much as 130 billion CFA Francs were embezzled annually and taken out of the country, the countless, multi-billion CFA Francs financial scandals involving governmental elites, including Bedié[51] that occurred before and during his presidency. Invariably, the actions taken by the soldiers throughout the 1990s, including the fatal blow to the Bedié regime, were justified by the disparities between their destitute living conditions and those of the elites. It is certain that the rather politically absurd advertisement of President Laurent Gbabo's monthly salary (nearly US$ 8,000) did not sit well with the mutinous soldiers whose monthly salaries are, on average, one hundred times less.

For years, through undemocratic means and an elaborate clientelist scheme, Houphouet-Boigny managed to enlist the loyalty and devotion of large segments of the intellectual and business classes. He used the *Parti Démocratique de Côte d'Ivoire* (PDCI) and its organs to maintain firm control over the state apparatus. Only in 1990, when violent demonstrations by the opposition threatened the very existence of the regime, was Houphouet-Boigny forced to introduce multi-party elections. While the introduction of multi-partyism and other trappings of democracy constituted a step toward increased government responsiveness and legitimacy, it did not guarantee free

---

49. Yves Faure, "Côte d'Ivoire: Analyzing the Crisis," in Donald Cruise O'Brien, John Dunn and Richard Rathbone eds., *Contemporary West African States* (59–73), Cambridge, Cambridge University Press, 198; Teya 1985; Toungara 1995; William, 1988.

50. William, 1988 5.

51. George Ayittey, *Africa Betrayed*, New York, St. Martin's Press, 1992, 241–42; Gaillard, 1995, vol. 2, 286.

and fair elections or democratic practices. The lag effect of 30 years of authoritarianism was felt throughout the 1990s.

Immediately after succeeding Houphouet-Boigny, with the tacit but firm support of France, Bedié displayed unmistakable authoritarian tendencies.[52] The multi-party elections of 1990 and 1995 were no more free and fair than the previous elections when the PDCI monopolized political life. In this respect, President Bedié seems to have mostly replaced the last resort strategies of subtle repression and co-optation characteristic of the pre-1990 period with heavy-handed, crass repression. Despite some limited progress since the 1990 reforms, Ivory Coast's record of respect for democratic rights and freedoms, measured by diverse organizations and observers, tends to indicate that these rights were often violated. Since 1991, every Amnesty International annual report describes the detention, mistreatment (including torture) and, in some instances, killing of hundreds of political opponents and several journalists. In 1991, members of the military were detained and tortured after an alleged coup attempt,[53] and significantly, two years before the coup, at least 10 members of the military figured among those detained and mistreated.[54]

Despite the promises of the 1990 reforms, the situation in Ivory Coast continued to decline. By the time the 1999 coup occurred, the disastrous policies of Houphouet-Boigny and his successor had damaged already poor economic conditions as well as exacerbated human, civil, and political rights violations. The seemingly irreversible wave of democratization and demilitarization of African politics notwithstanding, the stage was set for the military takeover. While a rapidly deteriorating situation, a series of fateful events, and the outright foolish behavior and attitude of President Bedié were precipitants of the coup, the civil-military relations brought about by flawed coup prevention strategies and other related policies are its root causes.

---

52. Howard French, "No More Paternalism but Public Executions," *New York Times*, 15 May 1995, A4.

53. Fall, 1991, 10.

54. Amnesty International, *Amnesty International Report*, New York, Amnesty International Publications, 1997, 129.

The Coup and Its Aftermath

With their decision to oust Henri Konan Bedié and to constitute a military junta, the *Comité National de Salut Public* (CNSP), to run the country, the Ivoirian military ushered in a new era of civil-military relations and political development in Côte d'Ivoire. The success of a group of non-commissioned officers in almost effortlessly displacing one of the longest running civilian regimes on the continent without bloodshed is an eloquent testimony to the utter failure of the coup prevention strategies and overall regime legitimizing policies of the PDCI regime. In particular, it illustrates the failure of the external guarantor strategy and officer corps manipulation/co-optation schemes to anticipate two critical phenomena. First, military interventions in African political processes are increasingly spearheaded by commissioned or non-commissioned junior officers, and no longer by the top brass. President Bedié's lament that all his generals had fled as the coup unfolded,[55] is instructive in this regard. Second, like the 1994 coup in The Gambia, the failed coup in Guinea in 1996, and, more recently, the failed coup in Burundi (2001) illustrate, these military incursions are no longer the planned, by-the-book, "full-blown" coups d'état of old. However, they can, in the heat of an 'ordinary' mutiny, achieve the same outcome. Though there seems to be evidence that other more 'typical' coups attempts may have been in preparation,[56] what started as a mutiny of soldiers to call attention to their precarious conditions and to the corrosive political situation in the country rapidly escalated into the ouster of the head of state.

According to General Robert Guei, who was brought out of retirement by the mutineers to lead them, in a statement on December 24, 1999, there were two reasons for the coup:

> There are problems which are strictly of military order which concern the restoration of their dignity; that is, the im-

---

55. Statement to the press by general Guei, on December 26, 1999, reproduced in *Fraternité Matin*, 10556, December 27, 1999.

56. Albert Bourgi, "Entre Militaires," *Jeune-Afrique/L'Inteligent*, 2066–67, 15–28 August 2000, 34–39.

provement of their equipment, salary increases and some
problems peculiar to the military profession...The other
problems are political, since they called for the unconditional
release of elements currently imprisoned at the Abidjan Central Prison for political reasons.

During his meeting with the mutineers, Bedié allegedly used foul language and displayed an arrogant and insulting attitude, in reaction to
which it was decided to remove him from power.[57] Just two days earlier,
in a speech to the nation, a defiant Bedié had stubbornly refused to heed
the insistent calls for moderation of friends in the international community. He had rejected pleas to free the jailed militants of the main opposition party (*Rassemblement Des Républicains*, RDR) and to lift the
ban imposed on Alassane Dramane Ouattara, the former Prime Minister. Ouattara had been excluded from the upcoming presidential election under the pretext that he was not a citizen of Côte d'Ivoire. As if
nothing could ever change in the basic nature of his relations with
France, Bedié relied almost blindly on the French military umbrella. This
attitude blinded him to noticeable changes in French policies on military intervention to rescue friendly regimes, in general. It certainly
blinded him to unmistakable signals that the French authorities (in a
stalemated socialist government/right-wing president situation) had
grown irritated by his drift toward autocratic rule, in particular. French
"preoccupation" with his handling of his political opponents (particularly the disenfranchisement of Alassane Ouattara) and the injection of
virulent xenophobia in Ivoirian politics through the crooked concept of
'*Ivoirité*' (Ivoiry-ness), was expressed in the form of polite public pronouncements as well as blunt private warnings. He had forgotten that
already in 1990, on the wake of promulgation of the *La Baule* doctrine,
President François Mitterrand had stunned Houphouet-Boigny by re-
fusing to intervene against mutineers who had occupied the Abidjan airport. Furthermore, as recently as 1997, France's foreign minister specifically told the Organization of African Unity (OAU) that henceforth his

---

57. Statement to the press by general Guei, on December 26, 1999, reproduced in *Fraternité Matin*, 10556, December 27, 1999.

country refused to "be dragged in internal conflicts" in Africa.[58] Finally, his almost defiant mismanagement of the economy brought the country very close to bankruptcy and alienated the European Union, the World Bank, and the IMF. The embezzlement of billions of CFA Francs from the EU aid destined for the health sector was still fresh in the news.

After a moment of confusion and a futile attempt to reverse the course of events, Bedié and his family fled the country after seeking refuge in the French embassy in a strange twist of irony. He had appealed directly on a French radio to loyalist forces and the general population to resist the coup. On the contrary, the population and the political class seemed to have almost unanimously been relieved to see the political impasse come to such a decisive, if unexpected, end. The statements of general Guei were reassuring enough as he declared that he had no ambition to remain in power and that the soldiers have taken power to "clean up the house" and that, as soon as this is done, they will abandon power.[59]

The shock and later the protestations of the international community, were somehow muted by the collective sigh of relief and even jubilation which emanated from the Ivorian people and its political class. Acceptance of the *fait accompli* was soon evident even as foreign governments and international organizations called for a speedy transition to constitutional rule. This was particularly true of the Organization of African Unity (OAU), which had, a year earlier decided to refuse admission to any government that comes to power through a coup d'état. After the initial puzzle as to why French troops stationed in Port-Bouet didn't intervene to save Bedié's regime, the real question turned to how long the military would stay in power, and what political situation was likely to emerge after the transition period.

As the military junta and the segment of the political class that objectively benefited from the ouster of Bedié started to prepare for the transition to new institutions and rules of the game, few foresaw the dangerous course Côte d'Ivoire was about to embark on. For however

---

58. Fraternité Matin, December 27, 1999.
59. Arnaud de la Grange, "*L'Afrique Doit se Gendarmer Seule*," Le Figaro, October, 1997, 4C.

welcome and even salutary it may seem sometimes, the intervention of the military in the political arena invariably brings about an array of uncertainties and dangers. Not only is the potential for deep divisions within the military a very likely outcome with a chain of coups and counter-coups, but the potential for violence as the preferred means to solve contradictions increases sharply. The experience of military rule in Côte d'Ivoire, although it lasted less than a year, brought all the possible twists and turns that can be expected from an inexperienced and divided military institution purporting to set up a democracy for a country. A deadly mix compounded to produce the most startling military regime interlude in African modern history. Its main ingredients consisted of General Guei's awakened personal political ambition, his inept leadership, and the effects of the tensions of the confusing role thrust on the military as a corporate institution and as government. Finally, the effects of the political manipulation of ethnicity, regionalism, and religion in the Ivoirian body politic also played a significant role. In spite of these pitfalls, the military hiatus constituted also a unique opportunity to right the wrongs of the PDCI regime and accelerate the country's farewell to autocratic politics. This was not to happen.

The Military Interlude and Beyond

For nearly forty years, power in Ivory Cost was certainly civilian as opposed to military. It was definitely not democratic. As Robin Luckam has stated, there is more than a nuance in the distinction.[60] Given the circumstances that led to the present political situation in Côte d'Ivoire, it is not farfetched to argue that the military interlude failed to usher in a democratic civilian regime, if this ever was its objective. In many respect President Laurent Gbagbo, just as Presidents Houphouet-Boigny and Bedié before him, does not owe his position to the express will of the Ivoirian people, at least in this respect, we are 'back to square one.' When the unsolicited "military experiment"

---

60. Robin Luckham, "Taming the Monster: Democratization and Demilitarization," in Eboe Hutchful and Abdoulaye Bathily, eds., *The Military and Militarism in Africa*, Dakar, CODESRIA, 1998.

Côte d'Ivoire underwent started, the odds seemed good enough. A political impasse was finally unblocked, the military leader dragged against his will from retirement unambiguously stated that he had no interest in power and that, once an orderly transition was completed the military would withdraw to its barracks. The euphoria in the population and in the overwhelming majority of the political class rapidly vanished when general Guei, without ever stating his intentions until the very last constitutionally mandated moment, revealed his true agenda. His intention to use the transition to fulfill a suddenly awakened presidential ambition became clear when, after decrying in his first pronouncements the political blunder Bedié had committed in injecting the poisonous concept of "*Ivoirité*" (Ivory-ness") in Ivorian politics, he embraced it and wrote it in article 35 of the new Constitution. Next, came the elaborate use of the judicial system to eliminate cumbersome opponents from running (another Bedié antic). And finally, in the face of electoral defeat by a "light weight" candidate, came the blatant attempt to perpetrate a "coup in a coup" by attempting to cancel the election altogether and proclaim himself president. Very few foresaw this evolution although, early in the transition, general Guei had started to wrap himself in the mantle of a still much revered Houphouet-Boigny. In hindsight, given his thorough cooptation in the political circles of the PDCI, between 1990 and 1997, when he was unceremoniously forced into retirement by Bedié, the opportunity to take his personal revenge on the political system and on Bedié himself would have been too tempting to let slip by. An element of what N'Diaye called the "De Gaulle complex" may have also played a role in his decision to want to stay in office.[61] His decision may as well have been simply the result of the corrupting influence of power. Whatever motivated it, this decision proved to be an unmitigated disaster for Côte d'Ivoire. And, as the frantic but failed efforts of the OAU to craft an acceptable political solution indicated, it also threatened to pull down the entire Sub-region into chaos and violence. When this sad episode was all over, the country was in economic

---

61. See Boubacar N'Diaye, *The Challenge of Institutionalizing Civilian Control*, Lanham, MD, Lexington Books, 2001, 161.

shambles. It was badly divided and in an advanced state of decomposition due to centrifugal forces of all sorts. Ominously, the same could be said of the military as an institution as well. Hundreds of peoples were killed, chaos loomed, and Ivory Coast was no closer to democratic civilian control or real political stability than it was on December 24, 1999. Arguably it was far worse off.

While the military institution was not a model of unity or professionalism when the coup took place, partly due to divisive tactics Both Houphouet-Boigny and Bedié carried out to maintain power, the experience of ruling the country deepened the cleavages along service, political, regional, religious, and even rank lines. Very early in the military administration, the *gendarmerie* believed to be more loyal to Bedié was pitted against the army. Similarly, northern high-ranking officers, particularly Generals Lassana Palenfo and Abdoulaye Coulibaly respectively second and third ranking members of the CNSP, who are Muslims and putatively close to Alassane Ouattara, seemed to be at odds with General Guei himself, and other Christian southern or western officers in the CNPS. To complicate this situation further, the same corporatist and materialistic-cum-political reasons that motivated the coup in the first place, led to a large-scale mutiny on July 4, and 5, 2000. In addition to asking millions of CFA Francs, the mutineers demanded no less than a pledge by General Guei that he would not run.[62] After fierce fighting quieted down, General Guei needed all the deal-making skills he could muster and sweeping promises of material reward to end the mutiny. Evidently, the 40% increase of the soldiers' salaries the junta had decreed earlier[63] was apparently not enough to assuage the military's assertive claims to a bigger slice of the shrinking financial pie. It was, however, all but certain that General Guei's candidacy to the presidency was an important reason for the restiveness in the ranks. It was soon evident that a widening rift existed in the ruling junta as well. The September 17, 2000 attack on general Guei's residence, whether real or faked, was another manifestation of the deep divisions in the military. As a

---

62. Francis Kpatindé, "l'Éléphant Malade," *Jeune-Afrique/l'Intelligent*, 2061, 11–17 July 2000, 8–11.
63. *Ibid.*

direct result of this attack, generals Palenfo and Coulibaly fearing for their safety had to take refuge in the Nigerian embassy to escape arrest. As their open letter to General Guei from their hideout revealed, the main reason for the rift was General Guei's decision to run for the presidency and their opposition to it.[64] Their trial under the Gbabgo regime confirmed their allegations, as General Guei through an envoy, urged the military tribunal to release them "because they had no hand in the attack."[65]

These developments confirm that it is indeed a difficult gamble for the military, by definition a non-democratic, hierarchical, conspiracy-prone institution to be in charge of transforming an authoritarian political system into a real democracy. It is not sure, however, that even a unified and efficient military would have been able to carry out successfully this task after forty years of PDCI rule. The task was made singularly more difficult after the divisive policies of Bedié fragmented so deeply the political elite and, generally, the Ivoirian people. Furthermore, there are objective social and political problems associated with the dozens of ethnic groups comprising Côte d'Ivoire, the worsening economic conditions, and the fact that up to one third of its population are immigrants from all the states of the sub-region. In addition, Ivory Coast has also had a history of economic and political disenfranchisement of the northern, predominantly Muslim part of the country by the predominantly Christian southern and western elites.[66] After the succession struggle in which Bedié prevailed, a split in the PDCI led to the creation of the RDR (*Rassemblement des Républicains*) around Alassane Ouattara, Houphouet-Boigny's last Prime Minister. While the 2001 municipal elections revealed its solid urban and national implementation, the RDR is widely believed to represent mainly northerners. The strength of the RDR and, over the last decade, the demographic shift in Côte d'Ivoire in favor of north-

---

64. See "Cher Robert," *Jeune-Afrique/l'Intelligent*, 2075, 17–23 October, 2000, 22–23.

65. See "Strange Case of Two Generals," *West Africa*, 26 March–1st April, 2001, 18–19.

66. See Zyad Limam, "La Guerre des Chefs," *Jeune-Afrique/L'Intelligent*, 2060, 4–10 July, 2000, 8–10.

erners, has, for the first time, made it possible for a northerner, namely Ouattara, to have a definite chance of being elected head of state. This prospect, and its potential for upsetting the economic, ethnic, religious, and political arrangement crafted by the PDCI regime, seems to have been at the heart of the efforts by Bedié and his circle to prevent Ouattara from running. As generals Palenfo's and Coulibaly's letter suggests, these considerations may have also influenced General Guei's advisors[67] in getting him to bar Ouattara one more time,[68] and to run for the presidency himself. A Supreme Court General Guei had made sure to pack with his cronies found legal reasons to eliminate any candidate likely to make the race competitive for the Junta leader. The former President Bedié still in exile in France, Emile Constant Bombet, his former senior minister, Mohamed Lamine Fadiga, another former minister were all disqualified for one reason or another.[69] General Guei also sabotaged the various initiatives of the international community, singularly the OAU's efforts, to find an acceptable solution to a situation with potentially grave implications for the entire West African sub-region.[70] Nothing was to stop his plans to remain head of state. However, these plans failed, when, on October 22, election day, the electorate voted massively for Laurent Gbagbo, the leader of the *Front Patriotique Ivoirien* (FPI). A long time opponent to the PDCI regime, he, like General Guei, is from western Côte d'Ivoire. Gbagbo too seemed to have accepted the "*Ivoirité*" thesis, if only tactically in order to eliminate Ouattara. It is widely believed that Gbagbo's candidacy was validated by the Guei controlled Supreme Court only because he was thought to be weak enough to allow and make more legitimate a first round victory for General Guei. To Laurent Gbagbo's credit, he called his supporters to refuse to accept Gen-

---

67. See "Strange Case," 18.

68. See also Jonathan Derrick, "No Way Ouattara," *West Africa*, 31 July–7 August 2000, 20–21.

69. Francis Kpatindé, "Les Jeux Sont Faits," *Jeune-Afrique/L'Intelligent*, 2074, 10–16 October, 2000, 16–18.

70. See Cersko Omunizua, "Hovering on the Brink," *West Africa*, 2–8 October, 2000 20–21.

eral Guei's electoral putsch and to replay the Yugoslav scenario that drove Slobodan Milosevic from power only a few weeks earlier.

To be sure, the lesson of the popular movement that chased General Guei from power is not likely to be lost on civil-military relations in Ivory Coast and elsewhere in the sub-region. However, as the unfolding events demonstrate, it was a grave mistake to overestimate its dissuasive effect for military men bent on asserting the power conferred by the gun and playing a role in the political arena particularly in a context where a deficient political leadership worsened various lingering crises. The ongoing crisis is but the patent manifestation of Côte d'Ivoire slow *adieu* to deeply flawed post-colonial political system and its authoritarian practices.

The Aftermath

After desperately attempting to cling to power by force of arms, in addition to sequestering the electoral commission members and using the troops, General Guei had to flee the palace when it became evident that the military, both officers and the rank and file had abandoned him *en masse*.[71] After a few days, he recognized Laurent Gbagbo as the head of state, thereby closing the disgraced military regime interlude. In a surrealist media event, president Gbagbo traveled to meet General Guei in Yamoussokro to sign with him an agreement sponsored by common French friends.[72] Power was back in the hand of a civilian, but it was by no means democratic. The new political dispensation was not to address, as a priority, the flawed civil military relations nor the other conditions that contributed to the coup in the first place. For one, it was under the newly constituted civilian regime that hundreds of people were massacred by security forces in *Yopougon*, a predominantly poor and northerner neighbor-

---

71. For a chronological account of the events that led to Guei's ouster see Albert Bourgi's "J'ai Vu l'Histoire Basculer," *Jeune-Afrique/L'Intelligent*, 2078, 7–13 November, 2000, 20–28; also Cersko Omunizua, "Chaos in Abidjan", *West Africa*, 30 October – 5 November, 2000, 9–12.

72. Francis Kpatindé, "Guei-Gbagbo: Les Secrets d'une Rencontre," *Jeune-Afrique/L'Intelligent*, 2080, 21–27 November, 18–21.

hood in Abidjan.[73] In the early days and weeks of the Gbagbo regime, dozens of opponents and nationals of Burkina Faso and Mali, Côte d'Ivoire's neighbors to the north, were tortured, raped, harassed, and imprisoned in various detention centers. While the failed military transition can be blamed for some of these events, for most it cannot. The discrimination against the RDR supporters and their harassment continued long after the new regime could have prevented or stopped them. It was under the civilian regime that Ouattara was, once again barred from running for parliament under the same pretexts as previously, and most leaders of the RDR arrested and charged with various crimes. A sure sign that the crucial civil military relations have not yet been addressed is that, amid rumors of impending military intervention, at least two serious coup attempt occurred since October 2000. Meanwhile, after the Guei debacle, countless soldiers were said to have simply vanished, among these the famous mastermind of the December 24,1999 mutiny, Boka Yapi. These soldiers were also said to have stashed large quantities of weapons. The September mutiny and its subsequent degeneration into a civil war with distinct regional and religious overtones have deep roots, but they are also the direct outcomes of the commissions and omissions by the post-October 2000 regime led by Laurent Gbagbo.

High Hopes and Missed Opportunity

When the flawed civil-military relations (broadly construed) that prevailed in the Ivory Coast are closely examined, the coup that toppled one of the longest running civilian regimes in Africa will no longer be viewed as a surprise. Reflected in the blind reliance on the presence of French troops and military advisors or the political, the ethnic and inter-service manipulation of the Ivoirian military, among other nefarious policies, they are the root causes of the coup. The coup itself, precipitated by the inept leadership, mismanagement and

---

73. See Assou Massou, "Abidjan en État de Choc," *Jeune-Afrique/L'Intelligent*, 2097, 7–13, 2000, 32–33.

crass behavior of president Bedié only brought to the surface, and in fact exacerbated the serious political and social crises that have been brewing in Côte d'Ivoire during the forty years of PDCI rule. The military intermission, supposed to prepare the transition to a truly democratic civilian regime did no such thing because of the equally disastrous leadership of General Robert Guei, and his murderous will to retain power. As mentioned earlier, the task the military junta, the CNSP, assigned itself was to "clean-up the Ivoirian house," hold free and fair elections after outfitting the country with a new functioning political system. Neither the constitution, nor practices or policy initiatives addressed seriously any of the crises that helped to propel the military into power. The critical component of a democratic order, i.e., the civilian democratic control of the military institution and other security sector elements, its frameworks and basic rules (including the presence and role of French military personnel) were not given the keen treatment they deserve given the circumstances. These issues are critical to any democratic regime. Unless they are seriously addressed, the condition that led to the various coup attempts and mutinies of the last several years will linger. And with them the risk of perpetual unstable civil-military relations, thereby delaying the country's and west Africa's farewell to instability.

Although short-lived and not expected to address seriously most of Ivory Coast's ills, the military interlude proved to be an unmitigated disaster. When he acceded to power after General Guei's debacle, Laurent Gbagbo had to his credit unquestioned political courage and acumen (mixed with troubling deceitfulness). However, he did not seem to measure the enormity of his task and the necessity to take advantage of the window of opportunity afforded him to carry out a far-reaching transformation of the political system whose defects he decried and fought against for decades. Unfortunately for Côte d'Ivoire, in light of his record, he never was able to graduate to the stature of statesman and remained stuck at the level of what can be labeled 'political adolescence' with a propensity to 'play politics' in the most objectionable and reckless meaning of the phrase. Laurent Gbagbo had the merit, however, to organize the "National Reconciliation Forum" in which all protagonists in Ivoirian politics were given a podium to vent their various grievances and to push various agen-

das on the state. Under the able leadership of Mr. Seydou Elimane Diarra a long time high level official, cabinet member under
Houphouet-Boigny, and Prime minister under General Guei, this
forum modeled on the South African Truth and Reconciliation Commission, overcame many obstacles. One of these was to convince the
major leaders, Bedie, Guei and Ouattara to participate. The much-
heralded forum allowed the airing, in a cathartic and therapeutic way,
of painful events and taboos in an effort to exorcise the demons that
seemed to have taken over and transformed the politics of the country. Not surprisingly, the nationality of Ouattara took center stage in
the Forum, one of the conclusions of which was that he should be issued a nationality certificate. The Forum also allowed the airing of
numerous other problems Ivory Coast has to address, including the
issues of ethnicity, regionalism, and prerequisites for national reconciliation. The Forum and other appeasing measures President Gbagbo
shrewdly took definitely seemed to reduce the level of political tension and enabled the much needed resumption of economic dealings
with France (which eagerly obliged), the E. U. and the IMF and World
Bank. A false note to what appeared as an important and necessary
step back from the brink of disaster was the acquittal of suspected
perpetrators of the massacre of *Yopougon* in which dozens (possibly
hundreds), were executed by security forces as Gbagbo came to
power. Soon it became evident that it was a mistake to underestimate
the risk of breakdown by equating the reduction of tensions with a
return of stability. The easing of tensions was brought about mainly
by symbolic measures and various international pressures. It was not
due to a genuine and sustained effort by President Gbagbo's regime
to stamp out the dangers of further destabilization or make strides
toward democracy and stability. A telling dimension of the impending Ivoirian tragedy in the early 2002 was played out in the fact that,
the president of the forum, and former Prime Minister, who is from
the north, had difficulties obtaining a national identity card, because
his name did not sound "Ivoirian" enough.[74] This and similar mani-

---

74. See Francois Soudan,"L'Homme qui Veut Sauver la Côte d'Ivoire," *Jeune-
Afrique/L'Intelligent*, 2001, September 11–17 2001, 30–33.

festations of this absurd reality did not bode well for many of the RDR militants and northerners generally and, sure enough, sharply increased tensions when the electoral lists were due for renewal, and a new national identity card created. When President Gbagbo, for self-serving reasons and under the pretense of reducing the cost of running the state had some military units slated for discharge, the stage was largely set for the full-blown national crisis Côte d'Ivoire has been grappling with since September 19, 2002. There is no evidence that the late General Guei was personally implicated in the September 19 events. However, he was believed to be still bitter and humiliated although he had converted into an old-fashioned party leader. Guei had stated in an interview that all he needed was a telephone call to "burn Côte d'Ivoire" if he so wished.[75] His words proved prophetic since one of the rebel groups now fighting the Gbagbo regime, the *Movement pour la Justice et la Paix* (MJP), claims to want to avenge his death. Many of the original mutinous soldiers now organized under the political movement (*Movement Patriotique de Côte d'Ivoire*) were allegedly recruited by General Guei.

The prevailing situation amply confirms the analysis developed above. As the crisis unfolded, coming very close to escalating into a full blown civil war, horrendous human rights abuses, were committed by both sides to the conflict continuing a troubling feature of Ivoirian practices. The orgy of violence against civilians and, ominously, the appearance of death squads on the side of the Gbagbo regime are troubling signs for the future of a truly democratic political system with a subordinated military in a unified and peaceful Côte d'Ivoire. Consequently, Côte d'Ivoire has moved dangerously close to an even worse breakdown than Liberia and Sierra Leone experienced. Up to now these two countries were considered the worst possible scenarios in West Africa. Only a swift French intervention prevented the collapse of Gbagbo's regime, stabilized the situation and forced the rebels and Gbagbo to negotiate. For now, the risk of an imminent outbreak of fighting has considerably receded and thanks to

---

75. Francois Soudan, "Que Veut Guei?" *Jeune-Afrique/L'Intelligent*, 2097, 20 March 2001, 24–25.

the combined efforts of the ECOWAS, the U.N., and France have produced following compromises in Marcoussis, Lomé, and Accra, a government of national reconciliation. However, the situation has by no means normalized as the stalemate over the appointment of the ministers of Defense and the Interior indicates. A severe test to this arrangement will come as the 2005 election approaches, even sooner if President Gbagbo reneges on his commitments as he has done already during the negotiations. Whatever the outcome of the Ivoirian crisis, even if the sub-region is ultimately spared humanitarian, economic, and political catastrophes, it will scar the country forever and will postpone by several years the ushering in of a truly democratic system. It would have been another missed opportunity to overhaul radically a deeply flawed system.

CHAPTER II

THE MILITARY AND "DEMOCRATIZATION" IN THE GAMBIA: 1994–2002

When junior officers of the Gambia National Army overthrew[1] the democratically elected government of Sir Dawda Jawara on 22 July 1994, they ended the longest surviving democracy and the tenure of the longest serving head of state in Africa. Under the leadership of Lt. Yahya Jammeh, they created the Armed Forces Provisional Council (AFPRC), and promised to restore democracy, transparency and accountability to government. Jammeh charged that Jawara had presided over a system that was riddled with corruption and that as "soldiers with a difference" they would protect human rights and govern under the rule of law. As is often the case, the coup generated considerable excitement and high expectations among Gambians, especially the youth. Jammeh, who at the time was under thirty years of age, projected himself as a populist reformer whose sole objective was to clean up corruption and then return the country to civilian rule. In time, however, this promise appeared unconvincing as Jammeh's

---

1. At the time of his ouster, Sir Dawda ruled The Gambia for twenty-four years as President, from 1970–94. He was Prime Minister from 1965–70 and Chief Minister before independence in 1962–65, making him one of the longest serving leaders in Africa. For discussions of the coup. see, A. Saine, "The Coup d'etat in The Gambia, 1994: The End of The First Republic," *Armed Forces & Society*, 23, 1(1996), 97–111; Z. Yeebo, *State of Fear in Paradise: The Military Coup in The Gambia* (London: Africa Research & Information Bureau, 1995); J. A. Wiseman & E. Vidler, "The July 1994 Coup d'État in The Gambia: The End of an Era?" *The Roundtable*, 333, (1995), 53–63.

actions indicated that he would stay in power for as long as he could. Combined international economic sanctions and domestic pressure, however, cut a four-year transition timetable to civilian rule to two.[2] This culminated in presidential and national assembly elections on 26 September 1996 and 2 January 1997, respectively.[3]

Jammeh, having earlier resigned his commission, subsequently contested and won the presidential election as The Gambia's second president. However the elections were conducted under conditions that were deemed neither free nor fair by the Commonwealth and the rest of the international community. A plethora of irregularities, including a doctored constitution, the banning of major pre-coup political parties and politicians, a monopoly of the media, and acts of intimidation and violence against the opposition, seriously undermined the credibility of the electoral process. In the end, it was a transition program and in particular, a presidential election, that was manipulated from the very beginning to suit the political aspirations of Jammeh. The AFPRC was the sole arbiter and played by rules it created to tilt an already uneven playing field further in Jammeh's favor. Predictably, international condemnation of the election results was swift and severe and Ousainou Darboe, leader of the opposition United Democratic Party (UDP), refused to accept them "because they did not reflect the wishes of the Gambian people." Consequently, since 1996, The Gambia's political landscape has been mired in controversy over the legitimacy of the Alliance for the Patriotic Re-orientation and Construction (APRC) Government, rules of the game, in addition to allegations of corruption angled against Jammeh.

The primary objective of this chapter is to describe and analyze the process of "democratization" under a quasi-military regime in The Gambia. Additionally, it seeks to provide policy recommendations with the primary objective of helping to unhinge the current politi-

---

2. The results of the presidential elections were hotly disputed by the opposition parties and condemned internationally. A. Saine, "The Presidential and National Assembly Elections in The Gambia," *Electoral Studies*, 16, 4 (1997), p. 554–59.

3. A. Saine, "The Presidential and National Assembly Elections in The Gambia," *Electoral Studies*, 16, 4 (1997), p. 554.

cal impasse between the APRC Government and opposition parties. The latter was particularly important in helping Gambians evaluate the presidential elections of October 2001. Thus, the chapter is subdivided into four sections. Section one provides an overview of the Jawara years (1965–94) and the causes of his ouster. In section two, emphasis is placed on the transition program to civilian rule and the presidential and national assembly elections in 1996 and 1997, respectively. Section three evaluates human rights protection under the AFPRC and APRC regimes. The protection and/or abuse of human rights are a good litmus test of democracy and democratization. The fourth section provides a conclusion and relevant policy recommendations to enhance and accelerate the democratization process in The Gambia. An important assumption of this chapter is that while the 1996/1997 elections represented modest steps in the direction of democratic government from military rule, they did not mean a permanent military withdrawal from politics. Instead, political events following the elections, tended to increase military involvement in the political arena, which in turn had negative effects on "democratization" and the protection of human rights.

The Jawara Years: 1965–94

The politics of The Gambia since independence in 1965 are inextricably tied to the life and personality of its first president Sir Dawda Kairaba Jawara. A veterinarian by training, Sir Dawda crafted a political system in The Gambia that allowed for the protection of basic human rights premised on a free-market capitalist economy.[4] Additionally, a pro-Western foreign policy earned him the respect and financial support of the international community.[5]

Reviewing The Gambia's political history under Jawara, however, resembles a plateau occasionally marred by volcanic eruptions. The

---

4. For this see, A. Saine, "The Military and Human Rights in The Gambia: 1994–1999" *Journal of Third World Studies*, Vol. XIX, No. 2, 2002.

5. A. Saine, "The Foreign Policy of The Gambia since the Coup: 1994–1999," *Journal of Commonwealth and Comparative Politics*, Vol. 38, No. 2, 2000.

general image, as projected perhaps too often to the world outside, was that of a mini-state adept at survival, able, in spite of underdevelopment, to run an open society. With a multiparty democracy, The Gambia under Jawara also encapsulated both the problems and opportunities of small states.[6] In this picture the attempted coup[7] of 1981 and for that matter, the coup of 1994, were portrayed as aberrations. On the economic front, despite years of claimed economic success, The Gambia under Jawara continued to have one of the lowest living standards in the continent and ranked 163 in the world out of 174 countries according to the UNDP Human Development Index.[8] Thus, The Gambia's paradox under Jawara lay in the fact that it was a mini-state whose viability as a sovereign state at independence was in question. In spite of the odds, The Gambia managed to build a relatively open economy and a functioning democracy, yet achieved a very low level of development. Clearly, while part of the problem lay in elite corruption and enrichment, the overriding cause was, more generally, the poor performance of public institutions. Poor factor endowments compounded human shortcomings, which, in addition to a tiny size, and recurrent droughts in the 1970s, exasperated existing problems.

These challenges not withstanding, Jawara oversaw a country in which the respect for the rule of law and the protection of fundamental rights, even for those who opposed his rule were its defining qualities. Consequently, he engendered in Gambia's political culture a level of tolerance amongst the population that was the envy of larger and more economically endowed countries. Growing social cleavages and tensions were assuaged through an informal system of ethnic proportional representation. In addition, a relatively strong economy, heavily subsidized by external donors that deemed the cautious policies of Gambia's leadership worthy of emulation, worked in tandem

---

6. *Ibid.*, p. 4.

7. *Ibid.*, p. 5; also see, A. Hughes, "The Attempted Coup d'État of 30 July 1981," in A. Hughes (ed.) *The Gambia: Studies in Society and Politics*, (Birmingham: Centre of West African Studies Series 3, 1991), p. 101.

8. The Gambia Country Study: *Economist Intelligence Unit*, 3rd quarter, 1994, p. 20.

to pacify an increasingly restless population, but in doing so, gave the leadership a false sense of invincibility.

The immediate causes of the 1994 coup against Jawara are to be found, however, in the growing loss of legitimacy in the policies of the Peoples Progressive Party (PPP) Government. Together with internal party factionalism, growing social inequalities, and in particular, the disparity of living conditions between senior Nigerian and junior Gambian officers, in the end, proved decisive in Jawara's ouster. Thus, the coup was also led as much against the Nigerian officers, who headed the army, as against the regime itself.[9] The Gambia under Jawara maintained cordial relations with Nigeria and in so doing, Jawara supported Nigeria's military role in Liberia by providing Gambian troops. In fact, by the mid-1990s, Nigerian officers headed and trained the Gambia National Army (GNA).

The condemnation of the coup by the Commonwealth, Western financial institutions, the EU, the UK and other development partners of The Gambia, and their subsequent economic sanctions, had a chilling effect on the coup and the economy. A British Foreign Office "travel advise" in November 1994, four months after the coup, coupled with a similar travel advise issued by the Scandinavians urging their tourists not to visit The Gambia because of "political instability," almost destroyed the tourist industry. Also, the fact that 80 per cent of The Gambia's national budget was funded by the EU, Japan, the UK, and international financial institutions meant that the sanctions almost crippled the economy.[10] The sanctions had an immediate negative effect on the projects outlined in the development programs, in addition to low tax revenue, due in part to dislocation in trade caused by foreign exchange shortage.

Consequently, suspended bilateral aid and balance of payment assistance provoked two main reactions. The first was a defensive reaction from the AFPRC itself that "with aid or without aid, The Gambia would maintain an independent state, run by Gambians in the interest of Gambians." The second came generally from government

---

9. A. Saine, 'The Coup d'etat in The Gambia,' pp. 102–3.
10. *West Africa*, 13–19 February 1995, pp. 386–87.

officials and the public at large, who felt that the sanctions were un-justifiable.[11] However, with sanctions in place, government coffers were being quickly depleted. An alleged counter coup in November 1994 against the regime, combined with Western sanctions to create an atmosphere of growing AFPRC insecurity domestically.

The Military and "Democratization": 1994–96

Aware of mounting domestic and international pressure against a four-year timetable to civilian rule, the AFPRC agreed to a two-year timetable to culminate in presidential elections in June 1996. By December 1995, Chairman Jammeh appointed an eight-person Provisional Independent Electoral Commission (PIEC) charged with the tasks of organizing the presidential and national assembly elections, a referendum over a draft constitution and voter registration. However, an all-pervasive atmosphere of enforced silence engendered by a ban on political activity and political parties began to raise doubts over the AFPRC's commitment to democracy and the holding of elections. The passage of decrees 70 and 71 requiring all individuals wishing to start newspapers to execute a bond of D100, 000 (US $10, 000) and all existing newspapers to do the same, cast doubt on AFPRC intentions.[12] These decrees effectively gutted The Gambia's once thriving and critical independent press, a detailed discussion of which is undertaken in section three on human rights. AFPRC intentions and sincerity regarding democracy and democratization became increasingly suspect however, when it expelled the representative of the U.S. based National Democratic Institute. And when, on 12 April 1996, two months before the scheduled presidential election in June, the AFPRC announced that the balloting would be delayed by six weeks. The reasons regarding resource constraints and the EU's alleged failure to underwrite the cost of producing needed election material were seen generally by the public as delay tactics by the regime. Meanwhile,

---

11. *Ibid.*, p. 367.
12. A. Saine, "The Military's Managed Transition to 'Civilian Rule' in The Gambia," *Journal of Political and Military Sociology*, 26 (Winter 1998), p. 165.

with the ban on political activity still in place, the AFPRC's political wing, the July 22 Movement, had, with official blessing, been preparing for the presidential elections and campaigning since its founding on 15 July 1995.

With a doctored constitution[13] that was adopted in a referendum on 8 August 1996, it was clear that Jammeh would contest the presidential election, and would be the victor over hastily formed political parties and their leaders. Not withstanding, the recommendations of the Constitutional Review Commission (CRC) to have a forty-year age requirement for the president, Jammeh decided to keep it at thirty so that he could run. Additionally, in spite of the insistence of Gambians to have term-limits for the president, Jammeh ignored this important recommendation, even though he made much of the fact that Jawara had been in power for almost thirty years. Perhaps the most troublesome issue about the constitution is the disqualification from seeking the presidency of all persons who have been "compulsorily retired," "terminated" or "dismissed" from public office or have been found liable by a commission of inquiry for "misconduct, negligence, corruption, or improper behavior."[14] Such a sweeping clause left the door open for Jammeh to use and abuse the constitution to serve his political ends. In fact, this is exactly what he did. This sweeping clause was to be the precursor to Jammeh banning all the major pre-coup political parties and politicians on 12 August 1996. In addition, the $1000 deposit required of other presidential candidates and the risk of forfeiture if the candidate was to receive less than 40 per cent of the votes cast, meant that all but the incumbent's candidature would be viable. Flaws such as these and many more in the adopted constitution were ominous signs that Jammeh was consciously designing these policies to eliminate potential competition.

On 17 August, Jammeh lifted the ban on political activity, declared his candidacy for the 26 September presidential election, and launched his APRC party on 27 August, a month before the election. The only serious candidate was Ousainou Darboe of the UDP

---

13. *Ibid.*, p. 166.
14. *Ibid.*, p. 165.

(United Democratic Party). Darboe, a veteran lawyer, received considerable support from the three banned political parties and politicians, but not enough to ensure his victory. The remaining three presidential candidates were no match for Jammeh's war chest. In addition, Jammeh's monopoly of the national media outlets gave him an added advantage over the weak and poorly financed opposition. Predictably, Jammeh "received" 56 percent of the vote to Darboe's 35 percent.[15] It was an election process marred by violence and deaths of opposition party supporters. The Commonwealth and the West, in general, denounced the election results and a campaign process in which Jammeh's major political opponents were banned and in fear for their lives. In fact, when the polls closed at 9 p.m. on 26 September, Darboe, members of his family, seven party supporters, including Jammeh's former external affairs minister, the UDP's senior administrative secretary Sidia Sagnia, sought refuge at the Senegalese embassy in Banjul, The Gambia's capital. They vowed to leave the embassy only if assured of their safety.

In the end, the outcome of the national assembly election was predictable. The APRC won 33 seats to the opposition's combined total of 12 seats in the new national assembly. With four additional seats of nominated members, president-elect Jammeh received a majority and de facto control over matters of state.[16] Thus, a variety of defects and irregularities in the adopted constitution seriously affected the credibility of the transition program and the presidential election in particular. The transition program and its doctored outcomes represented a contravention of the law and made a mockery of the most basic principles of democracy. In so doing, the "democratization" process, was eclipsed by the APRC in its effort to hold on to power. It was another military intervention, but this time with the use of the ballot box to lend civilian trappings to a de-facto military regime. This process of "democratization" through civilianization, has been used frequently by incumbent military leaders in the West Africa subregion to cling on to power.[17]

---

15. *Ibid.*, p. 165.
16. A. Saine, " The 1996/1997 Presidential and National Assembly Elections in The Gambia," *Electoral Studies*, 16, 4 (1997), p. 556.

Perhaps the most immediate victims of this transition program were democracy, democratic principles and governance under the rule of law. The period 1994–96 was also characterized by human rights violations, the magnitude and intensity of which were never before seen in The Gambia. The muzzling of the press through intimidation, arrests, trials, detentions, the beating of local and deportation of foreign journalists effectively silenced opposition to the AFPRC. The "mysterious" deaths of key ministers of the AFPRC, deaths that have yet to be accounted for, have left a bitter taste in the mouths of most Gambians.[18] Added to these was the widespread beating and torture of ordinary citizens by the national Intelligence Agency (NIA), the repressive arm of the AFPRC. (It is on these rights violations that we now focus.)

Civil and Political Rights under the AFPRC: 1994–96

A clear and important example of the development of authoritarianism and the decline of democratic principles and freedoms under Jammeh, was the relationship between the AFPRC and the independent press. Since independence in 1965, an independent and critical press has existed in The Gambia. Independent newspapers such as *The Gambia Onward, The Gambia Worker* and the Government owned *Gambia News Bulletin* began a tradition of debate and critical analysis rivaled by few in the West Africa sub-region. In time, these debates engendered in The Gambian press a vigorous culture of dissent and criticism against state policy. In later years, *Foroyaa (Freedom)* emerged as a critical newspaper and an important outlet for the political party, the People's Democratic Organization for Indepen-

---

17. See A. Saine, "The Soldier-Turn-Presidential Candidate: A Comparison of Flawed 'Democratic' Transitions in Ghana and Gambia," *The Journal of Political and Military Sociology*, Vol. 28, No. 2, 2000.

18. Military rule in The Gambia has been a traumatizing experience for most Gambians. Insulated from the experiences of citizens of other military-run countries, Gambians have since lost their innocence with the brutality they are subjected to on a daily basis by the Jammeh regime.

dence and Socialism (PDOIS). Its leaders, Halifa Sallah and Sidia Jatta have been unflinching in their criticism of the AFPRC and the deposed Jawara regime. Consequently, both men have been the targets of AFPRC arrest and harassment. In the early 1990s, *The Daily Observer* and *The Point* newspapers added significantly to the exposure of corruption in government. These criticisms, in addition to revelations of corruption by the press, contributed in no small measure to Jawara's ouster from office. While government relations with the press were benign following independence, they became increasingly confrontational a few years prior to the coup.

Not withstanding Jammeh's call for the press to "criticize" him, according to Ebrima Ceesay, a former editor of *The Daily Observer*, living in exile in the United Kingdom, the first casualty of what was an eternal gagging of the press was Kenneth Best,[19] the Liberian proprietor and Managing Editor of *The Daily Observer*. On 30 October 1994, just three months after the coup, Best was deported from The Gambia. Since then, more than a dozen non-Gambian journalists have been expelled, simply for writing newspaper articles the AFPRC did not like. Many Gambian journalists were also arrested, in some cases detained and later tried in court for newspaper articles critical of the regime. The brutal beating of Abdullah Savage, arrest and detention of Ebrima Sankareh[20] and harassment of Momodou Kebbeh, both of whom were high school teachers and journalists and now living in exile in the United States ended the honeymoon between Jammeh and the press, as Ceesay noted.[21]

In late March 1995, a new round of arrests of journalists began after *The Point* carried a report on a riot at a jail where most of the regime's political prisoners were being detained. Three journalists from *The Point*, Pap Saine, Alieu Badara Sowe and Ebrima Ernest were taken into custody and charged with "publication of false news with intent to cause fear and alarm the public." They were later ac-

---

19. Kenneth Best now lives and teaches journalism in the United States of America.

20. J. Wiseman, "Military Rule in The Gambia: An Interim Assessment," *Third World Quarterly*, Vol. 17, (1996), p. 924.

21. *Ibid.*, p. 924.

quitted but Saine's passport was seized and Ebrima Ernest was deported to Sierra Leone. In March 1996 a renewed campaign against the press began with the regime's decision to order the Government Printing Department not to produce independent newspapers. A couple of days later, the editors of *The Daily Observer, The Point,* and *Foroyaa* were taken to court and charged with a technical breach of Decrees 70 and 71. These charges were later dismissed in court. Loraine Forster, the Advertising Manager of *The Daily Observer* was detained for reporting the defection of the regime's Spokesman's to the U.S. Additionally, Baboucarr Sankanu was detained for filing a report to the BBC, and a Nigerian journalist, Chikeluba Kenechuku, was arrested and beaten up.

Professional organizations such as the Gambia Bar Association (GBA), the Association of Gambian Journalists (AGJ), and the Gambia Worker's Union (GWU) have all been vocal in their condemnation of the AFPRC's draconian laws, human rights abuses and the arbitrary arrests of journalists and citizens. The National Intelligence Agency (NIA) established after the coup and currently serving as the repressive arm of the regime, routinely harassed journalists and dissidents. In effect, the NIA succeeded in engendering a "culture of silence," insecurity and suspicion amongst Gambians. It is also notorious for its brutal beating and torture of dissidents. Accordingly, the press has become more circumspect, but continues its attacks on the regime indirectly by highlighting human rights abuses in Nigeria or Sierra Leone.

Yet, AFPRC rights violations were not limited to journalists alone. The mass arrest of some ex-politicians and citizens, as well as the trials of Momodou C. Cham, Omar Jallow, and the ex-president's brother in law, the late Ousainou Njie, in October 1995, indicated a rising tide of rights violation by the AFPRC. These arrests were related to an alleged planned demonstration on behalf of the ex-president. In addition, the frequent arrests of Waa Lamin Juwara, a former Member of Parliament, Pa Modou Faal, president of the Gambia Workers Union, Ousainou Darboe, leader of the United Democratic Party and ex-ministers of the erstwhile Jawara government, continued through 1995 to early 1996. State capacity has been adversely affected by the premature retirement of seasoned civil servants, their termination from government service, and their departure for reasons of job insecurity. Consequently, the instability created by Jammeh's frequent dismissals of cabinet ministers, including individuals such as Fafa Mbye, Nymasata Sanneh, Kumba Ceesay-Marraneh, Musa Bittaye, Balla Jahumpha, Fatoumata Tambajang, to name a few, reflects growing splits between the Council's civilian members and Jammeh.[22] Dissent by military members of the council against Jammeh was also common.

The brutally crushed countercoup against the regime on 11 November, 1994 led to the deaths of about 40 soldiers and the alleged summary executions of many more. The arrest of Chairman Jammeh's closest associates, Vice-Chairman Sanna Sabally and Captain Sadibou Haidara in connection with an alleged assassination attempt against Jammeh on 27 January 1995 was evidence of severe divisions within the AFPRC. Also, the arrests and imprisonment of Captains Sheriff Mbye, Mamat Omar Cham and Samsudeen 'Sam' Sarr, who were appointed to cabinet posts after the coup, started a trend in regime insecurity. The sudden deaths of Interior Minister Sadibou Haidara and Finance Minister Ousman 'Koro' Ceesay 19 days later in a burnt-out car remains a mystery to this day, in spite of opposition demands for an investigation. The failure of the regime to investigate these deaths has resulted in mounting suspicion of Yahya Jammeh and Edward Singhateh. By August 1994, the arrests of Lt. Alhaji Kanteh and Captain Kambi had brought the number of military and police detainees to around thirty out of an 800-man army. These arrests were made based on Decree No. 3 which gave special powers to the AFPRC Vice-President "in the interest of National Security" to arrest anyone, including members of the AFPRC.[23]

Predictably, since its assumption of power in July 1994, the AFPRC regime had come under much attack for its poor human rights record

---

22. The civil service is now characterized by growing job insecurity. Jammeh has effectively fired all those he suspects of disloyalty. Many seasoned civil servants and technocrats have been forced to leave the country. In so doing, state capacity has been weakened further. The average tenure of ministers is about a year.

23. A. Saine, "The Coup d'Etat in The Gambia," p. 103.

and especially for its decisions to restore the death penalty. By October 1996, however, the human rights situation improved somewhat. Of the 30 military and police personnel detained since the coup, 11 were released unconditionally. A majority of the 35 political detainees arrested in October 1995 allegedly for organizing a demonstration on behalf of the ex-president were also released. The further release of 4 soldiers detained since 1994 and the granting of amnesty to 20 prisoners in February and 13 more in July signaled Jammeh's intention to contest the impending presidential election in September 1996. Yet on 12 August 1996, Jammeh again banned the three major pre-coup parties, including the PPP, from politics. The former President, former Vice-Presidents, Ministers and other politicians were also banned and Jammeh also imposed penalties of life imprisonment or a $100, 000 fine should they engage in political activity.[24] This, in effect, eliminated all the viable opposition candidates from contesting the presidential election.

While the AFPRC did not exile its opponents, three senior officials of the former government, ex-President Jawara, Vice-President Saihou Sabally and Secretary General of the Civil Service, Abdou Sara Janha, remain outside the country and under threat of arrest and detention should they return. In addition, The Gambia's former Ambassadors to the United Kingdom, the United States of America and the Kingdom of Saudi Arabia (Momodou Bobb, Ousman Sallah and Abdoulie Bojang, respectively), as well as other middle ranking government employees (such as Abdoulie Kebbeh), decided not to return for fear of arrest. The AFPRC also engaged in the seizure of private property and travel documents and often placed armed guards at homes whose owners were suspected or proven guilty of embezzlement or misappropriation of government funds. The AFPRC also froze financial accounts of individuals under suspicion and prohibited the transfer of their property. In particular, the former Auditor General, Abou Denton, and Modou Dibba, a former official of the now defunct Gambia Cooperative Union (GCU), were evicted from

---

24. A. Saine, "The 1996/1997 Presidential and National Assembly Elections," p. 555.

their homes. Denton in particular was found to have built several luxurious homes at government expense. These measures received mixed reactions, not so much to the seizure of homes per se, but to the manner in which these individuals were evicted and humiliated. These violations, property seizures and the subsequent release of dissidents occurred amidst preparations for the presidential election.

Social and Economic Rights

The claim that only more development can guarantee individual human rights is weak.[25] This is because development strategies in Africa and The Gambia, in particular, have generally enriched those in power at the expense of the citizenry.[26] Thus, such a claim cannot often be used as the basis upon which to justify the primacy of economic rights. Also, Africa's generally dismal record on human rights provides little evidence that the more affluent countries have done better in implementing human rights provisions.[27] In fact, despite The Gambia's material poverty, it had an unrivaled distinction in Africa for having protected its citizen's rights under Jawara. Yet, perhaps because of Jawara's emphasis on civil and political rights and an open market economy, he tended to partially relegate to the latter, the articulation of economic rights. In hindsight, this neglect proved damaging and made him vulnerable to criticism. After almost 30 years of Jawara's uninterrupted leadership, The Gambia still had only two government owned high schools and hospitals, which, incidentally, were built by the British during the colonial period.

---

25. S. Mahmud, "The State of Human Rights in Africa in the 1990s," *Human Rights Quarterly*, Vol. 15 (1993), p. 494.

26. J. Mbaku, "Democratization and the Crisis of Policy Reform in Developing Countries," in M. S. Kimenyi and J. M. Mbaku (Eds.), *Institutions and Collective Choice in Developing Countries: Applications of the theory of Public Choice* (Aldershot: Ashgate Publishing Company, 1999), p. 335.

27. S. Mahmud, "The State of Human Rights in Africa," p. 494. For a positive evaluation of the military and its contributory role to democracy and development, see, Phillip C. Aka, "The Military and Democratization in Africa," *Journal of Third World Studies*, Vol. XVI, no. 1 (1999).

Upon assuming power, the AFPRC further justified its coup on the basis of "corrective" rhetoric and appeared committed to improving the lives of Gambians and those in the rural areas especially. The regime's construction of two new high schools, five middle schools, a large rural hospital, several rural clinics, and a new television station (the first in the country), endeared Jammeh to the population at large. The AFPRC under Jammeh's leadership also refurbished The Gambia's only international airport and Radio Gambia's facilities. The AFPRC also resurfaced roads in urban areas, especially Banjul's, and rekindled a sense of seriousness toward government service seldom observed during the Jawara era. A University Extension-Program planned in the Jawara era with a Canadian University was given momentum. These were coupled with reforms in education, the major effect of which was greater access to high school education for The Gambia's growing primary school student population. Sanitation in Banjul improved and was accompanied by a beautification program. Markets and food stores were adequately provisioned with the basic staples: rice, cooking oil, tomatoes, etc.

Jammeh's rule also opened up access to government scholarships for study abroad among those most unlikely to win them, the poor. It was common knowledge in Jawara's time that these scholarships went predominantly to the children of elite and wealthy Gambians. Independence Day celebrations on 18 February at the State House became an affair not only of the elite but of common Gambians as well. An air of optimism and confidence filled these festivities. Indigenous music and guests clad in traditional garb added color, pomp and circumstance to July 22 Day celebrations. Branches of the July 22 Movement, the propaganda arm of the AFPRC, were established nationally, partly to give Gambians a sense of belonging to Jammeh's historic experiment in "populist social change." Former government dissidents were given positions of power or prestige. In fact, it seemed as though the only qualification one needed to be in a position of power or prestige was to have been a former dissident. Civil servants suspected of loyalty to the deposed government were sacked or prematurely retired. In the course of six months, the AFPRC succeeded in supplanting the civilian political class with a growing politico-military elite. Under Jammeh, the council included four women. This is an unprecedented number in The Gambia's political history.

However, Jammeh's detractors, mostly members of the elite, vilified him for his lack of social graces and his erratic cabinet changes and firings. Arch 22, a huge monument to the coup constructed at the capital city's entrance, was termed a monstrosity and an exercise in futility and waste. In time, however, the criticisms seemed appropriate. Jammeh and some of his ministers gradually adapted well to the lifestyles of those they deposed. The fancy cars, residence in the most affluent areas, frequent foreign trips and improved social and economic status, engendered suspicion and skepticism of the "soldiers with a difference." The rhetoric of probity, accountability and transparency began to fall on deaf ears and, before long, Jammeh's rule could not be distinguished from Jawara's. Indeed, Jammeh had become a politician, a member group he often castigated and called a "bunch of thieves, rogues and drunks."

The low level of economic development in The Gambia made the provision of economic rights and improved welfare conditions for the majority of Gambians difficult. In a country where 60 per cent of the population lives below the poverty line, of which 40 per cent is classified "food-poor," it would have required more resources and careful planning to achieve such welfare goals. While the provision of these rights is certainly long-term, their fulfillment seemed bleak. Cuts in international economic assistance[28] coupled with a high population growth rate of 3 per cent and rising external debt[29] made their realization difficult. Thus, "the right to development," which was a key goal of the AFPRC, appeared unlikely in the short-term even when its future realization seemed probable. Jammeh's critics also charged that these poorly conceived development projects were inappropriate and that he embarked upon them to muster support for himself should he decide to contest the presidential elections. These criticisms became increasingly more convincing as Jammeh campaigned for the presidency. He appealed to Gambians to support his development

---

28. *West Africa*, 13–19 February 1995, pp. 386–87.
29. *Economist Intelligence Unit*, 2nd quarter, 1995, p. 19.

agenda and compared his accomplishments to those of the previous regime.

However, it seems that collective rights showered from above without mass participation and input do not portend well for a sustained and just distribution of state resources.[30] This is because these policies are often driven by elite interests and do not have the lives they aim to improve at their core. Furthermore, the AFPRC's basis in the military did not augur well for collective economic rights protection as Jammeh and some of his Council members worked frantically to improve their otherwise poor economic status. In the end, it is this politico-military class, handpicked civilian supporters and building contractors that benefited more from the change of government. This outcome in particular was to deal a major blow to Jammeh's putative commitment to democracy, democratization and human rights.

Human Rights under the APRC: 1997–2002

The assumption of power by the Alliance for Patriotic Re-orientation and Construction (APRC) Government, an acronym suspiciously similar to AFPRC, in January 1997, saw a further deterioration in the human rights situation of The Gambia. In particular, the arrests and torture of 8 UDP supporters[31] in June 1997 by the NIA was condemned by human rights groups and opposition parties alike. A national uproar was similarly created when a group of security officers allegedly introduced a truncheon into the genitals of a woman detainee. To many observers, the change in government was only in name and not in substance. Yaya Drammeh's death while in detention in May of 1997 continues to be shrouded in secrecy. Drammeh was

---

30. J. M. Mbaku, "Bureaucratic Corruption in Africa," in J. M. Mbaku (Ed.) *Corruption and the crisis of Institutional Reform in Africa*, (Lewiston: The Edwin Mellen Press, 1998), pp. 33–35. Also see, J. M. Mbaku, "Making the State Relevant to African Societies," in J. M. Mbaku (Ed), *Preparing Africa for the Twenty-First Century: Strategies for Peaceful Coexistence and Sustainable Development* (Brookfield: Ashgate Publishing Company, 1999), pp. 299–333.

31. See, *The Gambia: Report on Human Rights for 1997*, (U. S. Department of State, January 30, 1998), p. 14.

one of five men accused of treason for his role in the attack of the Farafenni army barracks in November 1995, in which six soldiers were killed. Since Jammeh's coming to power in 1994, there were two other military incidents at army camps in Kartong, July 1997, and Bakau, January 2000.[32]

Journalists continue to be harassed and Decrees 70 and 71, introduced in 1995 remain in force. In January 1997, three foreign nationals, all employed by *The Daily Observer*, were deported. In November, the Editor-in-Chief, Ellicott Seade, a Ghanaian was expelled. In late 1998, an independent radio station, Citizen FM, belonging to Baboucarr Gaye, the owner of the now defunct *The New Citizen*, was confiscated, ostensibly to silence him. International pressure prevented the government from prohibiting the state radio from broadcasting programs critical of Female Genital Mutilation (FGM). The practice is common in The Gambia and there is mounting domestic and international pressure for its eradication. Meanwhile, the political rights of Gambians worsen, with diminishing prospects for improved living conditions.

The year 2000 was ushered in with blood and violence. Two military officers were killed and one severely wounded by security officers for allegedly masterminding a counter coup. One of the killed officers was pursued and shot dead at Banjul's crowded Albert Market, while helpless shoppers watched in dismay and disgust. The alleged counter coup turned out to be a hoax staged by the Jammeh regime in a desperate effort to neutralize potential and imagined enemies.[33] Also, on 10 April 2000, police in Banjul opened fire on a student demonstration killing at least 14 people, including a journalist. The students were protesting the recent death of a high school student, Ebrima Barry, who was allegedly tortured by fire fighters, and the reported rape of a 13-year-old girl by a police officer. Five more stu-

---

32. A. Hughes, "'Democratisation' Under the Military in The Gambia: 1994–2000," *Journal of Commonwealth and Comparative Politics*, vol. 38, no. 3, November 2000), p. 10.

33. This is indicative of the growing insecurity of Jammeh and his regime. While investigations into these shootings have been promised, they were not carried out.

dents were killed a day after in the provinces for staging demonstrations in support of their slain friends on 10 April. In all, 14 people, including a journalist, were killed and over sixty individuals received life-threatening injuries.[34] While Barry's death and the rape of a young girl were the immediate causes of the student demonstrations, the root causes were much deeper. A police state with unrestrained brutal repression of dissent, mounting economic hardship, societal frustration over official corruption and numerous deaths and "disappearances" yet to be investigated and accounted for, constitute the backdrop against which these demonstrations and subsequent slaughter occurred. The fact that security officers staged a counter coup and killed two fellow officers and defenseless school children, are testimony to the pervasive and perhaps perverse paranoia of Jammeh and his security forces. They are also indicative of the extent to which the latter will go to maintain a tight grip on power.

Recent events in The Gambia suggest a return to more authoritarian practices of the overt military rule period, when unrestrained state violence was used in a relentless effort to hold on to political power. Today, old demons of clientelism, corruption, arbitrariness, violence and the abuse of power haunt Gambians. This lack of restraint and oversight exhibited by the security forces attest to the need for citizen control of the state, but more importantly, for the state to control itself. Equally worrisome is the regime's insensitive unconditional indemnity of the security personnel responsible for the April 10 and 11 slaughter and the continuing detention and imprisonment of political prisoners such as Dumo Saho. The year 2001 witnessed the lifting

---

34. The APRC Government now denies having started the shooting and instead blames it on the students and so-called "unscrupulous" elements in society. In fact, there is an attempt to blame the killings on the opposition. The regime has been busy trying to deny its responsibility in the killings and blame the students instead. Gambians living overseas and mostly members of Gambia-L have organized demonstrations in London, Washington D.C., Oslo, New York and other major cities protesting the killings. Moneys have been collected to assist families of the slain in addition to retaining lawyers on their behalf. A petition drive was also undertaken and sent to the UN, OAU, the US Congress/State Department and other relevant organizations.

of Decree 89 in preparation for the October 2001 presidential and national assembly elections. Imposed shortly before the 1996 presidential election, Decree 89 effectively banned the three major political parties from political activity. Again, it took combined domestic and international pressure to force Jammeh to lift the ban. The passage of the Media Bill in the national assembly in 2002, which requires, among other things, for newspapers and journalists to reveal their sources is yet another blow to democracy and democratic principles. In many ways, the Media Bill is a reincarnation of Decrees 70 and 71, this time with greater punitive force. In effect, the bill sets a dangerous precedent and leaves political parties and their leaders vulnerable to further harassment and violence. But all hope is not yet lost. There has been a significant domestic and international outcry since the bill's passage in April 2002 and the regime may have to drop this latest coercive measure just as it did Decree 89. It is clear that The Gambia is not the functioning democracy that it once was. It is also clear, as we shall see in the next chapter, that holding regular but tainted elections such as the presidential vote of 1996 and 2001 is inimical to democracy or democratization. The rise of such a false-front electoral regime is perhaps the biggest threat to national peace and progress toward democracy.

The unconditional amnesty that ex-president Jawara received, and his subsequent return to The Gambia in June 2002, however, may indicate that President Jammeh hopes to promote national healing and reconciliation. This would be good for democracy, especially if the amnesty is extended to those former officials of Jawara's government who remain in exile. Perhaps the parties and the democratically inclined elements within civil society will even be able to nudge the political system in a democratic direction. This would be a welcome move at a time when the economy, national currency, and living conditions are all plummeting.

Policy Recommendations

Despite the transition to "civilian" rule in 1996, the aftermath of military rule (1994–96) in The Gambia continues to have a traumatizing effect on the lives of many Gambians. While the 1996/1997 presidential and national assembly elections initially reduced the more overtly repressive attributes of military rule and set in motion a process of limited "democratization," repression and military involvement in The Gambia's political process has intensified. Continued human rights abuses by the ruling Alliance for the Patriotic Reorientation and Construction Party (APRC) Government, including the killing of citizens and defenseless students, coupled with declining transparency and accountability in matters of governance, are dark reminders of the period of military rule. However, the era of post-military rule has simultaneously witnessed limited growth in freedoms for "legal" opposition parties and their leaders to sometimes criticize government policy and hold political rallies. Yet, in spite of this welcome "democratic" opening, the national press remains muzzled by undemocratic military decrees from the era of overt military rule. With a doctored constitution whose legitimacy remains contested, and the existing ban on the major political parties and politicians, The Gambia's political landscape has descended precariously into another form of structured, police-state authoritarianism. In such a system, the rules of the game remain poorly defined and are characterized by intrigue and political subterfuge of bizarre proportions. It is also a system where feelings of trust, tolerance and reconciliation, despite president Jammeh's call for the latter after the 1996 elections, are persistently undermined and secondary to the pursuit of power, survival and self-aggrandizement.

Clearly, such a political atmosphere does not lend itself to mass political participation and democracy, both of which are fundamental rights to which all Gambians are entitled. For democracy and democratic procedures to take root in The Gambia, citizens trust that those in power play by the rules enshrined in the constitution, despite its inherent weaknesses, and work to reform it. Barring this, those in power are likely to perpetuate themselves through violence and election engineering, as was the case in the 1996 presidential election. Gambians must maintain the right to choose the government of the day in free and fair elections, in order to avert a political crisis. The impending crisis stemming from The Gambia's current political stalemate must be resolved politically. It is also important that the APRC leadership, together with leaders of opposition parties, women's organizations, religious groups, trade unionists, student activists and elders, begin a dialogue whose aim would be to initiate the process of truth telling, national reconciliation and justice in The Gambia. This is because success in building a genuine participatory democracy, based on the rule of law, will depend upon a broad range of factors. These include participation of The Gambia's collective leadership, an active civil society, a reasonably free mass media and the existence of a supportive international political and economic environment.

The anticipated benefits of these recommendations are likely to be many. One overarching potential consequence that enjoys broad consensus, is that of helping to improve the lives of Gambians through economic empowerment and democracy. Unfortunately, post-independence government policy in The Gambia has created new and reinforced pre-existing social and economic inequalities. It would suffice to say that after almost thirty years of Peoples Progressive Party (PPP) rule under Jawara, only marginal improvements in the lives of Gambians were registered. Under Jammeh, initial declarations not withstanding, the state of democracy, democratization, human rights and economic well being of most Gambians has deteriorated. Thus, an important plank in building democracy in The Gambia involves truth telling and the acknowledgement of wrongdoing. Otherwise, these efforts would be of little consequence.

Similarly, since it seized power in 1994, a dark cloud of suspicion has loomed over the AFPRC and continues to affect public perceptions of the current APRC Government. In particular, the deaths of two former minister of state, the slaughter of about forty military personnel and the summary executions of many more in 1995 are cases in point. In fact, recent allegations by ex-captain Ebou Jallow, a former spokesman of the AFPRC now in exile in the United States of America, indicated an insidiously calculated murder of these individuals by some military members of the AFPRC. However, Jallow's allegations must be taken with caution, as he, the current president, Yahya Jammeh, and some military members of the AFPRC are implicated in a $35 million embezzlement of a Taiwanese loan to The Gambia. These deaths in particular, and the manner in which they occurred have left an indelible scar on The Gambia's post-colonial history and on the collective memory of Gambians. Broken promises of government investigation to families of the deceased recently prompted Sainey Ceesay, Korro's father, to urge government resumption of the investigations in good faith. The pleas by Cessay and others are indicative of national frustration and of a plea for justice for all the families who have lost loved ones. These instances of gross human rights violations, including the deaths of 14 students and other instances of brutality such as rape against ordinary citizens, must be investigated, acknowledged and punished. It is in this regard, that a *Truth and Reconciliation Commission*[35] could play a critical role in a country like The Gambia that is struggling to come to terms with a period of gross human rights violations in its history. Truth commissions, as they are generically called, are bodies set up to investigate a history of human rights violations in a country. In the end, they are set up to facilitate truth telling, national healing, reconciliation and justice.

A compelling concern, however, is whether truth commissions help promote healing and reconciliation or deepen resentment by digging up old issues. Some argue that national healing and reconciliation could occur in the absence of a truth commission and that those implicated in human rights abuses are likely to oppose its creation.[36] Many have cogently observed, therefore, that Jammeh will never set up a truth and reconciliation commission to investigate himself or members of his regime(s). This argument, however, does not diminish the need for a truth and reconciliation commission while Jammeh is in power or after he leaves office. Granted, the latter is more likely. Similarly, support is likely to be strong among those marred by human rights abuse(s). If judiciously conducted, however, truth commissions could empty old wounds of all infection and begin the healing process.

If Gambians were to establish a truth and reconciliation commission to investigate human rights violations under the AFPRC and APRC Governments, its success would depend on the role played by domestic actors and the support received from the international com-

---

35. P. Hayner, "Fifteen Truth Commissions — 1974 to 1994: A Comparative Study," *Human Rights Quarterly*, Vol. 16 (1994), pp. 595–655.
36. *Ibid.* p. 609.

munity. The limited availability of material resources in The Gambia could be a serious impediment to the creation of a truth commission. The commission, commissioners and their support staff must be availed the tools to do an effective job and must be adequately compensated. It is here that international and domestic organizations, both governmental and non-governmental, could play a decisive role and make a contribution to healing, reconciliation and justice. If a truth commission were to be established in The Gambia, it would have to be set up by these non-governmental bodies, and possibly, an act of the national assembly to ensure transparency. Nominations to the truth commission would be invited from all quarters of society.

It should be noted that truth commissions are only one avenue, albeit an important one, toward national reconciliation, healing and renewal. Also, for truth commissions to have a lasting effect, they must be accompanied by other institutional reforms in the judiciary, military and the constitution to reduce the likelihood of future abuses.[37] Truth telling, national healing, and justice must also be extended to the economic domain to investigate firms and/or persons that may have benefited illegally by their association with the regime or government officials. Conversely, individuals and firms that have been adversely affected economically by capricious government policy action(s) must be compensated for their loss. The Commonwealth Ministerial Action Group (CMAG) contends that the closure by the Jammeh government of Citizen FM Radio in February 1998, the sacking of two leading journalists, Demba Jawo and Theophilus George and the purchase of the *Daily Observer* newspaper by Amadou Samba, a businessman believed to be close to the APRC, constituted gross violations of human rights. These contentions by the CMAG need to be investigated accordingly by a truth commission and those wronged compensated.

Alternatively, a *National Conference*,[38] alone or in conjunction with a truth commission, could be an important vehicle in resolving

---

37. *Ibid.*, p. 610.

38. A conference on Governance was held in The Gambia on March 14–16, 2000, sponsored by the APRC and the UNDP. It was however, not national in scope as it was limited to a few chosen participants. The opposition walked out

The Gambia's current political impasse. The national conference involves a broad coalition of leaders from all sectors of society. Like the truth commission, its members include elders, religious leaders, leaders of women's groups, labor activists, student activists and the ruling and opposition political leaders. Together, a national gathering is convened at the country's capital to debate and deliberate the contours of a new democratic political order. At its best, the national conference replicates at the national political level the ubiquitous *Bantaba* (meeting under a big tree) where mostly male participants have the right to voice an opinion. Decisions are made only when agreed upon by every participant. What follows is a summary of the proposals.[39] They are supportive of the call for truth telling, national healing/reconciliation and justice. They also support the concerns and sentiments expressed by the Commonwealth Heads of Government Meeting (CHOGM) held in Durban South Africa in November 1999 and call upon President Yahya Jammeh, his government, opposition political party leaders and members of civic and religious organizations to:

- Convene a *National Conference* to determine The Gambia's future political framework;
- Establish a *Truth and Reconciliation Commission* to investigate past violations of human rights in order to facilitate truth telling, national healing and reconciliation;
- Lift the ban all political parties and politicians to ensure free and fair elections in 2001/02 and a government based on the rule of law;
- Review the Constitution, and introduce a clause for term-limits for all politicians, including the president;

---

because The APRC representatives were not interested in creating a truth commission to investigate Jammeh for alleged corruption.

39. These proposals were sent to President Jammeh, leaders of political parties, civic, religious, professional and student organizations. Consequently, Dr. Abdoulaye Saine was interviewed by the BBC regarding these proposals on 9 January 2000. Also see the April issue of *New African*, pp. 44–46.

- Obey electoral laws and regulations enacted by an Independent Electoral Commission that reflects diverse political views so as to ensure a level playing field for all political parties and their candidates;
- Provide equal access to media outlets such that all political parties have their platform(s) known to the public;
- Create an atmosphere where fear of retribution is not a constraint to the free expression of one's beliefs, in print and/or verbally; and
- Train army, police and other security agents of the state to both defend and promote the human rights of Gambians, other nationalities and specifically journalists.

In the long term, President Yahya Jammeh or the government of the day should

- Create an enabling economic environment such that Gambians and other nationalities resident in The Gambia can pursue a livelihood with dignity irrespective of ethnicity, gender, age, religion, political affiliation and social standing; and
- Work toward and vigorously support gender equality and other activities that empower women and young girls.

The Gambia's Development Partners, together with the United Nations (UN), the Commonwealth, the African Union (AU), the Economic Community of West African States (ECOWAS), the United States Congress, the Black Caucus of the United States Congress and Amnesty International must support and help to create a truly democratic political framework in The Gambia.

Conclusion

At a time when many countries in Africa are moving away from authoritarian rule in favor of democratization and democracy, The Gambia cannot remain isolated and insulated for long from this global wave. In light of the many social and economic challenges that face Gambians as a people, it is important that solutions be found to avert what could otherwise be a bleak and brutal future. While we cannot predict the future, we can begin to prepare for it. As a new millennium unfolds, our call for fundamental change, and an end to de-facto military rule becomes more urgent, especially given the recent massacre of students in Banjul and the provinces on April 10 and 11, 2000. The Gambia, already at a disadvantage because of its relatively small size and undiversified economy, must create a niche for itself in the global economy so as to attract needed investments from within and abroad. We must embrace the future in order to face, what in The Gambia's case are daunting challenges. Clearly, while the long-term policy recommendations herein would take longer to achieve, those of a short-term nature are more readily achievable. Together, these proposals harbor important ingredients for the much needed tasks of truth telling, justice and democracy.

CHAPTER III

THE OCTOBER 2001 PRESIDENTIAL ELECTIONS IN THE GAMBIA

Background

On October 18, 2001, The Gambia held its second presidential election since the 1994 coup d'etat. The first, held in 1996, was declared not "free and fair" by the international community. Since then, a soldier-turned-president has ruled the country. The Gambia, a former British colony, is a tiny West African country of 1.5 million people almost surrounded by Senegal. Since gaining independence in February 1965, it remained one of four democracies in Africa. The coup d'etat of July 22, 1994 effectively ended the longest continuously surviving multiparty democracy in Africa and the reign of Sir Dawda Jawara, who at the time was the longest serving, democratically elected head of state in Africa. With the Armed Forces Provisional Ruling Council (AFPRC) in place, the Constitution was suspended, politicians and political parties banned, and all semblance of the rule of law ended. Rule by decree became the mode of governance with predictable arbitrary arrests, detentions, torture, disappearances, killings and other flagrant abuse of fundamental human rights. Those who openly opposed or were thought to oppose the regime suffered innumerable atrocities.

However, combined international economic sanctions and domestic protests, led to a two-year timetable back to "civilian rule." This ultimately led to presidential and national assembly elections in 1996 and 1997, respectively. The presidential election was, however, neither free nor fair because the electoral process was engineered from the very beginning to enable the incumbent military-turned-civilian leader to win. Consequently, the results were widely disputed and condemned by the Commonwealth. In fact, leaders of the United Democratic Party (UDP) continue to contest the results to this day. Therefore, despite The Gambia's return to "civilian" rule under the Alliance for Patriotic Re-orientation and Construction (APRC) party in 1996, the country continues to be headed by a "civilianized" military government. In fact, human rights deteriorated further, leading to the deaths of many citizens, including the tragic deaths of 14 students who were killed while peacefully protesting government policy in April 2000. Leaders and supporters of political parties such as the UDP remain vulnerable to violence, torture and intimidation by the ruling junta. During the 1996 presidential campaign, several UDP supporters were brutally beaten by security forces and three of them died. In summer 2000, UDP leaders and supporters were ambushed and beaten by APRC militants sent by the regime to disrupt a political meeting. Several presenters received severe burns when a pro-democracy private radio station was set on fire. The fire is believed to have been set by APRC militants. In addition, the National Intelligence Agency (NIA), the official repressive arm of the regime continues to engage in torture of dissidents and those perceived as threats to the regime. Predictably, the justice system and the courts are not generally regarded as independent and serve the primary purpose of enforcing draconian laws and decrees. State-employed judges and attorneys are often summarily dismissed if they rule against the regime. Accordingly, the press remains severely constrained by military decrees and journalists are sometimes subjected to severe beatings and torture. In effect, a "culture of silence" has been made possible by repressive laws and decrees used to punish attempts at free expression.

The regime prides itself, however, on the numerous schools, hospitals, clinics and roads it constructed since coming to power in 1994. It is true that the regime also refurbished the national airport and government owned radio station, in addition to building the country's first university and only television station. This is a remarkable achievement which many Gambians take pride in. On this score, the regime's performance is relatively better than that of the civilian regime it replaced. These improvements not withstanding, the economy remains sluggish, in part, due to a cessation of aid from the country's major European donors. The primary consequence has been deepening poverty for the bulk of The Gambia's 1.5 million people. At a United Nations sponsored conference held in The Gambia on November 28, 2001, Gambia's vice-president, Isatou Njie-Saidy admitted to the country's worsening poverty.[1]

It is against this backdrop of state sponsored repression, violence, intimidation of political opponents and increasing poverty that the October 2001 presidential election must be situated and analyzed. Focusing specifically on the 2001 presidential election provides an important prism through which to assess democracy and democratization in The Gambia under Jammeh. Therefore, the chapter critically evaluates the lifting of Decree 89, the voter registration and campaign process, the role of the Independent Electoral Commission (IEC) and the roles of other actors within the country.

Lifting Ban on Decree 89

On July 22, 2001 president Jammeh was forced to lift the ban on the major pre-coup political parties and politicians imposed shortly before the 1996 presidential election.[2] It took the combined efforts of domestic and international pressure to force Jammeh to partially open the political process. Widely condemned by the Commonwealth, Decree 89 was imposed on August 12, shortly before the September 1996 presidential election to strengthen an earlier ban implemented following the 1994 coup d'etat. Under the provision, the three major political parties: the Peoples Progressive Party (PPP), The National Convention Party (NCP) and the Gambia Peoples Party (GPP) led by self-exiled ex-president Jawara, Sheriff Mustapha Dibba and Assan Musa Cammara, respectively, were banned, together with most ex-ministers of the previous government, from all political activity. The ban was imposed for periods ranging from five to twenty years.[3]

---

1. allAfrica.com, November 29, 2001.
2. Reuters, July 22, 2001.
3. *The Point*, 12 August 1996.

While the lifting of Decree 89 elicited mixed reactions, ranging from jubilation to condemnation, it nonetheless, set high public expectations for the formation of an alliance of opposition parties in a bid to defeat Jammeh. Yet, a rift among political leaders was rumored.

This rumor was confirmed when Dibba of the NCP refused to endorse Darboe's presidential candidacy under a limited coalition between the UDP/PPP/GPP. It was alleged that Dibba was offered considerable sums of money by president Jammeh to desert the proposed coalition. The more likely reason for Dibba's refusal to join the coalition and endorse Darboe's candidacy, however, lay in Dibba's desire to be the coalition's presidential nominee. In the end, a combination of personal ambition, irreconcilable ideological and personality differences could not be overlooked as these differences failed to rally the opposition around the overarching imperative of defeating Jammeh. Thus, the lifting of the ban had the effect of splitting the opposition and hence was a blessing in disguise for the incumbent. Meanwhile, Jammeh had all the advantages of a sitting president abundant personal finances, state resources and monopoly over state owned media outlets. Furthermore, his candidacy was bolstered, as in 1996, by acts of violence and intimidation committed by military personnel and members of the July 22 Movement against members of the opposition. This made him a formidable opponent. Therefore, even under the best circumstances of a total coalition of opposition parties, the battle for the presidency would be uphill and especially daunting for a splintered opposition.

Former PPP government ministers and other banned politicians regrouped in efforts to rekindle public interest for their future candidacy. PPP cadres met under the leadership of Omar Jallow, a former PPP Agriculture minister and invited Jawara to return home and lead the party.[4] In a BBC interview, Jawara vowed to return home "to end the suffering of the Gambian people" and expressed willingness to join a possible opposition alliance against Jammeh.[5] Despite implicit assurances of Jawara's personal safety by Gambia's secretary of state for foreign affairs, Sedat Jobe, veiled threats made by president

---

4. *The Independent*, August 3, 2001.
5. allAfrica.com, August 1, 2001.

Jammeh that "anyone who tries to undermine the security of the state will end up six feet deep," dissuaded the former president from returning as planned.[6] Not only did the latter contradict an earlier statement issued by the regime's foreign secretary but it also raised serious questions about Jammeh's intentions. It appeared that as he was, on one hand, bowing to domestic and international pressure, Jammeh was, at the same time, implicitly re-imposing the ban on self-exiled politicians, on the other.

This led many observers to wonder whether Jammeh would hold free and fair elections. More important, however, was whether the financially strapped opposition, splintered as it was, could marshal its forces in less than three months to run an effective campaign and contest the election against an incumbent president who had all the advantages of state and personal resources. While Omar Jallow continued to enjoy considerable popularity in his constituency and Serrekunda, in general, his charisma alone could not bring back the PPP to its pre-coup popularity. Many exiled PPP politicians would not risk possible abduction, arrest and torture following their return. Those at home while still popular, had lost their edge after seven years of the imposed ban.

Sheriff Mustapha Dibba, a former PPP vice-president and minister of finance under Jawara, left the PPP and formed the NCP in the aftermath of a currency smuggling scandal involving his older brother in the early 1970s. A strident critic of the PPP and Jawara, Dibba reemerged from seven years of silence to resuscitate his party. But his silence, lack of activity and failure to challenge the legality of Decree 89 in court or verbally, as Omar Jallow of the PPP had, left him vulnerable to charges of opportunism and cowardice. Since the ban, many of his party stalwarts and supporters shifted their allegiance to the United Democratic Party (UDP).

Formed shortly before the 1996 presidential election and led by Ousainou Darboe, the UDP was by far the strongest of the existing opposition parties. Assan Musa Camara, a septuagenarian, could not, under the current constitution, contest the next presidential election. Like Dibba, Camara served as Jawara's vice-president until his expul-

---

6. Reuters, July 22, 2001.

sion from the party following the aborted 1981 coup d'etat. Yet, as an elder statesman, his presence strengthened the united opposition alliance. The Peoples Democratic Organization for Independence and Socialism (PDOIS), a pre-coup party not banned by Jammeh, appeared open to a united opposition party, but set preconditions that seemed unacceptable to the slowly coalescing UDP/PPP/GPP umbrella. The National Reconciliation Party (NRP), under its charismatic leader, Hamat Bah, also appeared open to an alliance of all the political parties. But emergence of the UDP/PPP/GPP alliance, following a meeting in which Darboe was elected the coalition's presidential candidate, dashed what hope there was for a united opposition party. Dibba, suspicious all along of the PPP's intentions, stormed out of the meeting and Bah, who was out of the country, could not be consulted. PDOIS, whether by design or default, never received the letter inviting it to the meeting. For PDOIS and NRP, however, the UDP/PPP/GPP limited coalition appeared to be controlled by the PPP, thus their reluctance to join it. Darboe, therefore, took a major risk in not trying to woo Bah and Jatta of PDOIS to his side and paid for it dearly.

Campaign and Issues

Jammeh, the incumbent president, ran a vigorous campaign that hinged concretely on his seven-year development record in The Gambia. He dismissed the limited UDP/PPP/GPP coalition leadership as a sinister front for the deposed PPP government bent on returning ex-president Jawara to power. Jawara's leadership of thirty-two years, he charged, brought nothing to the Gambian people but poverty. This he contrasted with his development of roads, hospitals, and better access to education and medical care, especially for the disadvantaged and rural poor. Jammeh vowed that his reelection would usher in more development and prosperity and used ex-PPP stalwarts, now in his camp, to further discredit Jawara and Darboe. Like during the 1996 presidential campaign, Jammeh accused Darboe of seeking to restore years of institutional corruption and poor performance. Darboe countered with charges of more corruption, murder, and a lack of both transparency and accountability under Jammeh's tenure. However, he could not successfully break out of the definition or box which he was trapped in. The appearance of a sweetheart deal between the UDP and the PPP in Darboe's election as the limited coalition's presidential candidate was not lost to the electorate either.

The limited coalition under Darboe ran a relatively strong campaign but not strong enough to overcome these negative public perceptions. Darboe focused on the April 10 and 11 slaughter of peacefully demonstrating students, a sagging economy characterized by growing misery and a plummeting currency, human rights abuses, and a bleak future under an APRC led government. Darboe promised that, under his leadership farmers would be paid a fair price for their groundnuts, and not with the useless promissory notes Jammeh gave them as payment. But more importantly, Darboe promised that his tenure, unlike Jammeh's would be one based on the rule of law. Yet, in spite of "these philosophical pronouncements and overview of their intentions, the coalition fell short in coming up with specific solutions where the APRC government was found wanting.[7] A catchy campaign slogan, Jammeh "jippo" (Jammeh, step down), did not, in the end, help the limited coalition capture enough votes to make their slogan come true.

But perhaps the most troublesome issue leading up to the election was Gabriel Roberts' reappointment to the Chairmanship of the IEC. Following the 1996 elections, Jammeh had summarily dismissed Roberts for reasons of alleged incompetence. Many, however, reasoned that Roberts was, in large measure, instrumental in Jammeh's tainted victory in 1996. And that his reappointment as head of the IEC, a Commission that for all intents and purposes lost its independence and credibility, would again make it possible for Jammeh to win. Roberts' return was, therefore, perceived as yet another ploy by the APRC to engineer the elections in Jammeh's favor. The rejection by Jammeh of the on-spot counting of ballots for logistical, security and financial reasons was perceived as another effort to stuff the ballot boxes. The resulting debate over the number of counting stations

---

7. *The Point*, October 9, 2001.

and their reduction muddied the waters further.[8] While rejection of spot counting appeared reasonable on grounds already given by Jammeh, it was not in his purview as a candidate, but Roberts' to make that decision.

A more nettlesome issue leading up to the polls had to do with those entitled to vote on election day. On the eve of polling, the opposition scored a victory when the IEC Chairman accepted a demand that only people whose names appeared on the main voter registers could vote. The previous regulation allowed voters to only show their identity cards.[9] President Jammeh took issue with the decision and worked to get it overturned. The decision by Roberts to rescind this decision on election day, allowing voters to show only a voter's card to vote, confirmed to many the underhandedness of Roberts and his resolve to see Jammeh reelected. The concern over the question of who should vote in the election is important, because of allegations of cross-border registration, and voting on election day by some thirty to seventy-five thousand Senegalese from neighboring Senegal's Casamance region. Countless refugees and other foreigners from the sub-region were added to this number. It was, in fact, alleged that the campus of Gambia College harbored some thirty to forty thousand of Jammeh's Jola ethnic kin from Casamance. The confiscation of voter cards and arrest by Senegal's border police of returning Senegalese two days after the Gambian presidential polls raised serious concerns over the fairness of the elections. In addition, a voter turnout of 105% in the Niani Constituency, in particular, raised more questions and increased suspicions of cross-border voting.

Also troubling during the campaign leading up to the elections were rising political tensions that resulted in two deaths and the arson attack by UDP supporters on the house of an APRC member of the national assembly.[10] Earlier arson attacks by APRC militants on houses of UDP supporters and a pro-democracy private radio station added to ongoing tensions. A political observer noted, the "political atmosphere is threatening the peace, stability and even the founda-

---

8. *The Independent*, August 10, 2001.
9. BBC World Service Africa/news/, October 18, 2001.
10. BBC World Service News, October 16, 2001.

tions of our nation. Our society is becoming dangerously over-polarized."[11] The houses of Lamin Juwara and Shyngle Nyassi were attacked.[12] The deployment of heavy anti-craft weaponry as well as visible police support and presence, also added to an already charged pre-election political atmosphere.[13]

Gambians abroad played a more active role in the 2001 presidential election compared to 1996. Several conferences were held in London; Washington, D.C.; Atlanta; Raleigh, North Carolina; and in parts of Europe to which party leaders or their representatives were invited. At these meetings, political parties presented their platforms and solicited funds. The February and July 2001 London Conferences held by the UK-based Movement for the Restoration of Democracy in The Gambia (MRDGUK) was attended by several British members of Parliament, exiled politicians, former civil servants living in the UK, and opposition party members from the Gambia. The New York based (MRDGNY), a movement similar in its goals to the UK's, held several meetings as well. They also organized several demonstrations against Jammeh and his entourage during the leader's visit to New York to address the UN's General Assembly. A similar conference held in May 2001 in Washington, D.C., by the Committee for Concerned Gambian Citizens (CCGC) was yet another forum. These meetings were indeed historic as they were the first attempts to assemble various party representatives to discuss The Gambia's future and a total coalition of all opposition parties. MRDGUK in fact, spelt out a comprehensive blueprint that was to serve as the basis for a united opposition party but, in the end, it could not achieve its noble aim. Together, these organizations lobbied for the annulment of Decree 89. In fact, U.S. president Bill Clinton responded favorably to a letter written to him by the Washington based CCGC.

Perhaps, for the first time in The Gambia's political history, political campaigning extended beyond the confines of The Gambia's geographic boundaries. Equally important was the extension of the campaign to cyberspace. The UDP, PDOIS and APRC leaders or their

---

11. *The Independent*, August 6, 2001.
12. *The Independent*, October 7, 2001.
13. BBC World Service News, October 17, 2001.

representatives were able to discuss their party platforms with Gambians on-line and through party web sites on the internet. Gambia-L, (G-L) a U.S. based internet mailing list with members throughout the world and devoted to the discussion and debate of issues relevant to The Gambia, was also a forum used by all the political parties and their representatives to reach Gambians in the Diaspora. Though Gambia-L is non-partisan, many of its 800 members are. Here, rife and generally constructive debates occur between different party supporters. It appears that the critics of Jammeh and his government have been more successful in dominating the forum. Government supporters, including civil servants in The Gambia and abroad have also used it to counter criticisms leveled against Jammeh and his government. Articles critical of Jammeh's policies written by its more erudite G-L contributors were often printed and circulated in The Gambia during the campaign. Ebrima Ceesay, a leading critic of the regime, now in exile in the U.K., wrote regular campaign messages as did Karamba Touray and Jabou Joh. Thus, the G-L has come to be recognized as a powerful voice and force in The Gambian political landscape. In fact, it is believed that the president and his cabinet are members of G-L.

Perhaps the most bizarre occurrence during the campaign period happened in early October in Brikama, a town about twenty kilometers from Banjul. Here, angry women danced naked in the streets in an effort to break a spell. The spell in the form of a slaughtered dog was wrapped in white cloth. Jammeh's opponents were believed to be responsible for casting the spell so as to negatively impact his bid for reelection.[14] This action was widely criticized by politicians and clergy alike. Another bizarre occurrence involved a lame four-year-old boy who was reported to have miraculously recovered and walked after Darboe and his entourage arrived in the village of Kumbija.[15] But the expulsion of Bharat Joshi, a British diplomat in August, underscored the growing tension between incumbent president Jammeh and Darboe. Joshi, an affable person, was expelled for attending an opposi-

---

14. allAfrica.com, October 16, 2001.
15. *The Independent*, October 12, 2001.

tion press conference to which he was invited.[16] The incident led to the expulsion of a Gambian diplomat of comparable rank from the UK and ultimately, to the resignation of Sedat Jobe, Jammeh's secretary for foreign affairs.

The Election Results

Contrary to public fears in The Gambia and abroad, the presidential election was peaceful. With a voter turnout of approximately 90%, Gambians lined up under a scorching sun to vote for their next president. Jammeh's APRC won 52.84 percent of the vote, (55.76 percent in 1996) as opposed to the coalition's 33.67 percent in 2001, and (the United Democratic Party's 35.84 percent) in 1996. Hamat Bah (NRP) polled 8%, Sheriff Dibba (NCP) 4%, and Sidia Jatta (PDOIS) polled 3% of the total vote.

Table 1. Voting results 2001 presidential election

Candidate(s)	Party	Votes	%
Yahya Jammeh	(APRC)	242,302	(52.96%)
Ousainou Darboe	(UDP/PPP/GPP)	149,448	(33.67%)
Hamat Bah	(NRP)	35,678	(7.80%)
Sheriff Dibba	(NCP)	17,271	(3.78%)
Sidia Jatta	(PDOIS)	13,841	(2.86%)
Total		458,540	(80%)
Total (electorate)		509,301	

Source: *The Point*, October 20, 2001

Voting appeared to have gone in an orderly manner, despite tensions in the run-up to the poll that left two opposition supporters dead. International observers declared the elections "free and fair" and Darboe later conceded defeat to president-elect, Jammeh. He said: "apart from the inducement factor (the plying of voters with cash by competing parties), I cannot complain much. The Gambian people are ready to suffer for another five years and there's nothing we can do

---

16. *The Independent*, August, 24, 2001.

about it."[17] Accordingly, Darboe praised the IEC for an excellent job and dispelled claims that it connived to rig the election in Jammeh's favor.

The voting pattern indicated that Jammeh won forty-one of the forty-eight constituencies nationwide, including former opposition strongholds of Jarra East, West and Central, Kiang East and Kiang Central, and Darboe's home constituency of Upper Fulladu West. Of the seven remaining constituencies, Darboe won six and Bah (NRP) won one, his home constituency of Upper Saloum, the only presidential candidate to do so. Jammeh also defeated Dibba (NCP) and Jatta (PDOIS) in their home constituencies. Even more interesting is that Jammeh also swept the constituencies of Banjul South, North and Central, once opposition strongholds. Many expected that the vote against Jammeh would be overwhelming in these constituencies, in part, because of increased urban hardships, high youth unemployment and the killing of fourteen students by government security forces on April 10 and 11, 2000. The voting pattern also suggests that Jammeh's support was broad based, especially in the rural areas. Here, it was expected that Jammeh would not do well because of dissatisfaction over the government's poor handling of a bumper groundnut harvest and rocketing food prices. In fact, it seems that even if the opposition parties had managed to form a single opposition party, they would have still lost to Jammeh. While Darboe won Bakau and Basse, two major towns, Jammeh won the more densely populated urban centers of Serrekunda and Brikama. Darboe's win in Basse has been attributed, in part, to the important role played by Omar Sey, a former minister for foreign affairs under Jawara, and Ousainou Njie, the ex-president's brother in law, played during the campaign. Both Sey and Njie hail from Basse, originally. Yet, despite Omar Jallow's popularity and charisma in Serrekunda, he could not deliver the vote. Jammeh's victory would, however, be haunted by accusations of cross-border voting and allegations of inflated voter rolls, despite commendations from the Commonwealth Observer Group. Less than a week after conceding defeat, Darboe strongly attacked the IEC and

---

17. allAfrica.com, October 19, 2001.

its Chairman for what he called "inept and corrupt" handling of voter registration in which non-Gambians were issued voter cards.[18] As proof, Darboe presented a Senegalese national who possessed both a Senegalese ID card and a Gambian voter's card to the press. In fact, it is alleged that over forty to seventy-five thousand foreigners, mainly from Casamance, voted in the election. The data also indicate a discrepancy in the number of registered voters and votes cast in Niani Constituency on election day. The IEC published results show a total of 7877 votes cast against a total number 7464 registered votes. This, Darboe contends, is proof that the IEC actually carried out "extra registration of non-Gambian voters who were then sent to various constituencies throughout the country to vote. This gave the APRC an unfair advantage over the opposition parties."[19]

Kemeseng Jammeh, (no relation to the president) the National Assembly's minority leader, similarly accused IEC Chairman Roberts of issuing voter cards to non-Gambians. Jammeh cited the dramatic change in the total number of votes cast in Karantaba and Soma in which 459 people cast votes in 1996 compared to 1331 in 2001. Soma, a growing urban center and residence to many citizens of Senegal, Guinea, Mali and Guinea Bissau, is a case in point. Jammeh contends that there were only two polling stations there in 1996 combining for a total vote of 1408. In 2001, by contrast, Soma had four polling stations with a total of 3,254 votes. Similar electoral mal-practices were also alleged by Jammeh in Jenoi, Pakalinding, Toniataba and Karantaba.[20]

While the proof shown by Darboe and allegations by Jammeh (the minority leader) of non-Gambian participation in the 2001 presidential elections raise serious doubts about the "free and fair" conclusion of international observers, the accuracy of the 40,000 alleged voters is difficult to substantiate empirically. It is true that Senegalese returning from The Gambia following the elections were arrested and their Gambian voter cards confiscated. But the number of reported cases appears negligible.

---

18. *The Observer*, October 25, 2001.
19. *The Observer*, October 25, 2001.
20. *The Independent*, November 12, 2001.

Post-Election Violence, Intimidation and Job Dismissals

Jammeh's victory celebrations were suddenly dampened by arrests, the beatings of opposition members, and the dismissal of civil servants perceived to be opposed to his rule. There appeared to be an organized attack on the opposition. Lamin Juwara, the UDP propaganda secretary's house was attacked together with Omar Jallow's and Dembo Bojang's, all of the coalition. The NIA arrested and detained other members of the opposition. Momodou Manneh, a former minister of Trade under Jawara, was among those who were brutally beaten by APRC militants.[21] Dominic Mendy, secretary of state for Trade under Jammeh until 1999, was arrested and put in custody for four days by the NIA on allegations of possessing "official documents."[22] Muhammed Lamin Sillah, Amnesty International's representative in The Gambia and president of a coalition of human rights defenders, was picked up by the NIA following comments he made to the BBC. Sillah alleges that he was "detained in conditions that amounted to mental torture."[23] Alhagie Mbye, a reporter with *The Independent* newspaper, was also brutally tortured by the NIA.[24] Instances of alleged APRC violence against opposition members in the provinces were also reported. In particular, APRC militants allegedly poisoned cattle belonging to a member of the opposition. Since the declaration of the results, harassment, intimidation and physical assault of coalition supporters have been common. It appears that Jammeh's 5% margin of victory has not reassured him of his mandate or, conversely, the mandate itself is taken to mean a continuation of his repressive practices.

The violence visited on the opposition by the regime and its militants has been accompanied by dismissals and retirements of senior

---

21. *The Observer*, October 25, 2001.
22. *The Independent*, November 9, 2001.
23. BBC World Service/Africa/news, October 29, 2001.
24. *The Independent*, December 13, 2001.

and junior civil servants thought to be disloyal or unsympathetic to Jammeh's government or bid for reelection. However, his attempt to purge the civil service of his opponents is rationalized along lines of "professionalism." If one is deemed "unprofessional," often analogous to "non-supporter," it could mean being dismissed. A visit by Juka Jabang, managing director of The Gambia's Management Development Institute (MDI) and her staff, however, was used by Jammeh to dispel the notion that he dismisses civil servants on the basis of their political affiliation. Jabang is married to a former PPP minister for external affairs.

Jammeh's frequent "hire and fire policy," as an astute political observer termed it, is nothing new, but represents a pillar in his repertoire to maintain power. In this regard, an average of one secretary of state is dismissed every six months. Since coming to power in 1994, Jammeh has fired, changed, or redeployed fifty-nine secretaries of state to other ministries.[25] One died under mysterious circumstances, another while in police custody allegedly of complications arising from hypertension. The latter's widow denied that her husband had hypertension. Foday Makalo, an opposition politician, disappeared more than three years ago and is presumed dead by his family. However, not all dismissals have been over political disloyalty and some who were dismissed earlier have since been reemployed.[26] The subsequent termination of Tombong Saidy as director of Gambia's Radio and Television Services (GRTS) has been attributed to Saidy's alleged incompetence and corruption. Others allege that Saidy's sacking had to do more with his less than enthusiastic support for Jammeh's bid for reelection to a second term. Despite his ouster as a leading propagandist for the regime, Saidy maintains his unwavering support for the president. Demba Njie, a military colleague of Jammeh's who served him loyally as protocol officer for many years, has been retired. It is not clear how many civil servants have been terminated or retired since October 19, 2001. A conservative estimate is that as many as thirty to forty junior and senior civil servants have been dis-

25. *The Independent*, July 24, 2001.
26. *The Point*, November 30, 2001.

missed.[27] What is clear is that the immediate effects of these dismissals, other than the obvious loss of state capacity and policy coherence, are the economic hardships these individuals, together with their immediate and extended families, will endure. As the State is the main employer in The Gambia, loss of state employment could mean a sudden decline into poverty. Assuming that each civil servant supports on average six to ten individuals, the consequences could mean increased hardship. Consequently, Jammeh has capriciously used this "hire and fire policy" to both punish and intimidate those employed by the state in order to ensure compliance and support.

By breeding insecurity among civil servants and critics alike, Jammeh believes he can engender compliance and support. The immediate effect of this "hire and fire policy" could ensure compliance, but only for a short time. The long-term consequences for state capacity and state building could be catastrophic. Jammeh's "hire and fire policy," like his campaign rhetoric regarding Jawara's thirty-two years in power, appears to have all the trappings of a continuing war against the relatively more educated, perhaps principled few, in the civil service. The flight by this group from both state service and the country will diminish the state's readiness to tackle the daunting economic and social challenges the regime currently faces. In spite of political rhetoric, reasons related to regime political expedience and longevity are likely to inform Jammeh's future policy directives.

Analysis

The limited coalition under Darboe and the other political parties were doomed from the start in their bid to defeat Jammeh, individually or as a collective. The fact that IEC Chairman, Roberts, changed the rules of the game in mid-stream, undermined the very essence of electioneering and fair play and ultimately called into question the "fairness" of the elections. But even if the vote itself had been properly conducted, some domestic observers contend, "the election could

---

27. *The Independent*, November 26, 2001.

not be described as free and fair. Apart from the fact that Jammeh does have some support, his victory is largely a result of his carrot and stick policy. The widespread dishing out of money to voters throughout the country, combined with his threats of exclusion from development programs for those opposed to his presidency must have given him the vote."[28]

Additionally, Jammeh is reported to have spent over two million Dalasis (over $122,000) on his campaign.[29] If this is true, and from all indications it seems so, it is a flagrant violation of election laws. It appears, therefore, that the political terrain was not only uneven but that the rules of the game were framed to favor Jammeh. Thus, the process was engineered from the beginning, with the assistance of a hand-picked IEC Chairman, who not only presided over a flawed 1996 presidential election, but also colluded with Jammeh in the latter's bid for reelection in 2001. Predictably, a level playing field did not exist as the rules of the game and a political atmosphere and campaign marred by violence and intimidation worked in tandem to favor Jammeh and oddly against the opposition parties. The concern over cross-border voting severely tainted the "fairness" of the election. It made "Jammeh the first truly elected president of Senegambia," noted an observer.

The coalition also appeared to have lost supporters on the last few days leading to the elections as clashes between security officers and July 22 militants led to two deaths. Crowd control punctuated by firing in the air had a heavy psychological toll on a generally peaceful population. This could have swayed the vote in Jammeh's favor.[30] These acts of violence and intimidation, as in 1996, were strong indicators of what was to follow if Jammeh lost the elections. Many Gambians reasoned then, and perhaps in 2001, that Jammeh would not step down and concede defeat peacefully were he to loose to Darboe. Fear of escalating violence and instability forced many to vote for Jammeh. An astute political observer noted, " indeed in a political culture such as The Gambia's, where politicians with power like

---

28. allAfrica.com, October 19, 2001.
29. allAfrica.com, October 19, 2001.
30. *The Point*, October 23, 2001.

Jammeh can use the resources at their disposal—both coercive and persuasive—with reckless abandon, it is not a great feat to win elections."

Dibba, leader and presidential candidate of the NCP, by contrast, saw the election as the "freest and fairest since independence" and observed that it had contributed to the "strengthening of the democratic process in The Gambia."[31] These comments were made in the aftermath of a meeting with Jammeh at the State House in which Dibba left open the prospect of allying with Jammeh or other political parties in the forthcoming National Assembly elections in February 2002.[32] According to his detractors, Dibba's comments were self-serving. But some of his supporters contend that they reflected his pragmatic approach to politics and his desire to serve the nation. Still yet, influential party members see his words as a betrayal of everything Dibba stood and fought for since independence. More importantly, noted a party leader, joining forces with Jammeh "is tantamount to slaughtering the spirit of the party."[33]

The reasons why Dibba left the option of allying the NCP with the APRC open were mixed. As an astute politician with a wealth of experience, Dibba could be an asset to Darboe, not Jammeh. Allying with the APRC, the party in power, appears more likely, for obvious reasons, than joining the UDP/PPP/GPP coalition that he had earlier rejected. Dibba could benefit from such an alliance, win a seat in the national assembly and, as an elder statesman, play a pivotal role in the newly elected national assembly and government. But this is only possible if Jammeh does not see him as a threat. But, by defecting de facto to the ruling party, Dibba stands to loose more than he could possibly gain if he chose to associate with Jammeh instead of forming an alliance with Darboe. Within the Darboe coalition, Dibba would readily be a power broker, a role he would not be granted within an APRC led government. Put another way, Jammeh does not need Dibba as much as Darboe does. Yet Dibba's new role could usher in unexpected power reconfigurations in the short-term and in doing so, inject a dynamism and stability to the status quo.

---

31. Gambia Radio & TV News, November 25, 2001.
32. *The Daily Observer*, November 26, 2001.
33. *The Independent*, November 30, 2001.

But more fatal to Darboe's bid for the presidency was not Dibba's refusal to join the coalition, but his failure to focus concretely on the issues or respond pointedly to Jammeh's charges. More importantly, Darboe failed to disassociate himself with the popular perception of him as a front for the PPP. It is this lingering public perception, dating back to the 1996 presidential election, that primarily doomed Darboe's race for the State House. This popular perception will haunt him for some time to come. Also, the fact that the issues in the campaign generally focused on Jawara and defense of his thirty-two year record by ex-PPP ministers in the coalition did not win him much public confidence. It appeared, in fact, that Darboe's campaign was unwittingly eclipsed, perhaps dominated, by PPP elements in the coalition who used it as a platform to vindicate themselves and their party. This did not help Darboe, as it appeared to confirm public perceptions of him. In reality, Darboe is an independent thinker who has run a successful private legal practice for over twenty years while resisting co-optation by the former government to serve as minister of Justice.

Nonetheless, the UDP/ PPP/ GPP coalition, in the end, hurt Darboe's bid for the presidency. This is because in 1996 Darboe alone won 35% of the popular vote to the coalition's 33% in 2001. In retrospect, it seems that if Darboe had instead aligned himself with NRP and PDOIS and ran on his own accord, he would have stood a better chance of winning, if not in the first ballot, in the second. Conversely, if Darboe was able to bring the NRP and PDOIS on board the limited coalition, he could have countered the public's negative perception of him. Ultimately, it seems his campaign promises as well as his indictments of Jammeh and his government did not matter much to the Gambian majority that voted.

But perhaps the most daunting challenge that dogged the limited coalition from the very start was its lack of financial resources. While Darboe made several overseas trips to make his platform known to Gambians in Europe and North America and to raise funds for his candidacy, the funds were not enough to make any lasting effect. The fact that the coalition did not include all the opposition parties coupled with the popular perception in the Diaspora that Darboe's presidency could be a comeback for the PPP and ex-president Jawara, led many to withhold financial support. Furthermore, the entry of Sheriff Dibba as a presidential candidate split what little money that was raised in the US into several donations, the larger share going to Darboe. Dibba's candidature appeared doomed from the start, however. His seven-year absence from the political scene, public perceptions of him as power hungry, limited resources and allegations of being sponsored by Jammeh to split the opposition further, did not help his cause. In the end, his candidature inadvertently helped Jammeh and hurt the coalition. PDOIS's Sidia Jatta, in spite of his record as one dedicated to principled politics and his reputation for donating a portion of the salary he earns as a member of The Gambia's national assembly to his constituency, ended up last but increased his total votes from 1996. PDOIS's insistence on issues rather than sentiment-based politics, though commendable, did not, in the end, attract many voters. Their failure to engage in usual campaign techniques and, in turn, urging voters to vote for the person(s) they deem the "right person" limited their appeal considerably.

Politics in The Gambia, as elsewhere, involves presenting an embellished platform to the electorate who then sift through the information and then decide on a candidate.

The Gambian electorate is, therefore, not as gullible or uninformed as PDOIS's leadership and others assume. In fact, their conservative reputation at the polls, generally voting for incumbents, owes more to their savvy for economic gain than their desire to maintain the status quo, per se. In this regard, the Gambian electorate is not qualitatively different from many of their counterparts in Africa and other parts of the Third World where voting patterns reflect not ideology, but a cost-benefit construct.

Of all the opposition candidates, however, it would seem that Hamat Bah of the NRP emerged as the clear winner, even if trailing behind Darboe. Dismissed as "a no-starter," he retained his constituency unlike Darboe and Jatta. In the intervening years since 1996, Bah sharpened his debating and oratory skills, impressing many Gambians nationally and in the Diaspora.[34] His ability to reach the rural populations whose concerns formed the cornerstone of his pro-

---

34. *The Point*, October 20, 2001.

gram and campaigns, paid off at the polls. Like Jatta of PDOIS, he has a clean image, one that is not tainted in the public's mind. It seems that a coalition of PDOIS and NPR in the last presidential election would have yielded more votes than their separate ventures. Clearly, this would have been a more viable duo than the rumored alliance between NRP and NCP.

If there is a single overriding set of reasons that explains the opposition parties' loss at the polls, it is their lack of unity in the face of Jammeh's more impressive war chest. A united opposition would have pooled its meager resources, improved and expanded individual party agendas, rendered propaganda and campaign machinery more effective, harmonized and reduced duplication of tasks and ultimately attracted more support both nationally and internationally. Together, opposition parties could have won decisively or at least forced Jammeh into a run-off election. In this case, they would have been the party to beat.

Why then, did Darboe acknowledge defeat? Perhaps the single most important reason for Darboe's acknowledgement of defeat has to do with concerns over the security of his supporters, The Gambia, and himself. This is because in 1996, Darboe, members of his family, seven party supporters including Jammeh's former external affairs minister, Bolong Sonko and the UDP's senior administrative secretary, Sidia Sagnia, sought refuge at the Senegalese embassy in Banjul and vowed to leave only if assured of their safety. The prospect of post-election violence could not be taken lightly given the violence leading to the elections. The peace and calm during the vote was underpinned by tension and hostility. All that was needed to set it off was a little spark.

Jammeh's threat to "shoot on sight" members of the opposition wielding weapons during and after the election could not be taken lightly.[35] The threat came in the aftermath of alleged violence by Darboe supporters. It appears that for Darboe to contest the legitimacy of the elections at the time could have plunged the country into violence, disorder and increased the loss of life. The spate of arrests following Jammeh's victory lends credence to this contention. Additionally, in-

---

35. *The Independent*, October 15, 2001.

ternational monitors had already pronounced the exercise "free and fair"; anything uttered to the contrary would have been seen as a case of sour grapes. It is also conceivable that, upon a few days of reflection on the process and outcome of the elections, Darboe saw the bigger picture and then decided to contest the legitimacy of the outcome.

Yet, despite certain electoral malpractices, it is unclear whether electoral discrepancies alone were as widespread as alleged. Jammeh's support appeared broad based; he defeated all but one presidential candidate in their home constituencies. From these constituencies, there were few reports of inflated voter rolls or participation of non-Gambians. Could Jammeh have won without these tactics? This is the fundamental question. It is likely that president Jammeh would not have won the elections, all things being equal. But all things are seldom equal in elections especially in Africa. Incumbents the world over have added advantages and resources at their disposal. In addition, Jammeh launched an effective campaign and stayed focused on Jawara's record, development successes under his rule and promises of a better future. The majority of Gambians who voted were convinced by Jammeh's campaign. And by his use of patronage, such as sending supporters to Mecca, Jammeh was able to further increase his popularity and appeal in many quarters.

Yet, if the allegations and Darboe's evidence of non-Gambian participation are accepted, approximately 30, 000 votes would have to be discounted from Jammeh's total of 242, 302 votes. If this were the case, Jammeh would not have earned the required 50% of the electoral vote. Thus, assuming that Jammeh received a total of 212, 302 (minus 30,000) votes to the total combined 216, 231 votes of the opposition, there would have been a run-off between Jammeh and Darboe. If this had occured, Darboe would have most likely defeated Jammeh.

However, both Jammeh and Darboe appeared to have overestimated their popularity. Jammeh vowed to win 80% of the vote while Darboe predicted that he would sweep the polls by a similar count. In the end, however, Jammeh was forced to go on the campaign trail as negative reports about his reduced chances of winning continued to reach him. Similarly, Darboe's teeming rallies did not translate readily into a winning count. The rally in Brikama launching the coalitions campaign kick-off in August and the march into Banjul on the eve of the elections heightened expectations of a victory. But the size of the crowds was not a good indicator of future voter behavior. However predictions of landslide victories by politicians and their political parties are common. They are part of the political game, intended to woo new and especially uncommitted voters to their party ranks.

But does Jammeh's mandate to rule for the next five years suggest a latent, perhaps overt contempt for the PPP and the things it stood for? Are Gambians not concerned about their individual/collective human rights and the events of April 10 and 11? Anecdotal evidence suggests that Jawara is still loved in The Gambia as a father of the nation, but despised by many for his poor performance generally, and official corruption specifically. To many Gambians his rule engendered "peace and tranquility" but also visited much misery on the populace, especially in the rural areas. Thus, human rights and democracy, as conceived in the more traditional sense and made popular by Jawara, meant little to the average Gambian concerned with the next meal. To that effect, debates over human rights during the campaign were only philosophical debates among well-fed elites who use a language and frame of reference to which the majority of Gambians had little organic connection.

While the bulk of Gambians regret and mourn the deaths of the students, they were, like many of their counterparts elsewhere, more concerned with bread and butter issues, or put another way, rice and stew issues. Comparatively, in the eyes of the average Gambian, Jammeh despite his faults, has delivered results. He is preferred to the thirty-two years of Jawara or to any who wish to bring back his type of political and economic dispensation. This specter will continue to haunt any politician associated mildly or even remotely with the ex-president and his party. This could change in time, however. Yet, Jammeh's humble beginnings, his relative lack of formal education, finesse and his bold entry into the political scene (taken by many of the elites as stigmatizing the country) may in fact, have some appeal with the average Gambian. In the end, it appears that the Gambian people (assuming the absence of gross electoral mal-practices), made a strategic choice and decision for the next five years in voting for Jammeh. Not that they do not value peace and tranquility, but because peace and tranquility without sustainable development, however defined, is tantamount to continued poverty. Paradoxically, increased poverty and poor economic performance characterize Jammeh's tenure. At the time of the coup in 1994, the dalasi, The Gambia's national currency unit, was about 8 (dalasis) to 1 American dollar. Today it is D17. 65 to $1 US. Yet the perception that Jammeh's rule is relatively better earned him the vote, in part.

Recommendations

The effects of a weak economy and deepening poverty in The Gambia suggests that, without major financial support from outside or electoral reforms to fund political campaigns, opposition parties are unlikely to be effective participants in the political process. The introduction of party web sites is an innovative development especially for their supporters and would be supporters outside the country. Thus, it is vital that these parties and their representatives be more aggressive in seeking alternative sources of funding or support the passage of funding legislation to finance the campaigns of recognized political parties. This should ensure a more even playing field. The IEC's mandate must include the provision of these funds to all recognized parties and set limits on party and candidate spending. The IEC must also make a more concerted effort to enfranchise overseas Gambians, who have, over the years, come to constitute an important source of foreign exchange for the country through their remittances and investments. Thus, they are an important political constituency. The alleged logistical difficulties given as reasons to deny Gambians in the diaspora the right to vote in the last elections must be contested by the opposition in addition to the issue of term limits for the president. With growing computer technology and competency among Gambians, legitimate means can be found to have their votes counted.

Additionally, the IEC must find more innovative ways to ease difficulties associated with voting and vote counting to engender more transparency. Vote buying and other illegal strategies to win voter support must be penalized. Security forces must also be trained in techniques of crowd control, especially during campaigns, in order to prevent the deaths. In doing so, the IEC and all political parties must dissuade the use and or display of lethal weapons at political rallies to safeguard life and limb. This calls for better training for the security forces. Too much is at risk when security officers are poorly trained to manage what sometimes can be excited and/or excitable crowds. The combination of large, excitable crowds and guns in the hands of poorly trained security forces is a recipe for disaster.

But these reforms are possible only if the armed forces and the IEC, specifically, maintain a genuine sense of autonomy and are not seen as tools in the hands of the regime used to engineer elections. Therefore, the IEC, army and police must reestablish their independence and credibility. Furthermore, opposition political parties must reform their structures to include more women to both run as candidates and help lead and set party agendas. The centrality of women in Gambian society and the subsistence economy, in particular, must be felt as well in the political arena. This is an important resource base as well as a reservoir for votes and goodwill. However, all these must be cultivated and nurtured over time. While women's grassroots leadership roles ("yayi-kompin") have their place, many committed Gambian women must be brought into the fold as candidates and leaders. They bring to the table perspectives that are often over looked by most men in The Gambia. The recruitment of new members to political parties must not be limited to female elites, however. In fact, if a party were to focus on the concerns of the rural electorate, it would probably gain crucial votes. Thus, the urban bias of the opposition parties must be overcome in order to make inroads throughout the country. Furthermore, unofficial campaigning must be ongoing, not something to be entered into at intervals of five years. There must also be a quicker response time between the presidential and national assembly elections on the part of political parties, so as not to loose momentum. A more pragmatic alternative to holding these elections separately is to run them together. Holding these elections in tandem could save limited state resources and those of financially strained opposition parties.

The need for an open and stable democracy in The Gambia cannot be overemphasized for its obvious and positive socio-economic benefits. So much time, creative energy, and precious lives are lost when the art of politics is reduced to bickering over the rules of the game or to self-serving manipulation of these rules. Needless to say, it deflects attention from the pressing economic challenges and hardships that face the country and its people. Gambians have little time to waste, as continued instability will only deepen the current economic and social crisis, the consequences of which are a spiral into more instability, poverty and political violence.

Conclusion

The October 2001 presidential election in The Gambia was riddled with several problems, ranging from a truncated campaign period, which favored the incumbent, to instances of intimidation and violence against the political opposition. In addition, a hand picked IEC Chairman, not only colluded with the ruling president to have himself reelected, but Roberts also single-handedly reversed an important ruling made earlier that contributed significant to the incumbent's victory. Accordingly, Decree 89 had the added effect of further dividing the opposition, which now had the daunting task of regrouping under short notice to contest the elections.

In hindsight, the short time allocated to campaigning following the repeal of Decree 89, appears to have been a calculated decision by Jammeh and perhaps the IEC Chairman. As a result, the opposition's limited time, financial resources and access to state owned media outlets meant that unseating Jammeh would not be an easy task. His plying of votes, carrot and stick campaign style, abundant financial resources and unfettered access to state owned media meant that the political terrain was uneven and favored Jammeh. Thus, Jammeh strengthened his advantage over the opposition.

Yet, at one level, the repeal of Decree 89 represented a tentative, though limited, step toward democracy and democratization of the political process. It was a "triumph for democracy" noted Darboe. This is because it enabled the opposition to overcome another hurdle in the political process in their efforts in ensuring a relatively more free and fair election. In 1996, not only was the ban in effect but the opposition, then consisting of PDOIS and the newly formed UDP and NRP, had barely three weeks to contest the September 26 presidential election. The opposition in 1996 also had less access to state-owned media. This improved marginally in 2001.

The private media, though still constrained, enjoyed some independence and freedom of expression in 2001. More importantly, the Commonwealth, other international and some national observers declared the election free and fair, unlike in 1996. But this declaration was based largely on the orderly and peaceful atmosphere on election day, which had been preceded by a less than conducive atmosphere for free and fair elections. The private media's autonomy was also short-lived as Baboucarr Gaye, a veteran journalist, was arrested and kept in custody for several days. His radio station was likewise closed by the NIA—the National Intelligence Agency—under the pretext of failure to pay taxes. This was the second time that Gaye's radio station had been impounded by the regime.[36]

In addition, in lifting Decree 89, Jammeh literally opened the door to the prospect of a more democratic future with more closely contested free and fair elections. This result was not necessarily of Jammeh's making, but the consequence of combined domestic and international pressures. This step forward must be maintained through pressure as democratic rights are never given on a silver platter. They must be struggled for with dedication. Yet, Jammeh can midwife these changes and use them to gain momentum or try to contain them as he has in the past, with unbridled repression of opposition parties and dissidents. The passage of a repressive Media Bill by the national assembly could signal what is to come in the near future. If Jammeh is short-sighted enough to continue in this illiberal direction, he must remember that change and freedom, as history has show countless times, cannot be contained forever.

It is also clear that holding regular but tainted elections is inimical to democracy. In order to have any legitimacy, Democracy and democratization must also include, among other things, respect for the rule of law. The prospect for peaceful regime change, protections for the opposition and dissidents, must also be part of the democratization process, otherwise democracy becomes a façade for authoritari-

---

36. BBC World Service, October 29, 2001.

anism. In the absence of these, elections become just another way of consolidating the power of the incumbent president. This perhaps, is the biggest threat to national peace and to democracy itself.

CHAPTER IV

MAURITANIA 1991–2001
Regime Rearrangement and "Consolidation" of Instability?

Introduction

Like many African states, the Islamic Republic of Mauritania jumped on the bandwagon of multiparty politics when it became fashionable, at the beginning of the 1990s. Yet, this country, which straddles Sub-Saharan and Northern Africa, has been nearly absent in the otherwise numerous country studies[1] on the processes and effects of "democratization" in Africa. For most of its recent history, the politics of Mauritania made it almost invisible on the continent. Its recent withdrawal of ECOWAS, the West African regional organization, will not reduce the propensity of most observers to leave it out of most analyses of African politics. However, Mauritania's mutation from a country reeling under overtly repressive military rule into a self-portrayed tolerant multiparty polity,[2] can add insight to the ongoing debate on the democratization of Africa. In fact, no country in West Africa is arguably more symptomatic of the slow farewell to po-

---

1. Since 1990, a copious literature have emerged on the democratization process (or lack thereof) in Africa. Mauritania has been generally absent as a case study. A 2001 special issue of the *Journal of Democracy* 12 (3) devoted to the state of democratization in former French colonies did include an article on Mauritania.

2. See Anthony Pazzanita, "The Origin and Evolution of Mauritania's Second Republic," *Journal of Modern African Studies* 34(4), 1996, pp. 575–96.

litical repression and authoritarianism than Mauritania. This chapter sheds light on the political developments since April 15, 1991 when reforms were introduced, up to Mauritania's first ever, reportedly free and fair, general (municipal and parliamentary) elections in 2001 and their aftermath. The circumstances that led to these developments, their dynamics, the weight they carried and their consequences are also analyzed by focusing on a number of critical factors that underpinned Mauritania's convoluted and, indeed, slow farewell to authoritarianism. Before these variables are examined, a brief historical background to this little known country may be useful.

Historical Background

Mauritania became independent on November 28, 1960. Claimed by Morocco as part of its territory, it needed all the backing of its former colonial power, France, to impose its international sovereignty. Domestically, French trained barrister Mokhtar Ould Daddah, Mauritania's first president, was confronted very early on with the daunting task of holding together centrifugal ethnic, cultural and political forces[3] while building, from scratch, the infrastructures of a modern state. Mauritania's estimated 2.5 million people are made up of three major ethno-cultural groups. The first group is comprised of four black ethnic groups (the *Halpulaar, Soninke, Wolof,* and *Bambara*) who live mainly in the south and make up roughly one third of the total population. Mauritania's recent political history has been marked by cyclical attempts by these groups to assert their (non-Arab) cultural identity, and insistent claims to a more equitable share of political and economic power.

The second group is the nomadic Arab-Berber (*Beydane* or 'White' Moor) tribes who live mainly in the North, the West, and in the East. They also make up about one third of the population but monopolize all facets of political and economic power. Finally, the *Haratines* and *Abeed,* the largest group, are (freed or still enslaved) descendants

---

3. For an expert analysis see Philippe Marchesin, *Tribus, Ethnies et Pouvoir en Mauritanie,* Paris: Khartala, 1992.

of enslaved black Africans, who identify culturally and psychologically with their former or current *Beydane* masters with whom they share the same language and Arab-Islamic culture and orientation. One of the most significant developments in Mauritania politics in recent years has been the emergence of the *Haratines* as a potential social and political force. The movement *El Hor*,[4] elements of which lead "*SOS-Esclaves*," has been the foremost symbol of the *Haratines*' fight against the persistence of slavery, the exploitation of former slaves, and for a political space.

Until he was overthrown in a bloodless coup on July 10, 1978, Mokhtar Ould Daddah had succeeded in forging a national identity. Thanks to a consummate policy of ethnic and regional balancing, he had deftly kept the underlying ethnic and political tensions in check. He also made headway in establishing a viable, internationally respected state and launching a promising economic development program. Weary of a war it was fighting (and losing) against the independence movement of the Western Sahara, the army took power, and withdrew from the ruinous territorial conflict. Soon thereafter, dissension and personal ambitions within the military led to a series of coups and countercoups. The latest coup was staged on December 12, 1984 by Ould Taya who was allegedly aided by France. Ould Taya remained Chairman of the restructured military junta, the *Comité Militaire de Salut National (CMSN)* (Military Committee for National Salvation), until the first multiparty presidential election was held in 1992 under a new political dispensation. In 1987 and 1989, ethnic tensions flared up once more. In 1987, three black officers, alleged conspirators of a plot for a military coup, were executed. In 1989, a border incident with neighboring Senegal escalated and resulted in the massacre of

---

4. "El Hor' means freeman. It is a semi-recognized political movement formed by the Haratines to fight the manifestations and legacy of slavery and for the improvement of the lot of the Haratines in Mauritanian Society. While many have adopted a moderate stand and collaborated with the political authorities, the most radical wing is in the opposition and has pursued in international fora the politically embarrassing issue of slavery. *SOS-Esclaves* is a Human Rights organization set up to monitor the issue of slavery and assist slaves to attain freedom.

hundreds of black Mauritanians, both military and civilian. Tens of thousands more black Mauritanians were deported to neighboring countries between 1989 and 1992. These events marked the end of the traditional role of Mauritania as the "*trait d'union*" (hyphen) between Sub-Saharan and Arab oriented North Africa, as its subsequent withdrawal from ECOWAS in 2000 substantiates.

External Pressure and Its Outcome

In one of the first studies of political reforms introduced by authoritarian regimes in Africa, Michael Bratton and Nicholas Van de Walle suggest that these reforms have come primarily as a response "to active demands, spontaneous or organized, from a loose, multi-class assemblage of indigenous groups."[5] A few years earlier, Abraham Lowenthal also noted in all the cases he studied the preeminence of domestic forces and actors in the move toward more openness.[6] A similar argument is forcefully made by Guillermo O'Donnell and Philippe Schmitter who insist that it would be "fruitless to search for some international factor or context which can reliably compel authoritarian rulers" to open up their political systems.[7] However, in Mauritania, the decision of the *Comité Militaire de Salut National (CMSN)*—more accurately its leader Colonel Ould Taya[8]—to embark on a process of instituting multipartyism defied this conventional wisdom. To be sure, Mauritania was not immune to the con-

---

5. Michael Bratton and Nicholas van de Walle, "Popular Protest and Political Reform in Africa," *Comparative Politics* 24 (4) July 1992, p. 420.

6. Abraham Lowenthal., "Foreword," in Guillermo O'Donnell and Philippe C. Schmitter, eds., *Transition from Authoritarian Rule: Tentative Conclusions About Uncertain Democracies*, Baltimore: The John Hopkins University Press, 1986, p. IX.

7. O'Donnell and Schmitter, eds., *Transition from Authoritarian Rule: Tentative Conclusions About Uncertain Democracies*, Baltimore: The John Hopkins University Press, 1986, p. 18.

8. See Francois Soudan, *Le Marabout et Le Colonel: La Mauritanie de Ould Daddah a Ould Taya*, Paris: Jalivres, 1992. Soudan suggests correctly that the decision was Taya's and his alone.

tagion[9] of demands for democracy that were being articulated throughout the world and, after the 1990 La Baule summit, in West Africa as well. However, in 1991, the street by no means threatened the survival of the military regime.[10] Shrewd safety measures and a ruthless state security apparatus had made the threat of coup or destabilization "from the street" highly unlikely.[11] Nothing suggests that there was a breakdown of the consensus of the ruling military junta as to the urgency or the desirability of altering the political status quo. Rather, the evidence indicates that the impetus for opening up the political system came entirely from international factors.

Mohameden Ould Mey has convincingly argued that the decision to introduce multiparty politics in April 1991 came almost exclusively as a result of intense Western pressure.[12] Janet Fleischman put it best when she observed that "[a]fter siding with Iraq in the Gulf War, thereby losing the economic support of the Gulf and much of the West other than France, the Ould Taya regime was desperate to rebuild its international credibility."[13] Ould Mey credits France in particular for pressuring Mauritania to reform. A few days after emerging from a marathon meeting with France's foreign minister, Taya surprised everyone when he announced his intention to introduce

---

9. As Bratton and van de Walle, 1992 (pp. 430–32) have acknowledged, the "diffusion effect" of the democratization process elsewhere cannot be dismissed as a contributing factor to the political developments of the early 1990s in Africa.

10. Bratton and van De Walle observed that Mauritania was among the countries in which no major political protests were held by the opposition, see table page 432; Francois Soudan has pointedly noted that Mauritania, due to its comparatively small urban population, advantageously lacked the "urban logistics" for riots associated with large crowds, p. 115.

11. Ould Taya had created a special unit made up of his Smassid kinsmen in charge of his personal safety. See Africa Confidential, 29 June 1990 and 8 February 1991; also Philippe Marchesin, *Tribus, Ethnies*, 1992 pp. 294–97. A longtime close ally Ely Ould Mohamed Vall has been also running the state security paramilitary bureaucracy with ample discretion.

12. Mohameden Ould Mey, *Global Restructuring and Peripheral states: The Carrot and the Stick in Mauritania*, Lanham, MD: Littlefield Adams Books, 1992, p. 225–28.

13. Janet Fleischman, "Ethnic cleansing," *Africa Report* 39 Jan–Feb. 1994, p. 45.

major policy changes.[14] The image the post-1992 regime advertises of Mauritania is that of a multiparty, tolerant polity in which basic civil, political, press and other freedoms are respected. The number of opposition newspapers and political parties contesting episodic municipal, legislative and presidential elections, and the absence of permanent political prisoners are underscored to support this claim.

This picture perfect democracy is highly misleading, however. Things are almost never as they appear to be in Mauritania. Even an astute and long time observer of Mauritania, Anthony Pazzanita, was misled by this façade.[15] In fact, the conclusion Mohameden Ould Mey reached in his study of the political economy of Mauritania aptly captures the political reality of the country.

> [T]he structure of power survived (almost intact) the transition from a military regime to a civilian regime based on multipartyism, free election and free press. To caricature it, the colonel took off his military fatigues and wore a business suit as a cosmetic constitutional reform designed more for appeasing Western pressure and disarming the opposition than genuinely empowering the people...[16]

Keen observers of Mauritania would agree that, more than ten years later, the regime's basic characteristics have persisted under the veneer of a serene and tolerant democracy. Even the October 19, 2001 elections where the opposition captured a few parliamentary seats and municipalities, do not fundamentally alter this statement. As the opposition strenuously contends, Mauritania is a long way from the pluralist and open democracy Ould Taya's regime is eager to project to the world.[17] Kevin Bales, a scholar who conducted an undercover investigation in Mauritania for his book on slavery, observed perceptively that Mauritania's outwardly "Alice in the Wonderland charac-

---

14. Ould Mey, p. 228.

15. Pazzanita, "The origins…" 1996.

16. Mohameden Ould Mey, p. 256

17. See, for example, Jemal Ould Yessa, "*Façade de Pluralisme et Dérive Autoritaire en Mauritanie*," Demain Magazine 30, 9/15–9/21, 2001.

ter" concealed a ruthless "police state."[18] For example, while the military as an institution is no longer in power, military officers, transformed into wheelers and dealers, have continued to run major state-controlled enterprises and wield power behind the scenes. Another feature is that despite the existence of formal institutions, procedures, and mechanisms, Ould Taya with a restricted group of advisors, kin and kith essentially monopolize the bulk of the state apparatus. Critical questions, then, are why did the military regime in place follow the "non-democratization" path it did, what variables account for this outcome, and how did it go about it?

To answer this and related questions one must initially closely examine three critical, interrelated variables. The first is the metamorphosis in Ould Taya's personality and worldview and his display of theretofore unsuspected political skills. The second is the reverberations of the massive human rights abuses perpetrated under the military regime mainly between 1986 and 1992. The third critical variable needed to understand the dynamics and outcome of the regime rearrangement process launched on 15 April 1991, is the *de facto* transfer of the bulk of the national economy and of the state apparatus to a mostly Smassid (Ould Taya's tribe) business class. Finally, a close look at the regime's responses to various challenges from the opposition as it scrambled to reduce its international vulnerability while strengthening its hold on power, is indispensable to shed more light on the recent evolution of the political system.

Ould Taya's Personal Evolution

Scholars of democratization have not always paid sufficient attention to the political, psychological variable involved in the array of factors that determine the evolution and nature of a democratization process. To understand the process that led to Mauritania's demand for multiparty politics, one must consider Ould Taya's personality and psychological make-up in 1991. In their widely quoted discussion of

---

18. Kevin Bales, *Disposable people: New Slavery in the Global Economy*, Berkeley, University of California Press, 1999, 80–83.

the characteristics and exigencies of "personal rule" in Africa, Robert Jackson and Carl Rosenberg insist that, given the uncertainty and the highly personalized nature of such political systems, retaining power becomes the highest priority of the leader.[19] The political developments in Mauritania between 1986 and the October 19, 2001 parliamentary and municipal elections must be traced to the amazing transformation in the personality and world view of colonel Maaouiya Ould Sid'Ahmed Taya as well as his determination to cling to power. In less than a decade, he went from a political non-factor to a savvy political manipulator who consolidated and legitimized his power at almost no cost to himself or his regime.

Before the 1984 coup that propelled him to power, Ould Taya was generally perceived by many Mauritanians as a member of a despised group of officers without political agenda or ideals, more concerned with partying and enjoying the spoils of power (or the association therewith) than the political orientation or the well-being of the country.[20] Unlike the other officers, he sought no political base among his kin of the Smassid tribe, nor belonged to any of the numerous Arab nationalist groups that competed within the army.[21] When he acceded to power, Ould Taya had a reputation of a "detribalized" Moor in a society where ethnic and tribal affinities are determinant. The failed coup attempt by a group of Halpulaar officers in 1987 and racial tensions in 1989 were turning points in Ould Taya's metamorphosis. The international isolation that resulted from Taya's government's handling of these events added to what Habib Ould Mahfoudh has called "his pronounced persecution complex and feeling of isolation."[22]

---

19. Robert Jackson and Carl Rosenberg, *Personal Rule in Black Africa: Prince, Autocrat, Prophet, Tyrant*, Berkeley: University of California Press, 1982.

20. Mohamed Nassirou Athie, "Il y a Onze ans, le 16 Mars," *Al Beyane* No. 14, p. 8.

21. For a very informed discussion of the proliferation of Arab nationalist groups in the Mauritanian army see Anthony Pazzanita, "Mauritania's Foreign Policy: The Search for Protection," *Journal of Modern African Studies*, 30 (2), 1992, pp. 288–300.

22. Habib Ould Mahfoudh, "La Tension," *Al Beyane*, No. 6 January 22–28, 1992 (Supplement) p. 2.

A slow and profound transformation of his outlook on Mauritania, its politics, its problems and the most appropriate ways of handling them was taking place. The consciousness of his isolation and the necessity to go back to the tribal fold started to crystallize as his manichaean view of the "national question" (Mauritania's intractable and intertwined ethnic, racial, cultural and political woes), in particular, developed. A formerly "detribalized" Ould Taya soon became a born again Arab nationalist championing the Arab character of Mauritania. He started to see his mission in life as the rescue of the "national unity" and the defense of the "Arabness" of his country against the "permanent plot" of its enemies.[23] The subsequent decisions he made stemmed, to a large extent, from this personal evolution and the willingness to go to any length to retain power. One of the most unwieldy consequences of this mind-set was the brutal repression he visited on non-Arab Mauritanians.

Human Rights Abuses

The process of political and economic marginalization of Mauritania's non-Arabic speaking populations has been amply documented by foreign governments and non-governmental organizations alike.[24] These practices were so uncommon even by African standards of political exclusion and repression that they were labeled an informal apartheid.[25] Between 1989 and the end of 1992, 50,000 to 100,000 black Mauritani-

---

23. Ould Mahfoudh, p. 1; see also Francois Soudan, "Maaouiya Ould Taya: 'Le Sénégal nous Veut du Mal'," *Jeune Afrique*, No. 1513, Jan. 1 34–37.

24. See for example *Mauritania's campaign of Terror: State Sponsored Repression of Black African* Human Rights Watch/Africa, New York, 1994 and U.S. Department of State, *Country Report on Human Rights Practices for 1992: Mauritania* Washington, D.C. US Government Printing Office, February 1992 pp. 162–70; and *Country Report on human rights Practices for 1993*, pp. 177–85.

25. The oppressive practices of the Ould Taya regime in particular were not as sophisticated or as codified as those of apartheid South Africa. However, some opponents and neutral observers have made a strong case as to the similarities between the effects of the repression of Blacks in both countries. See FLAM Manifesto "Mauritanie: 30 ans d'un apartheid meconnu," October 1989 (pamphlet), Dakar and *Hearing before the Subcommittee on Human Rights and International*

ans were stripped of their citizenship and deported or forced to flee to Senegal and Mali.[26] Human Rights observers have also documented the extrajudicial killing of (at least) 500 black Mauritanians most from the ranks of the military. These events resulted not only in what was described as, a "psychosis of fear in the black community"[27] but also in a tremendous amount of anger and resentment in that community. Any truly democratic government elected in from fair elections would have had to address this issue for the country to stand a chance to finally rid itself of the demons of race and ethnicity.[28] Genuine democratization was bound to fail as long as the incumbent regime remained in power. The outcries of human rights organizations and the opposition were unable to force Ould Taya to bring to justice the perpetrators of even the most egregious of these crimes. In fact, the law number 23/93 of 14 June 1993 granted a "complete pardon" for all the crimes committed between 1 January 1989 and 17 April 1992. This law shielded high-ranking officers in the military, high level civil servants and powerful businessmen from prosecution. O'Donnell and Schmitter identify such a measure as "the worst of bad solutions" for democratization prospects because of its inevitable negative repercussions on the military and the entire society.[29] Punishment for those who perpetrated the most heinous crimes was a major stumbling block to genuine democratization. The conditions for removing it were never met.

Organizations and on Africa, 19 June 1991, Washington, DC: US Government Printing Office.

26. The UN high Commission for Refugees estimates at the number at 65,000 as of June 1991 in Senegal and Mali. Other estimates are higher. See Fleischman, p. 45–46.

27. Rakiya Omaar, "Arrests and Executions," *West Africa,* 8–14 July 1991, p. 1124.

28. Statements by Ahmed Ould Daddah on the issue indicate a high level of awareness of the need to tackle the issue if only because the votes of blacks would have made the difference in any election. See "Ahmed Ould Daddah, un des Leaders de l'Opposition," Interview by Dominique David, *Le Courrier* 137 Jan–Feb. 1993, pp. 32–34.

29. O'Donnell and Schmitter, 1986, pp. 28–38.

The Economy: A Tribal Monopoly

Despite substantial national resources and assets (iron ore, fish, copper, a small population, etc...), sustained financial aid from rich Arab states and western financial institutions and states, the gross mismanagement by successive military regimes after the initial July 10, 1978 coup prevented any real economic development. An already bad situation has considerably worsened, however, under Ould Taya's watch.[30] Virtually all indicators were desperately bleak by 1991. The World Bank estimated that between 1986 and 1992 the average *per anum* and per capita percentage growth was a negative 0.1. The total external annual debt averaged over 2 billion dollars since 1986.[31] This amounts to more than one thousand dollars for every Mauritanian, the fourth worse debt predicament in Africa.[32] In essence, despite turning over the national economy to the international financial institutions and thereby gaining access to millions of dollars to supposedly to several development projects in all sectors of the economy, the regime does not have much to show for itself after twelve years of more or less faithfully executed structural adjustment programs.[33] Mauritania ranked 149 out of 174 countries on the 1996 UN Human Development Report, despite receiving close to one quarter of its GNP in development assistance, about 153.2 dollars per capita.[34]

However, beyond the damning economic indicators, what could be called the "Smassidization" of the Mauritanian economy following Ould Taya's accession to power better accounts for thwarting genuine

---

30. The following data pertain mainly to the Ould Taya era which started in 1985. They are drawn from the World Bank Report *African Development Indicators 1994–1995*, Washington, D.C., The World Bank, 1995, unless otherwise indicated.

31. World Bank, 1995, p. 6.

32. World Bank, 1995, p. 178.

33. For a thorough and well done study of the economic policies of the Ould Taya regime and the involvement of the IMF and World Bank, see Ould Mey, *Global Restructuring*, especially chapters 4, 5, and 6.

34. UNDP, *UN Human Development Report 1996*, Washington, D.C., United Nations Development Program, 1996, p. 173.

democracy. Starting in 1987, Ould Taya turned virtually the entire economy over to the Smassid, his tribe, represented by three families in an almost Mafioso sense.[35] The Ehel Abdallahi, Ould Noueiguet and Ehel Maham who were already active in the retail business, suddenly saw their fortunes turn for the better after Ould Taya's tribal instincts were awakened by the 1987 coup attempt led by a group of Halpulaar (non Arab) officers.[36]

With the exception of the mining sector, which has been monopolized by a state controlled company headed by Ould Taya's cousin since 1984, these three families together, with their members interlocking in a large business, political and bureaucratic network hold a virtual monopoly on most sectors of the national economy. "They have a presence in everything that moves, from the import-export sector to the retail of charcoal, from banking to agriculture."[37] These families and their economic allies exercise a near complete control over the most lucrative sectors of the national economy. The new land tenure reform allowed the collusion of the Arab-Berber public servants and businessman to lawfully dispossess black communities and individual landowners of lands they have held for centuries.[38] The intense involvement of the Ministry of the Interior and businessmen from the north occurred against the background of the near comple-

---

35. See Marchesin for a discussion of the distribution of economic strength between the different tribes of the north in the early years of Ould Taya's rule, pp. 380–85. The distribution has considerably shifted in favor of the Smassid. A recent opposition document stresses this shift. See Front Arabo-Africain du Salut, "*Lettre Ouverte au President*," Paris, October 26, 1996.

36. See Ike Onworki, "A question of Race," *West Africa* No. 3719 October 24–30, 1988 p. 1984 for a discussion of this watershed event and its implications for Mauritanian politics.

37. Interview on July 18, 1997, with an official in the Ministry of Finance who is not a member of the Smassid, requested anonymity. See also Marchesin (1992) for a discussion of the very close relationships cultivated between the Ould Taya regime and the increasingly politicized merchant class issued mainly from the major Arab-Berber tribes of the north, singularly the Smassid, Ould Taya' tribe.

38. See Thomas K. Park et al *Conflict over Land and the Crisis of Nationalism in Mauritania*, Madison: Land Tenure Center University of Wisconsin-Madison, 1991, for a particularly well done study of this issue and its ramifications.

tion of major agriculture related development projects in the Senegal valley region. Many have argued that the construction of two internationally financed dams on the Senegal river and the prospect of very lucrative exploitation of thousands of hectares of land in an area mostly inhabited by blacks Mauritanians were the real reason for the displacement and repression visited on the landholders of the area.[39] The stakes this new class has in the perpetuation of the regime made many of the other Arab-Berber tribes almost as resentful of the Ould Taya government as the non-Arabic speaking (black) Mauritanians. This, in turn, meant that genuine democratization would entail the near certainty of losing power, a risk the main beneficiaries of the regime were not about to take. Colonel Ould Taya was left with no other choice than to engage in survival maneuvers based on a calculated legitimizing strategy destined primarily for international consumption. While by necessity this process had to encompass a break from the openly repressive practices of the past, a genuine democratization was not intended and, quite logically, did not ensue.

The "Programmed Electoral Putsch"[40]

With the crushing defeat of Iraq in early 1991, the external vulnerability of the Ould Taya regime was palpable, as Janet Fleischman has pointed out.[41] It had managed to alienate its Arab and western financial backers and friends by siding with Iraq in the Gulf crisis. Throughout Africa, Ould Taya had observed his colleagues' desperate maneuvers to hang on to power being reduced to pitiful sideshows. He witnessed the unhappy fate of his friend Moussa Tra-

---

39. See Park et al., 1991; also Elimane Fall, "*Sénégal-Mauritanie: Le Dossier du Conflit, Les enjeux de l'après Barrage*," *Jeune Afrique* # 1491, August 2, 1989, pp. 39–44.

40. This phrase was used by the main opposition leader to characterize the event leading to the first election of Ould Taya. See *Livre Blanc sur la Fraude ou Chronique d'un Putsch Electoral Programme*', *Direction de la Campagne du Candidat Ahmed Ould Daddah aux election Presidentielles du 24 Janvier 1992 an Mauritanie*, Nouachott.

41. Janet Fleischman, "Ethnic Cleansing."

ore of Mali, who was ousted under the pressure of popular unrest.[42] Hence, his challenge was to be responsive to Western pressure, and adapt to a new worldwide reality without losing power in the process. That he outmaneuvered those who all but buried him when he announced new multiparty elections is a testament to Ould Taya's ability to learn quickly and his uncanny speed at preempting the moves of the opposition

While still convinced that the country was not ready for democracy,[43] he nevertheless drafted a Constitution styled after that of the French Fifth Republic. He also made sure that the opposition had absolutely no input in the process. To mute the protest of an embryonic but growing opposition emboldened by the regime's international isolation, he put its major leaders under house arrest and exiled them to remote villages.[44] They were freed only after the Constitution was passed—as originally drafted, without term limits. On 12 July 1991 a draft of the Constitution was submitted to a referendum and ratified with 97.9% of the vote cast amid the opposition's calls for a boycott. However, only 8% of the registered voters participated in the poll.[45] Taya's ability to stay ahead of the opposition characterized the entire transition process. *After* the Constitution was adopted, article 104 was added to it. This article, conspicuously absent in many English versions of the Mauritanian constitution, reads: "All the laws and regulations currently applicable in the Islamic Republic of Mauritania remain in force as long as they have not been duly modified in conformity with the present Constitution" (authors' translation). This addition all but emptied the Constitution of any substance. In practice, it annulled all the basic freedoms of assembly, association, etc. that the new Constitution was supposed to guarantee. Article 104 reinstated (supposedly as a transitory measure) the same restrictive decrees governing these matters as enacted under the military regime.

---

42. For an account of the overthrow of Moussa Traore, see Pascal James Imperato, "Downfall," *Africa Report*, 36 (4) July–August 1991.

43. Soudan, p. 112.

44. *Ibid*, p. 113.

45. Peter Da Costa, "Democracy in Doubt," *Africa Report* 37 (3) May–June 1992 p. 59.

A multitude of parties, most of which were very close to if not created by the government, were allowed to operate. To avoid a risky two-way race between Ould Taya and the opposition's candidate Ahmed Ould Dadddah (the first civilian president's brother), the military junta instigated additional candidacies.[46]

When the presidential election was held on 24 January, 1992, the end result of the entire process was a foregone conclusion. Colonel Ould Taya was declared the first round winner by 62.65% of the votes cast. The opposition and neutral observers pointed to massive election fraud calling it a "democratic farce."[47] Massive irregularities were documented in the establishment of electoral lists as well as in the actual conduct of the election.[48] The opposition had just lost the first and decisive battle. Like many others, it had collectively underestimated Ould Taya and, in this instance, his determination to remain in power at all cost. He had pulled off one of many tricks that left his opposition baffled and always one step behind him. This made the subsequent consolidation of his power easier and pushed the prospect of a complete break with authoritarianism back even further. Only a few months earlier, many thought genuine democratization (which to many implied regime change) inevitable given the situation in which Mauritania's Colonels found themselves after the defeat of their ally Saddam Hussein in the Gulf War. A telling indication of the success of the regime's overall strategy was the continuing split of the opposition on the eve of the 12 December, 1997 presidential elections (which occurred, not coincidentally on the 13th anniversary of the regime). While some opposition figures joined the party in power,

---

46. Mohamed Vall Ould Oumere, "Il évite le Face à Face," Al Beyane 11–17 Dec. 1991.

47. Jacques de Barin, "Mauritanie: La Démocratie a l'épreuve des Tensions Raciales," Le Monde (Paris), March 6, 1992; also Africa Research bulletin (Political, Social and Cultural Series) 29 1–31 January 1992 p. 10414–15.

48. Da Costa, p. 59. It was common knowledge that the Moor-looking Touareg refugees from Mali were allowed to vote and that the electoral lists were inflated just as many blacks were prevented from voting. Those in refugee camps in Senegal and Mali were not acknowledged much less allowed to vote. See also Rakiya Omaar and Janet Fleischman, "Arab Vs. African," Africa Report 36 (4) July–August 1991 pp. 35–38.

others formed a coalition…only to run against Ould Taya despite the boycott decided by the major opposition parties.[49] This added legitimacy to an election whose script closely resembled that of the 1992 election. This time, challenged only by minor candidates, Ould Taya was elected by more than 90% of the vote.[50]

The "Consolidation" of Instability

At the end of the Cold War and with the general movement toward the end of repressive political systems, there was a palpable euphoria among practitioners and students of democratization. There was a sense that the triumph of western liberal democratic forms of political and economic organization was ineluctable. In such an atmosphere of the "end of history,"[51] the flawed processes that led to the "legitimization" of once oppressive regimes were generally overlooked. In many instances continent-wide and singularly in West Africa, issues of transitional justice and the substance of the reforms introduced have not been given all the attention they deserve from either the West or academics and observers of these processes. With the caveat that liberalization must be qualitatively distinguished from democratization, it was often presumed that once blatant repressive practices were abandoned, an irresistible movement toward democratization would ensue using western style liberal democracy as the model and end goal. For example, the moral and political obligation to provide justice to the victims of atrocious human rights violations and, for the sake of democracy itself, to see to it that the principles of accountability and due process were upheld, were not given seri-

---

49. Hamdy Ould Mouknass, the former foreign minister of the pre-1978 regime decided to back Ould Taya. The other major parties joined together to boycott the election citing the lack of transparency in the logistics of the polling and the total government control over the media, among other grievances. See *Africa Research Bulletin*, "Opposition Boycott," July 1997.

50. *Africa Research Bulletin*, "Taya Reelected" December 1997, p. 12928.

51. See Francis Fukuyama, "The End of History," The National Interest 16, 1989, 3–4.

ous consideration in most cases. Mauritania is a particularly poignant example.[52]

As made evident in the foregoing discussion of Mauritania's post 1992 evolution, "consolidation" in this context by no means refers to the critical stage of a democratization process abundantly addressed in literature. That is, a stage of institutionalization and routinization of democratic practices and ethos "by which [a newly found] democracy becomes so broadly and profoundly legitimate [...] that it is very unlikely to break down" as a theoretician defined it.[53] To elaborate further, Juan J. Linz and Alfred Stepan posited three "minimal conditions" that must be fulfilled before a regime can be considered a consolidated democracy.[54] The first of these is the existence of an autonomous, authoritative, impersonal, central authority that protects the rights of its citizens. The second precondition requires competitive, inclusive and generally fair elections. The third minimal condition for a regime to be democratic is for democratically chosen leaders to adhere to the scrupulous respect of the established constitutional and legal norms. None of these conditions have been obtained yet in Mauritania today. Nevertheless, Mauritania is no longer the clumsy authoritarian state that for years deported thousands of its own citizens and imprisoned, tortured and killed hundreds more.

As though the concept of consolidation applied only positively, the process, dynamics and outcomes of what could be called "negative consolidation" whereby an authoritarian regime succeeds in strengthening its hold on power by "legitimizing" itself, has not been as systematically studied. According to Webster's dictionary, to consolidate is to "make firm and secure." This literal definition clearly applies to the post-1992 Mauritanian regime. Yet, even by the most minimalist definition of democracy, Mauritania's post 1992 political system does

---

52. See Boubacar N'Diaye, "The effect of Mauritania's 'Human Rights Deficit' on the Democratization Process: The Case Against to 'Forgive and Forget,'" *Journal of African Policy Studies* (8(1) 2002, 17–35).

53. Larry Diamond, "Toward democratic Consolidation," *Journal of Democracy* 5 July 1994 p. 15.

54. Juan J. Linz and Alfred Stepan, "Toward consolidated democracies," *Journal of Democracy* 7 (2) April 1996 pp. 14–15.

not qualify as democratic. In this case, a shrewd and calculated exploitation of a minimalist, procedural (mis)reading and perversion of what democracy entails, led to the strengthening of Ould Taya's grip on power, rather than a genuine transition to democracy and a clean break from the past. The state, its organs, and even the unilaterally crafted constitution were blatantly subverted. Initially, this robbed the opposition of its most powerful weapon, the broad consensus (domestically as well as internationally) that the regime was illegitimate, undemocratic and needed fundamental overhaul. It left the opposition lacking cohesion and a rallying cry powerful enough to even approach the one provided by the pariah status of the pre-1992 Ould Taya regime. It also made it easier for the regime, thanks to its total control of the state reward and sanction mechanisms, to freely pursue its strategy of co-opting or completely silencing the most vocal or threatening segments and leaders of the opposition (see below). As E. Gyimah-Boadi has pertinently observed, given the economic hardships suffered by precisely those segments of society most likely to spearhead the struggle for democracy, most individuals and groups in Africa find it difficult to resist the temptation of cutting deals even if this undermines the struggle against undemocratic governments.[55] The following discussion indicates that these practices have strengthened the hand of the post-1992 regime. At the same time, these practices are strong signals of the regime's inherent instability and the increasing probability of political violence as a likely feature of Mauritanian politics.

By all accounts, all the periodic elections held between 1992 and 2001 were not truly competitive. Both the whole process that led up to elections and the polling itself were fraudulent. The elections were held mainly for the eyes of the international community and to legitimize a paranoid, power-hungry, military leader unable to imagine his country without him at the helm. Mauritania has only gradually rearranged the political system. It has been what Larry Diamond would call a "pseudo-democracy" in his discussion of the state of the

---

55. E. Gyimah-Boadi, "Civil Society in Africa," Journal of Democracy 7, (2) April 1996, 126.

so-called "third wave" of democratization.[56] Terry Karl and Philippe Schmitter would label Mauritanina a "hybrid regime," "a polity which cannot meet the procedural minima of democracy but also does not return to the *status quo ante*,"[57] a familiar breed throughout West Africa even a decade after the so-called 'wave'. After the 1992 elections, there was no need for the regime to reverse to the *status quo ante* due in part to the prevailing mindset regarding democratization. That necessity may have arisen only more recently (see below).

Firmly in control of what Da Costa called the "paper democracy of his creation,"[58] Ould Taya was able to charm Mauritania's main providers of vital economic aid and political support while cleverly continuing to neutralize the opposition. Because of its economic and strategic interests, France was (and is) much more understanding—and protective[59]—of a regime it (in all likelihood) helped put in power. As to US administrations, they were seemingly more determined to punish the Ould Taya regime for its defiant alliance with Saddam Hussein than for any other reason. France left no doubt as to its stance when President Mitterrand received Ould Taya in a business-as-usual fashion just a few months after his inauguration following elections the French President knew were fraudulent.[60] Not coincidentally, European (mostly French) companies extracted in-

---

56. For a very useful discussion of conceptual and qualitative distinctions between the types of regimes resulting from the third wave of democratization, see Larry Diamond, "Is the Third Wave Over?" *Journal of Democracy* 7 (3) 1996 20–37.

57. Terry Karl and Philippe C. Schmitter, "Comparing Neo-Democracies: Origins, Trajectories and Outcomes," in Leslie Elliot Amijo, ed. *Conversations on Democratization and Economic Reforms*, (Working Paper on the Southern California Seminar) Center for International Studies School of International Relations University of Southern California Los Angeles, CA, 1996, p. 331.

58. Da Costa, p. 60.

59. See in this regard a clearly apologist interpretation of the 1992 elections by the representative of the European union in Mauritania, Jean-Michel Perille, "Entretien avec Jean Michel Perille," Interview by Dominique David, *Le Courrier* 137 January–February 1993 pp. 39–41.

60. See Francois Soudan, "Mauritanie: Le Bon Elève," *Jeune Afrique*, December 23, 1993 – January 5, 1994.

credibly lucrative deals with Mauritania in the fishing sector in particular.[61] Silencing the only critics who could jeopardize the legitimization and 'consolidation' of his power put the finishing touch on
Taya's efforts to retain power while rehabilitating himself. By the end
of Ould Taya's first term, Mauritania's Western partners seemed to be
satisfied indeed. In addition, the (legal or underground) political opposition, kept in check or neutralized, has not been able to seriously
challenge the peaceful and benevolent image the regime has assidu-
ously projected to the world.

Plus Ça Change...

There is no doubt that President Ould Taya has been successful in
achieving his main, concurrent objectives of maintaining his power
almost intact and neutralizing his opponents. His adroit maneuvering left his opposition, once confident in its ability to displace him,
baffled, divided, and in disarray. While on a few occasions Ould Taya's
regime appeared threatened and the opposition appeared in a position to seriously challenge his power, the essential elements of the post
1992 regime's *modus operandi* have remained remarkably constant, as
the recent evolution in mauritanian politics illustrates. Three critical
features characterize this evolution. The first is the extreme vigilance
and consummate ruthlessness of Ould Taya's government and its willingness to take drastic, often impulsive measures to prevent the emergence of any credible challenge. A second related feature has been a
policy of undermining, frustrating, and dividing the opposition in
order to keep it constantly off balance. Finally, Taya's shrewd diplomatic moves to remain in the good graces of western countries and
their lending institutions have helped him consolidate power.
Throughout its tenure, the overriding concern of the regime has been
to prevent any evocation of what was labeled Mauritania's "human
rights deficit" discussed above, which has also remained the sore point
in politics in the country.

---

61. Hamoud Ould Etheimine, "Un Marché de Dupes," *La tribune*, No. 17 July
3, 1996 p. 6.

Authoritarian governments strive on ensuring that even remotely potential challenges remain in check in order to prevent their growth and ability to exploit circumstances that may enable them to develop into a threat or an alternative to the existing order. As discussed above, this feature did not disappear with the formal demise of the military regime in 1992. Because of its isolation, unpopularity, and the political 'baggage' it carried (the 'electoral putsch' and massive human rights violations), the survival of the Ould Taya regime required that it left nothing to chance. The 'human rights deficit,' as the massive human rights violations committed between 1986 and 1992 are called, has become *the* single phrase in Mauritanian political lingo although the government never even acknowledged officially that massive human rights abuses were committed. The 23/93 law of 14 June 1993 granting a "complete pardon" for all crimes committed between 1989 and 1991 ended investigation into this 'human rights deficit' and, paradoxically, instead of occulting the issue, made it a permanent, albeit hidden, presence in the political discourse in Mauritania. Since the law was passed, a national silence has been imposed on the topic and any attempt to revive it is considered an attack against 'national unity.' A cornerstone of most of the political decisions made after 1992 has been enforcing this stance and preventing any evocation of the 'human rights deficit' and its consequences in the political arena. For example, the January 2002 decision to ban a leading opposition party, *Action pour le Changement* (AC), resulted directly from the freshly elected members of parliament of this party asking the Prime Minister pointed questions about this very 'human rights deficit' and the practice of slavery. This latest, abrupt, and certainly, anti-climactic decision, which followed the first free and fair polling, was, in fact, only one in a series of measures very much imitating the practices of the "transition" period to the post 1992 regime. The most conspicuous of these has been the constant harassment of leaders of the main opposition parties. For example, every opportunity was used to arrest Mr. Ahmed Ould Daddah, the leader of UFD/EN, for more or less brief periods. This was done a record number of times, with occasional trials on charges ranging from conspiracy to dissemination of false information. The harassment culminated in the ban of his party altogether, in an effort to curtail his growing stature as a potential alternative to Ould Taya. The leader of another opposition party, the *Front Populaire*, Mr Chbih Ould Cheikh Malainine was jailed in April 2001 on trumped up charges of conspiracy to commit violence following a trial widely believed to be political. Between 1998 and 2000, several party and civil society leaders were also detained or put on trial. On January 2, 2002, the Ould Taya government's first political decision of the new year was to ban *Action pour le Changement*. This was the only remaining viable opposition party widely viewed as a truly nationally based party where all ethnic and cultural groups in the country were represented. The pretext invoked in this case was the allegedly "racist and violent" nature of the party. In reality, its members of parliament and party leaders had dared to ask the Prime Minister questions regarding the fate of the victims of the human rights abuses and the taboo issue of continued slavery in the country. In fact, since its inception, *Action pour le Changement* (AC) has always viewed itself as an ardent advocate for both issues and has often raised them in political discourse. These ideas are central to the AC's purpose, as stated in its constitutive documents. Several independent papers were harassed, temporarily seized, and ultimately forced to closed down altogether. These actions were justified through a series of invocations of the infamous article 11 of the decree on the press which gives extensive discretionary powers to the Minister of the Interior over the press. Restrictive measures were also taken against international media such as *Radio France International* and the satellite television station *El Jazzeera*. In most cases, unfavorable coverage of policies or events related to human right abuses and slavery were behind government action. Simultaneously, the Ould Taya regime acted to prevent any coalition of the opposition susceptible to garner enough momentum to represent a challenge. This was accomplished mainly by pursuing elaborate renditions of the age-old strategy of divide and conquer.

Through infiltration and manipulation, Taya's regime first weakened the opposition by polarizing even further the Haratines (former slaves) and the non-Arabic speaking Mauritanians, the two groups most likely to provide significant electoral support to the opposition. Observers of Mauritania have argued that the *Haratines* were deliberately used by their former masters (often allies of the Ould Taya's regime) to commit the most vicious abuses against non Arabic-speaking blacks since 1989 and to occupy the land of deportees in an effort to make the prospect for an eventual alliance even harder.[62] The opposition is no less fragmented in the Arab-Berber population where attachment to tribe or region and personal enmities, combined with government tactics of divide and conquer, have prevented the formation of any significant coalition against the regime. For example, any attempt to build coalitions between the various ethno-social groups, even during the 1992 presidential election, was made to appear illegitimate. It was portrayed as an embrace of the radical theses of the sometimes violent *Forces de Libération Africaines de Mauritanie* (FLAM)—one of the outlawed, black, political movements committed to the destruction of Arab-Berber domination of Mauritania's political and economic systems.

In the same vein, a consummate mixture of co-optation and repression, succeeded in splitting the once promising "El Hor"[63] movement into feuding moderate, opportunistic, and radical wings. One of the most significant achievements of the Ould Taya regime has been to cleverly divide, and thus neutralize, this growing political force, the Haratines (freed slaves).[64] The most militant factions led by former government officials such as Bah Ould Rabah and Messaoud Ould Boulkheir (now leader of the banned AC and once nicknamed the "Mauritanian Mandela") have vigorously pursued, through *SOS-Es-*

---

62. See Omaar and Fleischman pp. 37–38.

63. "*El Hor*" is the political organization formed by the descendants of former slaves (Haratines) to fight against the manifestations and legacies of slavery in Mauritania and for the improvement of the conditions the *Haratines* in Mauritanian society. While a moderate wing was co-opted by the regime, the more radical wing is relentlessly ostracized even harassed.

64. Marchesin, 1992, p. 343, put the Haratines at 26% of the population in 1980 with an annual growth rate of 11%. The *Haratines* are today considered the largest ethno-political group. They make up more than one third of the total population. Although black Africans they speak hassanya (an Arabic dialect), the same language their former masters speak and are still attached to the latter by complex relations of economic and psychological dependence mixed with resentment. For an analysis of the rapidly growing clout of the *Haratines*, see Marchesin pp. 384–402.

claves, and more recently all the way to the parliament, the politically embarrassing issue of slavery. They succeeded in putting pressure on the regime where it is most vulnerable, its international image. Ould Taya once characterized Mauritanians who push this issue as foreign lackeys.[65] The ban of *Action pour le Changement* is directly related to this stance.

Third, still with the same objective of dividing the opposition, but also to bolster its credentials as a "fledgling democracy," the Ould Taya regime introduced limited electoral reforms and organized early municipal and parliamentary elections in October 2001. The reforms consisted essentially in the adoption of a partial proportional electoral system and a new system for financing political parties. Although these measures were built up as major strides toward anchoring "Mauritania's young democracy," they were made in the wake of the ban of a major political party, the arrest of its leader along with numerous other opponents, and the closure of independent newspapers. It was hoped that rival parties, starved for funds, would compete fiercely for funding, thereby reducing the pressure on Ould Taya's main party, the *Parti Républicain Démocratique et Social* (PRDS). Another anticipated outcome of this reform was the creation of incentives for the opposition parties to moderate their stance and collaborate with the PRDS in order to keep much needed funding forthcoming. Similarly, it was also anticipated that major rifts would occur in the opposition on the appropriateness of participating in the early elections (without enough time or means to prepare). In fact, these scenarios did materialize to a certain extent. However, to the government's surprise, thanks to the absence of widespread fraud and the unexpected cooperation among opposition parties in the second round, the election was a major victory for the opposition, particularly in major cities. For the first time, the parliament included 11 members of the opposition, enough to constitute a parliamentary group. While this unexpected outcome introduced a new equation into Mauritanian politics, and forced the government to eventually

---

65. See "Extraits du discours du Président Ould Taya," *Mauritanie-Nouvelles* # 234 January 12–19 1997, p. 10.

curtail the opposition's gains, it was in reality another (mis-) calculated attempt to divide and weaken the opposition and keep it off balance. Various repressive and anti-democratic strategies were effective enough in neutralizing the domestic opposition. It is evident that most of the decisions concerning the opposition made since 2000 were, in fact, to insure Ould Taya's reelection for a third consecutive term in 2003. However, since the impetus for the military regime to introduce multiparty politics came form the pressure of the international community, as discussed above, the post-1992 regime needed to make the "non-democratization" path acceptable to the West. This was achieved by introducing unabashedly accommodating policies toward western financial institutions and shrewd diplomatic moves destined to enlist the sympathy of major western countries and mute their criticisms of the nature and practices of the regime, particularly in the area of governance and human rights.

The post-Gulf War international dispensation made courting the favors of the West an attractive proposition for nearly all vulnerable regimes. However, Mauritania went arguably beyond any other regime in this regard. This was done to some extent to compensate for its alliance with Saddam Hussein in the conflict. The shrewd diplomatic moves Ould Taya made were unquestionably related to domestic politics and the necessity to mute criticism of his regime. France has been traditionally the protector of various regimes in Mauritania. It may have played a crucial role in bringing Ould Taya to power in 1984 and helped him maneuver the transformation of his regime in 1991. France's attitude, deferred to by the European Union members, is that the situation in Mauritania has been slowly but steadily improving. Quite willingly, although knowing better, France bought into Ould Taya's characterization of the state of affairs. This stance has shielded the regime from any pressure to engage in genuine democratization. Only Captain Ely Ould Dah[66] affair soured relations between the two countries and forced the Ould Taya regime,

---

66. For a discussion of the impact of this affair on Mauritanian politics, see N'Diaye, "The Effect of Mauritania's 'Human Rights Deficit" *Journal of African Policy Studies* 8(1) 2002, 17–35.

feeling threatened, to build even closer relations with the United States.

Mauritania's uncharacteristic embrace of closer relations with Israel, as early as 1995,[67] and its willingness to participate in the NATO-led efforts to fight Islamic fundamentalism in the Maghreb,[68] were clear indications of Ould Taya's readiness to pay his dues in order to gain international acceptance in the post Gulf-War world dominated by the United States. Before 1995, only the United Stated had maintained pressure on the Ould Taya regime citing the continued mistreatment of its citizens, including the institution of slavery. This changed when Mauritania displayed its eagerness to redeem itself after its disastrous support of Iraq in the Gulf War. In April 1999, the United States government awarded Mauritania trade benefits under the Generalized System of Preferences (GSPA). A few years earlier, the same vital privilege had been suspended because of human rights abuses, including slavery.[69] It is also significant that military maneuvers between Mauritanian troops and NATO were scheduled in April 2001 following a four year long military collaboration in fighting the possible rise of Islamic fundamentalism in North Africa. Some of these moves only accentuated the regime's isolation among its traditional allies in the Arab World and further distanced it from its own Arab-Berber base at home. In November and December 2000, daily confrontations between (mainly Arab-Berber) university students and

---

67. See *Africa Research Bulletin Political, Social and Cultural Series*, 32 Dec. 1–31 1995 p. 12101C. This shrewd move on the part of Ould Taya on behalf of a country such as Mauritania where deep seated anti-Semitic feelings prevail should put to rest the argument put forth by the president to explain his support for Saddam Hussein as reflecting the fear of "being swept aside" by the strong domestic support for Iraq.

68. See *Africa Research Bulletin Political, Social and Cultural Series* 32 March 1–31 1995 p. 11775B.

69. In 1993, President Clinton addressed a correspondence to Congress expressing his "intent to suspend indefinitely Mauritania from [its] status as GSP" beneficiary. Other forms of bilateral aid were also curtailed. However, many were then baffled by the State Department's decision, starting in 1996, to delete from its annual reports the critical paragraphs about human rights abuses, including the residual practice of slavery.

security forces over the government's Israel policies are both an illustration and a consequence of this shift in alliance. In 2000 still, suspected Islamists were rounded up, their political party (Attliaa) banned and, even before September 11, 2001, Mauritania collaborated ostensibly with the U.S. efforts against terrorism. However, the most astute and profitable move, was Mauritania's decision to establish diplomatic relations with Israel. It has remained the only Arab League and World Islamic Conference member, to maintain its ambassador in Tel Aviv and to send its Foreign Minister there despite the resolutions of these bodies to withhold normal diplomatic relations with Israel. This shrewd diplomatic move in total defiance of national, Arab and Islamic international public opinions has had the added benefit of attracting the favor of international financial institutions and muting US criticism of Mauritania's human rights practices especially, the persistence of slavery. The international community was, once again, reminded of these issues by a November 2002 special report by Amnesty International documenting their persistence and gravity.[70] This pattern of bizarre decisions in the international arena was capped by Mauritania's decision to withdraw from the regional organization (ECOWAS) it helped to found.

Starting in 1985, Mauritania entered various structural adjustment programs and loan agreements with the IMF and the Word Bank. It eagerly accepted the usual recipes of these institutions, particularly the privatization of parastatals, most of which were sold off to a coterie of businesses and individuals close to Ould Taya. The international financial institutions have based their continued engagement with Mauritania on the dramatic increase of its macroeconomic indicators of growth since 1996.[71] This blind reliance on the benevolence and tacit support of its Western partners confirm the regime's

---

70. Amnesty International, "*Mauritania, a Future Free from Slavery?*" Amnesty International, London, 2002.

71. Since 1996, World Bank annual reports have consistently lauded the performance of Mauritania's economy putting its annual GDP growth at more than 4% annually. This assessment of the macroeconomic indicators, is contested by the opposition. It certainly does not seem to have improved the dismal living conditions of the population.

emphasis on international acceptance and legitimacy at the expense of domestic legitimacy through free and fair elections, and democratic institutions and practices.

Opposition Radicalization and Uncertain Future

After the October 2001 early elections, many observers hoped that at last, a modest but irreversible step was taken toward introducing genuine democratic practices in Mauritania's politics. It was assumed that this first 'free and fair' election would make it very difficult to reintroduce the fraudulent practices used in past elections. The decision to ban *Action pour le Changement* seriously reduced the likelihood that this will happen peacefully. The main reason seems to be that Ould Taya cannot fathom not being in power, and that, in the present conditions, free and fair elections will undoubtedly result in his defeat. This results in a political impasse, a predictable outcome of which has been radicalization of the opposition, eager to replicate the democratic gains in neighboring countries, such as Senegal and Mali. The record-breaking and seemingly whimsical government reshuffles,[72] and the frequent, impulsive, overt reliance on a very active state security apparatus are clear indications of the lack of democratic ethos and practices. They are also indicative of the inherent instability of the regime. Furthermore, the still festering wound of years of repression of black Mauritanians symbolized by the continued presence of tens of thousands of refugees in camps in Senegal and Mali and of thousands of highly educated exiles throughout the world continue to estrange black Mauritanians from the government. In light of these conditions and the continued, if discreet, role of the army, the picture of a stable and peaceful evolution of Mauritania's political system in a troublesome region can be deceptively comforting. The role of the military and, most importantly, the state security infrastructure suggest that the essential features of the regime dis-

---

72. Since December 2001, Mauritania has had four Prime Ministers and countless entries and departures and permutations of ministers. These often pointless permutations are part of an elaborate maneuvering destined to keep everyone guessing.

cussed above are not about to change fundamentally. Ould Taya's persecution complex, palpable in the late 1980s and early 1990s has evolved into a bunker mentality.[73] He has set up a two hundred strong Praetorian Guard unit, the Brigade de Sécurity Présidentielle (BSP), as the centerpiece of an elaborate security apparatus. These well-paid and well-trained elite troops, recruited exclusively among the northern and predominantly Smassid tribes, are under the command of Ould Taya's cousin. His second in command is none other than Ould Taya's own thirty-year old son, said to be groomed to succeed his father. The current political impasse, characterized by sporadic but increasingly open recourse to blunt repression as an instrument of control, should only be seen as another manifestation of this instability. The latter can only be exacerbated when the opposition, shut off from any meaningful democratic and peaceful participation, sees no alternative to radicalization and possibly non-political means for action. Though many older opponents have rallied more or less discretely to the ruling party following promises of material rewards, several events are indicative of the radicalization of younger, educated Mauritanians and the increased probability of violence.

The current political situation could degenerate into political violence fueled by years of pent up frustrations of all kinds and origins and, notwithstanding much lauded macroeconomic statistics, harsh daily conditions. This will inevitably be compounded by ethnic and communal violence of an unpredictable scale. The still unknown factor could be a decision by the Haratines to side against their former masters. Already in 1997, Messaoud Ould Boulkheir, the foremost leader of the Haratines, made public statements widely construed as a call to violence against the government.[74] Before it was banned, the UFD-EN had adopted a defiant stance against the government punctuated by weekly rallies. In a 1999 joint public *communiqué*, the first civilian President (now deceased) and the then leader of the opposition umbrella organization (front of opposition parties) called outright for the overthrow of the government. The

---

73. This can be construed literally since he had a Saddam Hussein style bunker underneath his palace built by the Chinese in the late 1990s.

74. See "Messaoud en A Assez," *L'Eveil-Hebdo*, December 1, 1997 pp. 1, 6, 7.

latter, Chbih Ould Cheikh Melainine, was jailed following a trial for "conspiracy to commit violence." The head of state's November 28, 2002 statement confirming the presence of off shore oil and natural gas due for exploitation in 2005 only adds to the risk of violence by those who would want to share in the revenues and prevent their monopoly by Ould Taya's tribe and associates.

Alarmingly still, there is a proliferation of often feuding Arab nationalist groups (mostly Ba'athists, Iraqi affiliated, and Nasserists, Gamal Abdel Nasser's ideological heirs), within the armed forces.[75] Along with the renewed threat of a "politicized" Islam in the Maghreb and West Africa,[76] this situation could provoke yet another violent outcome. The frequent banning of Islamic political parties, even a decade after the institution of multipartyism, as well as the opportunistic embrace of the fight again Islamists, did not prevent a renewed activism by militant Muslims determined to implement the *Sheria* (Islamic law) in Mauritania. The continued relations with Israel (including in the security area) will undoubtedly be exploited by Islamists, eager to capitalize on a situation that was deeply resented by most segments of Arab-Berber society, particularly with the sharp deterioration of the situation in the Middle-East. The prospect of an alliance between an activist Islamist movement and Ba'athists and Nasserists (both well known for their putschist proclivities) could increase the regime's vulnerability and corollary reliance on more overt repression as recent events tend to indicate. A successful overthrow of the regime (though not likely given the deliberate operational weakening of the army) or widespread mob violence would undoubtedly open yet another era of perilous instability given the extreme polarization of the country. Ould Taya's deftness in strengthening and legitimizing his rule in the eyes of the West (mostly) without hardly any concessions demonstrates the limits of a flawed 'democratization process' undertaken under external pressure and primarily for external consumption. More than any other West African state, Mauritania's (very) slow farewell to au-

---

75. See Pazzanita, "Mauritania's Foreign Policy," 1992, pp. 288–300.
76. See Ould Mey, pp. 247–48.

thoritarianism stands as a vivid illustration of this political reality in the sub-region.

CHAPTER V

FRIEND OR FOE?
The Military and Democratic Transition in Benin and Togo

Introduction

In post-colonial Africa, the military has clearly assumed a new role. First viewed as a symbol of national sovereignty during the early years of independence, the military has become increasingly involved in politics. Both Benin and Togo experienced complicated patterns of interaction between civilians and military personnel. Despite their small size, the armed forces in these two countries used their control of weaponry to dictate their will to civilian leaders. Ethnic tensions, poor economic performance, and social cleavages interact with rank, service branch, personal factionalism and differential recruitment to boost the position of the armed forces within society. Consequently, the military remained *the* key actor of African politics until the wave of democratization. However, due to this checkered past, the military was, *a priori*, perceived as a potential foe of democracy rather than a friend or ally. Unlike in the West, the values of Puritanism, discipline, rationality and achievement orientation of the military were clearly missing in post-independence Africa. Because of the limited role of the authoritarian African state, the military became the most powerful single group within society. Unfortunately, the normative and prescriptive tone of the political role ascribed to the military derived from the Western conception of the duties and roles of the professional soldier as subordinate to and subject to civilian control, never took hold. The hope that the military was going to deliver its promises in "guaranteeing the political stability so necessary for economic development"[1] remained unfilfilled.

All over the continent, military interventions became endemic, and both Benin and Togo followed the rule rather than the exception.[2] Squeezed between two Anglophone giants, Nigeria and Ghana, Benin and Togo are two relatively tiny neighboring Francophone states in West Africa that share such similarities as climate, cultural composition, and pre-colonial history. Contrary to civilian leaders' expectations, the armed forces became a formidable political force to reckon with. As a political organization with its own agenda, the military managed to retain, until recently, political power in both Benin and Togo.[3] Political instability marked the first twelve years of Benin's independence, as the military intervened half a dozen times, "ostensibly to quell both incessant political bickering and the ethno-regional conflicts."[4] In Togo, the army struck also in the name of restoring order.

In the late 1980s and early 1990s, the African continent was still marred with corrupt and autocratic regimes, whether civilian or mil-

---

1. Olatunde Odetola, *Military Regimes and Development: A Comparative Analysis in African Societies*, London, U.K.: George Allen & Unwin, 1982, p. 5.

2. See William Gutteridge, *The Military in African Politics*, London, UK: Methuen & Co. Ltd, 1964; and *Military Regimes in Africa*. London, UK: Methuen & Co. Ltd, 1975; See also Robin A. Luckham "The Military, Militarization, and Democratization in Africa: A Survey of Literature and Issues." *African Studies Review* 37/2 (September 1994), pp. 13–76.

3. See Claude E. Welch, Jr,. "Soldier and State in Africa." *Journal of Modern African Studies* 5/3 (1967), pp. 305–22; Eric A. Nordlinger, "Soldiers in Mufti: The Impact of Military Rule upon Economic and Social Change in Non-Western States." *American Political Science Review* 64/4 (1970), pp. 1138–48; Alan Wells, "The Coup d'État in Theory and Practice: Independent Black Africa in the 1960s," *American Journal of Sociology* 79/4 (1974), pp. 871–87; Samuel Decalo, "The Military Takeovers in Africa." *International Problems* (September 1974), pp. 80–90; and *Coups and Army Rule in Africa*, 2nd Edition. New Haven: Yale University Press,1990.

4. Dov Ronen, "People's Republic of Benin: The Military, Marxist Ideology, and the Politics of Ethnicity," in *The Military in African Politics*, ed. John Harbeson. New York: Praeger Publishers, 1987.

itary.[5] But when the "wind of change" started blowing out of Eastern Europe, the attitude of the military *vis-à-vis* the process of democratization varied from one country to another. Whether out of concern for corporate interests or because of leaders' personal interests,[6] the armed forces in most countries were reluctant to embrace democracy. Only in a few countries was the military leadership genuinely willing to help the democratization process. These two contrasting views are well illustrated in the attempts to reform politics in Benin and Togo.

The Military and Politics in Benin

The Republic of Benin, formerly known as the Republic of Dahomey between 1960 and 1975, and People's Republic of Benin between 1975 and 1991, is one of Africa's tiniest countries with an area of 112,655 square kilometers. The pre-colonial history of Benin is that of the once-powerful kingdom of Danhomê. From Adja Tado, in contemporary Togo, the Agasouvi dynasty founded the traditional kingdoms of Abomey, Allada, Adjatchê (Porto-Novo), and Savi.[7] Although they were all settled in Allada initially, rivalries split the brothers. Tê-Agbanli migrated to Adjatchê, Do-Gbagri to Abomey, while Adjahouto remained in Allada.[8] The same political bickering allowed the military to become a prominent player in Benin's contemporary politics.

The army in Benin evolved out of the remnants of French colonial troops in Africa. Until World War II, the training of African armies had been rudimentary because of their limited role in quelling poten-

---

5. Pierre Dabezies, "Vers la Démocratisation de l'Afrique," *Défense Nationale* (Mai 1992), p. 21.

6. See Robert Jackson, "The Predictability of African Coups d'État." *American Political Science Review* 72/4 (1978), pp. 1262–75; also "Explaining African Coups d'État." *American Political Science Review* 80/1 (1986), pp. 225–32; see Simon Baynham, ed. *Military Power and Politics in Black Africa*, London: Croom Helm, 1986.

7. Samuel Decalo, *Historical Dictionary of Benin*, 3rd Edition. Lanham, MD: Scarecrow Press, Inc., 1995, p. 2.

8. Jacques Lombard, *Dahomey: Sa Géographie, Son Histoire, Son Ethnographie*, Dakar, Sénégal: IFAN, 1958, p. 78.

tial disputes on the continent.[9] Rapid expansion into the hinterland of Africa had imposed raising *ad hoc* units of troops and police to meet particular needs. However, World War II and the wars of Indochina and Algeria created new demands for "qualified manpower." Africans, from the colonial armies, were consequently selected to join French forces and received a much higher level of training. Upon their return to Benin, these officers waited for the opportunity to strike. Before being sent back to their countries, the servicemen enjoyed higher standards of living in Europe. When they returned home, a change in their lifestyle became inevitable, and it would not take long before signs of frustration appeared.[10] Yet, they resisted any outright display of anger and dissatisfaction. In the meantime, civilian leaders struggled to start the post-independence rebuilding process. Between 1960 and 1972, six military coups occurred, due to several factors, including ethnic rivalries, economic mismanagement, and political "rectifications."[11]

The First Military Coup of 1963

The October 1963 military takeover was perceived by some as the result of either personal ambition or ethnic rivalry.[12] Others saw it as reflection of the incapacity of civilian leaders to engage the country on an adequate development path. These assertions partially convey the truth.

At independence, Benin did not have a single charismatic leader, but three veteran politicians who controlled the constituencies of their respective regions of origin. Hubert Maga "owned" the North,

---

9. See Jean-Louis Martin, *Le Soldat Africain et le Politique: Essai sur le Militarisme et l'État Prétorien au Sud du Sahara*, Toulouse: Presses de l'Institut d'Études Politiques, 1990.

10. Samuel Decalo, *Historical Dictionary of Togo*, 3rd Edition. Lanham, MD: Scarecrow Press, Inc., 1996, p. 100.

11. See Samuel Decalo, *Coups and Army Rule in Africa*, 2nd Edition. New Haven: Yale University Press, 1990.

12. See Emmanuel Terray, "Les Révolutions Congolaise et Dahoméenne de 1963: Essai d'Interpretation," *Revue Française de Science Politique* 14/5 (1964), pp. 917–43.

Justin Ahomadégbé "commanded" the *Fon* of Abomey in the center, and Sourou Apithy "controlled" the destiny of southerners of Porto-Novo. The regional polarization of Benin politics submitted any coalition or partnership to intense negotiations, and the December 1960 elections displayed the complexity of political maneuverings in Benin. The victory of the Maga-Apithy coalition, interpreted as "two-against-one," was denounced by Ahomadégbé, who expected the traditional rivalry between the two sister kingdoms of the South, Porto-Novo and Abomey, to be put aside.

In such a political atmosphere, Ahomadégbé's arrest in May 1961 for an alleged plot against the government formed by Maga and Apithy, confirmed the *Fon*'s suspicion. Despite Ahomadégbé's release in November 1962, for "good behavior," the damage had been already done. There was a sense of humiliation shared by the *Fon*, among both civilians and military officers from the center. It was little wonder when the *Fon* officers used a simple civil protest to topple the government.

In the wake of widespread urban unrest against the excesses and corruption of the Maga-Apithy regime, two specific incidents triggered a great deal of resentment: the overspending on the presidential palace in Cotonou at a time of fiscal austerity,[13] and the Bohiki affair.[14] While exorbitant spending in the office of the president generated anger given the sacrifices and sufferings to which the austerity program subjected the populations, the Bohiki problem took the insensitivity of the regime in place to a higher level. Christophe Bohiki, a parliament member of Maga's ruling party was accused of the murder of Daniel Dossou (an Apithy's party activist). The National Assembly refused, on Maga's order, to lift Bohiki's immunity so that he could stand trial.[15] Because the victim was from Porto-Novo, ethnic strife burst out in that city and even the belated decision to bring Bohiki to trial could not appease the crowds. During those events, Apithy, the partner and Vice-President of Maga, felt obliged to support

---

13. Finer, *op. cit.*, p. 493.

14. See Maurice Ahanhanzo Glèlè, *Naissance d'un État Noir (L'Évolution Politique et Constitutionnelle du Dahomey, de la Colonisation à nos Jours*, Paris: Librairie Générale de Droit et de la Jurisprudence, 1969.

15. Decalo, 1995, p. 92.

his base, further straining the relationship between himself and the President.[16] The whole affair, quite legalistic in nature, was exploited for political purposes with heavy ethno-regional overtones appropriate to the Dahomean political scene.

Taking advantage of the tense political situation, the *Union Générale des Travailleurs du Dahomey* (UGTD), the trade union, a staunch supporter of Ahomadégbé, demanded the abolition of the five percent austerity tax. Faced with Maga's obstinacy, the union demanded his resignation, and staged massive demonstrations as well as a general strike.[17] Since no action was being taken, the army, conveniently moved in and dissolved Maga's regime on October 28, 1963. General Soglo's military coup opened the door to political instability in Benin.

The Military Coups of 1965

After the "October Revolution," Soglo approached Apithy and Ahomadégbé, asking them to form a coalition government to address the urgent needs of Benin. The unanimous vote confirming this decision, suggested that the population wanted some unity between the two sister regions: the Center and the South. Unfortunately, that golden opportunity was missed when the two rivals failed, once again, to reconcile their fundamental differences.

In the meantime, nothing seemed to "calm people down" in the North. In retaliation for Maga's dismissal, most southerners residing in the north were harassed, and some killed. Those who escaped death found their houses looted. Meanwhile, the country's overall economic situation did not and could not improve, simply because both leaders were rather preoccupied with their petty squabbles.[18] By June 1965, it became evident that something needed to be done if the government was to continue to fulfill such basic functions as paying civil

---

16. Dov Ronen, *Dahomey: Between Tradition and Modernity*, Ithaca: Cornell University Press, 1975, pp. 191–92.

17. Chuka Onwumechili, *African Democratization and Military Coups*, Westport, CT: Praeger, 1998, p. 43.

18. Maurice Ahanhanzo Glèlè, *Le Danxome: Du Pouvoir Aja à la Nation Fon*, Paris: Paillart, 1974, pp. 289–93.

servants' salaries. In July, even as living conditions worsened, the government decided to increase the austerity tax from ten to twenty-five percent.[19] Under a different government, that decision would have been accompanied by a general strike. But, because of the amicable relationship between the unions and the regime, the country, in general, and civil servants in particular, swallowed that bitter pill without noticeable reaction.

Despite the favorable context, President Apithy and his Vice-President Ahomadégbé remained on different wavelengths concerning the orientation Benin would take to resolve its urgent problems. Their antagonism reached its peak when the Vice-President pushed a bill through the National Assembly while Apithy was on a state visit in France. Apithy's refusal to sign this bill on his return prompted a serious constitutional crisis.[20] In spite of their common party's intervention, Apithy maintained his position and, rather, invited the military leaders to "take their responsibilities."[21]

Once again, Soglo became the "rainmaker," by demanding and obtaining the resignation of both Apithy and Ahomadégbé on November 29, 1965.[22] Following the provisions of the constitution, National Assembly President, Tahirou Congacou, was asked to assume the presidency. That provisional government was given the mission of supervising the drafting of a new constitution. Typical political turmoil in Benin prevented Congacou's government from reaching its goal. In a very peculiar move, the angry population, disappointed by both the behavior and performance of Apithy and Ahomadégbé, called for a military intervention, a welcome opportunity for the armed forces to once again "flex their muscles."[23]

On December 22, 1965, Soglo unilaterally ended Congacou's mandate and assumed full powers. His new government of "technocrats" included another *Fon* officer, Colonel Philippe Aho and a cohort of

---

19. Decalo, 1990, p. 103.
20. Ronen, 1980, p. 120.
21. Decalo, 1990, p. 103.
22. Ronen, 1975, p. 199.
23. See Samuel Decalo, "Regionalism, Politics and the Military in Dahomey," *Journal of Developing Areas* 7/3 (April 1973a), pp. 449–77.

civilians.[24] Given the sense of urgency to "fix" Benin's problems, it was widely perceived that the "technocrats" were going to put their skills to use. Their failure to attain the only stated purpose of the new regime—to improve the economy of Benin—made another coup unavoidable.

The 1967 Military Coup

For reasons still unknown to date, there was a widespread belief that, this time, General Soglo's government would address the economic ills of the country. However, the "technocrats" showed their hands early on when, instead of abolishing or suspending the austerity tax, the new regime, extended it to the private sector. With Ahomadégbé, the recipient of unions' support no longer involved in politics, unions felt free to take appropriate measures.[25] Their call for strikes was positively answered with civil disobedience and massive demonstrations, forcing Soglo to end his experiment with the "technocrats." Through shuffling and reshuffling, seasoned politicians entered Soglo's new cabinet. Meanwhile, within the army, there was an intergenerational problem. Young officers who had always regarded Soglo's avuncular administration as conservative and weak, had formed a *Comité de Rénovation Nationale*, a mixed civilian, clerical and military body to monitor the government's behavior.

Despite the formation of a "watchdog," Soglo's technocratic regime failed to follow agreed upon standards. In hopes of influencing events, the young officers of the military imposed a strictly military body to guarantee the execution of government decisions and to carry out periodic examination of state institutions. The new committee was known as the *Comité Militaire de Vigilance*.[26] That committee was made up of restless, more radical and younger officers, who were very unhappy with the handling of accusations of corruption within the Soglo government.

---

24. Decalo, 1990, p. 104.

25. See Francine Godin, *Bénin 1972–1982: La Logique de l'État Africain*, Paris: L'Harmattan, 1986.

26. Ronen, *op. cit.*, p. 122.

With the continued deterioration of the economy, Soglo flew to France for help. On his return he declared that "[he] did not come back empty handed,"[27] and, consequently, raised expectations. Wage earners read into that message the end of the austerity tax. Unfortunately, their sense of relief was short-lived. The Finance Minister soon declared France's aid insufficient to abrogate the austerity law. That declaration generated a strike by the teachers' union, which was followed by other corporations.[28] The government's maladroit handling of the movement when it arrested labor leaders led to general social unrest. Forced to retreat, the government freed the union leaders and promised to discuss the austerity issue with the workers. That situation precipitated the termination of Soglo's era. Gutteridge aptly sums up the looming crisis:

> The course of the Dahomey crisis as it developed displayed the full range of characteristics that tend to encourage the firm establishment of army rule. On December 8 1967 the union of primary schools teachers declared a forty-eight hour strike in support of salary claims. The Soglo Government's response was to declare all trade union activity suspended on the grounds of the misuse of trade union rights. This action originated with the Military Vigilance Committee and amounted to a declaration that the strike was illegal.[29]

Young officers of the *Comité Militaire de Vigilance*, who had been following the government's moves, realized the time was ripe for them to act. On December 17, 1967, "the young officers of the army" took over. Led by Major Maurice Kouandété, a group of officers attempted to arrest Soglo who only escaped through a back door of the adjacent U.S. embassy. A month after their takeover, "the young officers" announced their government and their plan of action. A cabinet headed by Colonel Alphonse Alley[30] announced that the military would transfer power to civilians within five months after the adoption of a new Constitution.

27. *Id.*, p. 204.
28. *Id.*
29. Gutteridge, 1969, p. 52.
30. Decalo, 1990, p. 102.

Upon the completion and adoption of the new constitution, the military decided to ban the three rival veteran politicians—Maga, Ahomadégbé, and Apithy—and their associates from running in the scheduled presidential elections.[31] The expectation was that the removal of these "old timers" would calm the political storm in Benin. Outraged, the former presidents called for a boycott of the elections, which were later found unconstitutional by the Supreme Court. However, the military regime overruled the highest court and proceeded with the elections, despite calls from other African leaders to re-evaluate the situation. Ultimately, an obscure candidate from Abomey, Dr. Basile Adjou Moumouni, won the "elections." Surprisingly enough, the military annulled the results of the elections, as if their "candidate" did not win.

Subsequently, the armed forces entrusted the reins of power to Dr. Emile Derlin Zinsou, another southerner. By then, tensions became noticeable among the "young officers." Those clearly in favor of a new head of state from the north resented Alley's attempt to place another *Fon* at the helm. With the traditional north–south divide back in play, the internal dynamic within the military leadership prompted another coup.

The 1969 Military Coup

Among the disgruntled officers, Major Kouandété, a *Somba* from the North, was clearly the most frustrated. Therefore, it was no surprise when he decided to take matters in his own hands by staging another military coup. However, his actions were neither a mere ethnic retaliation nor a simple corporate adventure. President Zinsou also simply failed to address the problems his predecessors had faced.[32]

The new constitution strengthened the military's hand by allowing the army to participate in the social, economic and cultural progress of the country. The new document also denied parliament members the traditional compensation and other benefits, remuner-

---

31. Decalo, 1995, p. 7.
32. Decalo, 1990, p. 114.

ating them instead for time actually spent in the Assembly. Despite the sense of a new beginning Zinsou's regime had brought, grim economic realities remained difficult to overcome. It was, after all, Zinsou's attempts to tackle daunting economic and political problems that resulted in his downfall. Dahomey seemed simply unmanageable.

Among his economic and fiscal measures aimed at balancing the budget, President Zinsou's regime had introduced new taxes that represented an additional burden for workers. His "backdoor" ascent to power and the ensuing resentment predisposed workers to be less tolerant *vis-à-vis* his administration. Because of the lack of support, and due to pressure from politicians, the unions called for strikes and demonstrations to clearly display the workers' anger. Within the army, rumors of coups and assassinations gained currency. All the preconditions seemed to be in place for a military action.[33]

Sure enough, on December 10, 1969, Kouandété led a small military group that toppled Zinsou's government on the pretext that the state had been paralyzed by corruption while the vigilance committee remained silent. After a commando kidnapped the President and took him to the north, Kouandété simply put the majority of Benin army officers before a *fait accompli*.[34] On Radio Dahomey, Major Kouandété declared, "the Dahomean army, conscious of its duties, carries out once more its responsibilities and decides that Dr. Zinsou, President of the Republic, is relieved of his powers." To further justify the army's action he stated that:

> The Army entrusted the government of Dr. Zinsou in July 1968, to reconcile all the people of Dahomey [*tous les fils du Dahomey*] and to maintain the unity achieved by the Army. An objective analysis of the situation shows not only that the regime of Dr. Zinsou created total insecurity, but that he also deliberately abandoned the guidelines set out by the proclamation of June 17, 1968, the task for which Dr. Zinsou was

---

33. See Séverin Adjovi, *De la Dictature à la Démocratie sans les Armes*, Paris: Éditions CP 99, 1993.

34. Samuel Decalo, *Historical Dictionary of Benin*, 3rd Edition. Lanham, MD: Scarecrow Press, Inc., 1995, p. 7.

designated by the Army... In light of this situation the Army
has, once again, assumed its responsibilities.[35]

According to the armed forces, the economic and social situation
of Dahomey had deteriorated while the government had become
"drunk with power," behaving like "veritable potentates."[36] Kouandété
announced the establishment of a constitutional committee leading
to a referendum and free popular elections. To reach these goals,
Kouandété set up a temporary Military Directorate (*Directoire Militaire*). But, once again the Directorate's actions, or lack thereof, failed
to save Benin from yet another coup.

The 1972 Military Coup

The *Directoire* was made up of the heads of the army (Major
Kouandété), the *Gendarmerie* (Colonel Benoît Sinzogan), and the department of national defense (Colonel Paul Emile de Souza) who, because of his seniority, became the Chairman. In its attempt to restore
some normalcy, the Directorate invited the "old guard," Maga,
Ahomadégbé, and Apithy, to participate in upcoming presidential
elections. The hope was that, after a bitter rivalry and its awful consequences, these former political leaders would bind together and se-
lect one of them to run. It turned out to be wishful thinking. All three,
plus former President Zinsou, who was bent on vindicating his term,
ran in the 1970 presidential elections.[37] After passionate campaigns,
the elections, marred by corruption, intimidation, and fraud, were
deemed unacceptable and stopped by the Directorate before any final
result was announced. The interruption of the electoral process provoked a serious political crisis, since Maga, the apparent winner,
threatened to lead the north to secede. Apithy replied by suggesting
the formation of a federation with Nigeria if Maga were to be declared the winner of rigged elections.

---

35. See *Le Monde*, December 11–17, 1969.
36. Gutteridge, 1969, p. 53.
37. Decalo, 1995, p. 8.

Faced with an extremely difficult situation, the Directorate urged the three main leaders to agree on a resolution of the crisis. Unfortunately, personal ego and ambitions made the situation more difficult, forcing the military to suggest a rotational body to take over from the military. A first in Africa, a Presidential Council (*Conseil Présidentiel*) was formed as a compromise. After weeks of deliberations, the first two-year term started with President Maga on May 7, 1970. While the early part of his term was without major incidents, the last days were quite tense. The deteriorating economic situation and ethnic or regional politics threatened the final days of Maga's term.

By the time President Ahomadégbé took over on May 1972, the country was experiencing both severe economic and political difficulties. The performance of Maga's administration left the impression that maybe a Presidential Council was not the right answer to Dahomey's problems. Disappointment set in. Civil servants were unhappy and schoolteachers were calling for massive strikes. Within both civilian and military circles, a great deal of anxiety prevailed. It was becoming clearer and clearer that unless some major moves were made to improve living conditions, Dahomey was set for yet another coup d'état.

By early 1972, two important mutinies had taken place within the army, a bad omen for days to come. While the first mutiny revolved around several non-commissioned officers' demand that their commander be replaced, the second involved an attempt on the life of the Chairman of the Directorate, de Souza. As one of the main perpetrators of the second mutiny, Kouandété was sentenced to death. That sentence not only enraged the northerners in general, and *Somba* in particular, but also heightened tension within the army.[38] At the same time, civilians, through President Ahomadégbé's administration, continued to display their inability to lead the country.

This continued display of deplorable performance by civilians and other political and regional reasons motivated the "young Turks" of the army to topple Ahomadégbé's regime. Led by a *Somba*, Major Mathieu Kérékou, the military ended the experimentation with a tri-

---

38. Ronen, *op. cit.*, p. 229.

umvirate on October 26, 1972.[39] Allen describes accurately the power struggle prevailing in Benin before the 1972 coup:

> As the instability induced by factional conflict within civil and military authorities prolonged itself, the bulk of the rural population, the urban workers and intelligentsia, and the rank-and-file in the army became alienated not simply from a given regime but from 'spoils politics' itself. The 1972 coup may be seen as an attempt to bring an end to spoils politics, and united the more radical among the junior officers in the army with union leaderships and the student groups based in the main towns. These groups saw the main defects of the former system as its elitism, its dependence upon and its subordination to France, and its elimination of political participation.[40]

That intervention, unlike previous ones, proved durable. If not for an economic downfall, the revolution might still be in progress. Besides injustice, torture, detentions without trials, flagrant human rights violations, declining living conditions made Kérékou's regime less and less bearable, making the military more amendable to the idea of a national conference. Faced with a bankrupt state and widespread anger as a result of their handling of the economy, the military was looking for a way out. The national conference became the golden opportunity.

The Military and the National Conference in Benin

The Second "October Revolution"

Contrary to expectations, Benin's second "October Revolution" came to stay. The 1972 coup turned out to be of a praetorian kind in that it marked the emergence of the armed forces as an autonomous political force, acting on its own behalf and according to its own po-

---

39. Decalo, 1990, pp. 116–17.
40. Chris Allen, "'Goodbye to All That': The Short and Sad Story of Socialism in Benin," *Journal of Communist Studies* 8/2 (1989), p. 65.

litical vision. In the words of one *junta* member, Major Koffi, "this time the armed forces have assumed their responsibilities. We do not intend to give up power to anyone...we must show our abilities."[41] Though some of the plotters were known to be supporters of members of the previous civilian triumvirate, and a few had acquired reputations as "conservatives" or "radicals," there was initially no indication that the coup was any different from others.[42] However, an ideological militancy and a quest for a radical socio-economic change soon emerged. It became gradually clear that this team, given the personalities of its leaders, and the nature of its early orientations, represented a radical branch of the army. The ideological stance of the new regime took Benin to the brink of economic and political bankruptcy,[43] and, ironically, brought it back to some sense of renewed hope. An understanding of the military's position towards the national conference can only be explained through the path of destruction taken by the leaders of the 1972 coup.[44] Under normal circumstances, the armed forces would have been less open to any dialogue between civilians and the military. If the past is any indication, the military in Benin has always been in control of the civilians and took no orders from them. Were it not for the failure of the military to fulfill its "revolutionary" commitment to redress years of mismanagement, corruption and incivility, the incentive to adhere to the concept of a national gathering to discuss critical issues would have been absent.

Although the main authors of the military takeover were believed to be Major Michel Alladaye, Captains Janvier Assogba, Hilaire Badjogoumê, and Michel Aïkpé, Major Kérékou emerged as the leader. Besides his known stubbornness, nothing in Kérékou's past prepared him for a political career.[45] He was a rather shy and reckless officer,

---

41. Quoted in Martin, 1986, p. 65.

42. Decalo, 1990, p. 117.

43. *Id.*, p. 119.

44. See Richard Adjaho, *La Faillite du Contrôle des Finances Publiques au Bénin (1960–1990)*, Cotonou: Éditions du Flamboyant, 1992 ; see also John R. Heilbrunn, "Social Origins of National Conferences in Benin and Togo," *Journal of Modern African Studies* 31/2 (1993), pp. 277–99.

45. Decalo, 1990, p. 118.

known only for his insubordination. However, Kérékou's speech on political framework—*Discours Programme*—of November 1972, had a clear tone of radicalism that only the true coup leaders could have initiated. The new leaders intended to fight corruption, disorder, and inter-tribal rivalry. In a fashion typical of coup rhetoric , the military embarked on an "impossible mission," promising to rid Benin of its economic, political and social ills. While they embraced a "new national independence," they denounced "foreign domination," and pledged to take Benin's economy to new heights.[46] There was obviously an anger toward past economic policies and those who engineered them. A sense of a new dawn was born and the new military leaders seemed, initially at least, to be motivated by the promotion of Benin's economic and social development. Westebbe is accurate in stating that:

> After 1975, the process of transforming Benin into a mini Marxist state on the eastern bloc model began. The rationale was to use the state to promote the welfare of the people by preventing their exploitation by domestic and foreign capitalist interests. The objective was to accelerate economic growth and development by the state dominance of the means of production. Most formal sector activity was brought under state control, including distribution, secondary-sector enterprises, and financial institutions. Public enterprises were created throughout the economy, with large industrial investments financed with foreign borrowing.[47]

Because they believed that economic planning would best achieve internally oriented economic growth, Kérékou and his colleagues allowed the Beninese state an indispensable role in the promotion of entrepreneurs. Unfortunately, their radicalism would blind their vision for a better society in Benin. With neither compass nor vision,

---

46. Martin, 1986, p. 66.
47. Richard Westebbe, "Structural Adjustment, Rent-Seeking, Liberalization in Benin," in *Economic Change and Political Liberalization in Sub-Saharan Africa*, ed. Jennifer A. Widner. Baltimore: Johns Hopkins University Press, 1994, p. 82.

the new leaders became simply lost in their own radical rhetoric, with consequences that went beyond their wildest imagination.

In the first two years of the *Révolution*, some hope remained that the hard-line rhetoric was just a façade that would be progressively diminished in the face of harsh economic realities. All hopes were dashed in 1974 when Marxism-Leninism became the fundamental tenet of the new regime. In an eight-point speech delivered on November 1974 at Goho (Abomey), President Kérékou announced that Dahomey would follow a socialist path of development, with Marxism-Leninism as the guiding philosophy.[48] A year later, the country was also re-christened as, *la République Populaire du Bénin* (People's Republic of Benin), with a single political party, the newly created *Parti de la Révolution Populaire du Bénin* (Benin People's Revolutionary Party). In retrospect, the proclamation of Marxism-Leninism tolled the death knell for Benin as a country with a viable economy. As a socialist society, several fundamental economic and political changes became inevitable. The country experienced a wave of nationalization. Several foreign-owned companies were simply confiscated. What ensued was a whole series of parastatal corporations that became "financial leeches" that sucked Benin's resources. The new state also monopolized the means of informing and educating citizens. In their attempt to alter the fabric of Benin's society, the military leaders embarked on important social reforms. A new school system, *l'École Nouvelle*, was to ensure an appropriate education to younger generations. The renamed national radio, *la Voix de la Révolution*, and the national newspaper, *Ehuzu* ("Change," in *Fon*), both contributed to the drastic alterations within Benin's society.[49] Even administrative and economic spheres were profoundly affected. Steps were taken to control the agricultural sector, primary industrial and commercial businesses, and the banking, trade, insurance and entertainment sectors.[50] Socialist Benin would leave no section of

---

48. Richard Banégas, "Retour sur une Transition Modèle: Les Dynamiques du Dedans et du Dehors de la Démocratisation Béninoise," in *Transitions Démocratiques Africaines: Dynamiques et Contraintes (1990–1994)*, eds. Jean-Pascal Daloz et Patrick Quantin. Paris: Khartala, 1997, p. 39.

49. *Id.*

50. Martin, 1986, p. 67.

society unchanged. To create the new society they envisaged, new military leaders showed their determination to reach their goals.

Overall, the vanguard party and its leftist members reached their goal: a *Perestroika à la Béninoise*. There was an obvious concentration of power, with an organic fusion between the party and the government, as well as a high degree of militarization.[51] But, all along, very few military leaders were really involved in the restructuring of Benin society. Faithful to their leaders, who, themselves trusted the "enlightened" civilian *idéologues* of the party, the armed forces simply supported the revolution. As an institution supposed to guarantee national integrity and order, the military was often called in to restore order. Despite the imposition of a single party, few pockets of resistance and resentment could be noticed within society.[52]

The National Conference

One such recalcitrant group was the National University of Benin, which battled the Marxist regime consistently to the very end.[53] In fact, a student movement prompted the massive demonstrations and strikes that brought the country to a standstill in 1988. After several years of lonely challenge to Kérékou's power, the students started searching for means to widen their actions. Through a campaign of "information" geared towards civil servants, businesses, and market women, the students managed to convey the urgency of action to the entire population. Ultimately, the decline of Benin's economy would become the students' best advocate, allowing the whole country to demand fundamental changes.[54]

After several months without pay, workers started paying some heed to the students' message: to rise up to get rid of Kérékou and his clique. The anger and resentment of the population increased among both civilians and the military. Sections of the military leadership

---

51. Banégas, *op. cit.*, p. 38.

52. See Dossou, *op. cit.*; also Adjaho, *op. cit.*

53. Decalo, 1997, p. 51.

54. See Kathryn Nwajiaku, "The National Conferences in Benin and Togo Revisited," *Journal of Modern African Studies* 32/3 (1994), pp. 429–47.

blamed the civilians for taking the country to an economic dead-end. It was time for decisions, rather than finger pointing. Consequently, both civilian and military *apparatchiki* embarked on the search for solutions to the severe economic problems Benin was facing. Clearly, the mood within the army ranks was one of frustration. The situation indeed seemed ripe for a military coup. Yet, the dynamics within the armed forces were not conducive to such an outcome. Therefore, when Kérékou decided to convene a national conference, the military leadership jumped on the opportunity to rescue the country, while simultaneously saving face.

Although the decision to open up the political system came out of a meeting of the ruling party, the intention was to initiate a merely cosmetic change. As an institution the military was feeling embarrassed, especially in light of Major Koffi's assertion about the armed forces' desire to stop Benin's descent into hell.[55] Judging by the state of the economy in the late 1980s, it is quite difficult to praise the "abilities" of the military. The armed forces simply failed to fare better than previous administrations. Everything seemed to have fallen apart around the armed forces, and resistance to democratization would have been illogical.

In the wake of a tense political atmosphere, Kérékou made an important first move, by allowing the formation of political parties. Through the national gathering, Kérékou expected "all the [active] forces of the nation, whatever their political sensibilities might be," to help find appropriate solutions to the severe crisis Benin was facing.[56] In a move similar to that of King Guézo, Kérékou was seeking an economic renewal with cosmetic change to his political system. While his kingdom was going through serious economic and political difficulties, King Guézo called upon "all the sons of the country to plug the holes of the punctured calabash [jar] with their fingers in order to save the fatherland."[57] However, Kérékou's ideological shift was not believed to be sincere, and threats of strikes were still present, until

---

55. Martin, *op. cit.*, p. 65.

56. Pearl T. Robinson, "The National Conference Phenomenon in Francophone Africa," *Comparative Studies in Society and History* 36/3 (1994), p. 575.

57. Robert Fatton, Jr., "Democracy and Civil Society in Africa." *Mediterranean Quarterly* 2/4 (1991), p. 88.

the national conference was actually convened. On February 19, 1990, a very important chapter was turned in Benin's history. The Hotel PLM-Aledjo of Cotonou became the locus of what *Béninois* thought impossible only a few months earlier. Although invitations were extended to all strata of Benin's populations, and even to *Béninois* abroad, the government was still hoping to welcome a token representation of the people, in order to avoid deep changes. Unfortunately for the government, and fortunately for the country, not only did the invited guests show up, they also organized bodies that demanded and obtained representation.[58] Participants included members of the ruling single party, trade unionists, civil servants, "political tendencies" (emerging political parties), students, religious leaders, farmers, and the military.[59] All former heads of state of Benin, including one sentenced, *in absentia*, for "subversive activities against the state", were also invited. To grant international status to the conference, the entire diplomatic corps gratified the gathering with its presence.

It was in a tense atmosphere that Kérékou took the floor that morning of February 19. In his traditional verbose style, he laid down his expectations for the conference.[60] Given the solemnity of the audience, his anxiety became apparent when he reiterated his guidelines to the conference: to "fix" the economic structure of Benin, with no substantial change to the political system.[61] Although he called for political renewal, and pledged to implement the IMF's Structural Adjustment Program, his focus was clearly on the country's critical economic crisis. In his address, he asked participants to draw up a list of urgent economic problems to solve.[62] Through an elaborate round of

---

58. Decalo, 1997, p. 54.

59. Walter S. Clarke, "The National Conference Phenomenon and the Management of Political Conflict in Sub-Saharan Africa," In *Ethnic Conflict and Democratization in Africa*, ed. Harvey Glickman. Atlanta: ASA Press, 1995, p. 234.

60. Decalo, 1997, p. 54.

61. Jacques-Mariel Nzouankeu, "The Role of the National Conference in the Transition to Democracy: The Cases of Benin and Mali," *Issue: A Journal of Opinion* 21/1-2 (1993), p. 45.

62. See Béatrice Gbado, *En Marche vers la Liberté: Préludes du Renouveau Démocratique au Bénin*, Cotonou: SYNES, 1991.

applause, more out of courtesy than anything else, the participants gave the impression of appeasing Kérékou, who left the audience filled with confidence. But, the participants had their own agenda. After so many years of unshared power, and mismanagement, the mostly former political opponents were determined to use this golden opportunity to settle, if indirectly, a few scores.

After a great start, the conference seemed to be proceeding smoothly under the leadership of the Archbishop of Cotonou, Monsignor Isidore de Souza, until its third day. On February 21, aware that the far-reaching changes they had in mind could not be suggested under the old regime, and after long deliberations, the participants declared the conference 'sovereign.' That move almost ruined the gathering, had it not been for the extraordinary negotiation skills displayed by the chairman of the conference.[63] The declaration of sovereignty by the delegates shocked Kérékou so much that he was willing to disband the meeting. Open threats of a military coup came from the abrasive Kouandété, who urged his fellow northerners in the armed forces to take over, if Kérékou were to be removed from office. Only De Souza, and pressure from France, saved the conference, and consequently, Benin. Drawing strength from their self-proclaimed sovereignty, conference participants embarked on a series of political transformations. The 1977 *Loi Fondamentale* (the constitution) was abolished, along with its institutions. Several ad-hoc committees were formed to look into different aspects of the crisis in Benin. After ten days of proceedings, the delegates agreed on sweeping reforms. Pending national elections to a new legislature, the functions of the former *Assemblée Nationale Révolutionnaire* (ANR) were to be assumed by an interim *Haut Conseil de la République* (HCR), which included the main opposition leaders.[64] As a reward for having allowed the conference to go on, Kérékou received the bonus of remaining in power during a transition period. He was, however, stripped of most of his power and executive authority.[65] As a 'sovereign and executive'

63. Clarke, *op. cit.*
64. *Id.*, p. 235.
65. Robinson, *op. cit.*, p. 576.

body, the conference's decisions superseded all existing laws, regulations and provisions. After a severe critique of Kérékou's tenure, delivered live on radio and television, the participants drew the necessary lessons, before taking appropriate actions. Dates were set for the election, by universal suffrage, of a president, who would have a five-year term, renewable once. To guarantee the implementation of its decisions, the conference elected an interim Prime Minister, Mr. Nicéphore Soglo, to serve during the transition period.[66] According to Westebbe:

> Soglo's mandate was to restore the structural adjustment process and create a consensus for its implementation. Soglo was committed to cleaning up corruption and introducing institutional reforms. His was a government committed to morality in public life, the rule of law, efficient use of public resources, and raising revenues to finance vital expenditures.[67]

However, the scariest part was yet to come, since the decisions still needed to be approved by Kérékou, who, at one point, blamed the conference for staging a "civilian coup."[68]

The atmosphere was unbearable that morning of February 28, 1990. Persistent rumors and speculations did not help the situation. According to what is known in Benin as *Radio Trottoir* (rumormongers), Kérékou, under pressure from his fellow northerners and his Marxist clique, would not go along with the decisions of the conference. That fear had been present all along. However, on the last day, it became real, to the point where, the president of the conference, Archbishop de Souza, urged the audience to invoke God's blessings.[69]

However, Kérékou, in an uncharacteristic brief address to the delegates, expressed his willingness to comply with all the decisions reached by the conference. The surprise was immense. Both the con-

---

66. Clarke, *op. cit.*, p. 234.
67. Westebbe, *op. cit.*, p. 96.
68. Nzouankeu, *op. cit.*
69. See Fondation Friedrich Naumann, ed. *Les Actes de la Conférence Nationale*, Cotonou: Éditions ONEPI, 1994.

ference participants and Kérékou's diehard supporters were amazed. Apparently, Kérékou had planned to reject, in a long diatribe submitted by the Central Committee of the single party, all the decisions, if not, at least some.[70] For whatever reasons, Kérékou decided to give democracy a chance. Magnusson aptly captures Kérékou's contribution not only to the success of the national conference, but also, and foremost, to the future of the fragile democratic transition in Benin, when he states:

> He [Kérékou] admitted that the Marxism-Leninism option had been a divisive failure, rather than the unifying, developmental ideology that he had envisioned. In local culture, the regurgitation of the sorcerer's wares must be accompanied by an admission of culpability in order for the victim to be freed from its power. Kérékou's admission, his acceptance of the National Conference decision as binding, and his 1991 acceptance of his electoral defeat proved to be the basis for his national rehabilitation among many people as a heroic figure who had paved the way for African democracy.[71]

Indeed, Kérékou's acceptance of the gathering's resolutions did usher in a truly new political environment in Benin. A new constitution was approved through a national referendum. Basic civic and political rights, restricted or banned for several years, became reality. New legislation was promulgated to permit the registration of political parties. Independent newspapers and journals flourished. In contrast, while Benin's national conference allowed for political renewal and hope, Togo's was characterized by uncertainty from start to finish.

Despite the open and obstinate desire to retain power displayed by civilian politicians, it is safe to assume that the military leadership, beginning with Kérékou himself, was looking for a way out. It became

---

70. See Dossou, *op. cit.*

71. Bruce Magnusson, "Testing Democracy in Benin: Experiments in Institutional Reform," in *State, Conflict, and Democracy in Africa*, ed. Richard Joseph. Boulder, CO: Lynne Rienner Publishers, 1999, p. 222.

evident this time that no foreign aid would be forthcoming until some reforms were undertaken.[72] Consequently, although the national conference stripped him of his powers, Kérékou, along with the majority of the army top brass, accepted the resolutions of the gathering.[73] With that bold move, both the army in general, and Kérékou in particular, redeemed themselves, while at the same time allowing Benin to enjoy the peaceful democratic transition, neighboring Togo is still seeking.

The Military and Politics in Togo

Togo is also a small West African country, forming a narrow strip of land stretching north from a coastline of 32 miles, and 320 miles inland. After a brief German colonization and a U.N. mandate, Togo became independent in 1960. However, a north–south divide and social stereotypes inhibited economic and political progress. For a country nicknamed the "Switzerland of Africa," the future turned quite bleak early on when the military assumed power in the first coup d'état in West Africa. Until 1963, Togo had no formal army. As a mandate under the League of Nations, and then a United Nations trust territory, to maintain civil order Togo had developed a small force of *gendarmes*, a police force and a colonial army.[74] Although these forces were, in theory, open to all, mostly northerners sought to join them to finally get an edge over the southerners. The colonial army gave northerners a perfect opportunity to level up socially with southerners and to escape poverty.[75] By 1963, what became the Togolese army, included a disproportionate regional representation, with eighty percent of northerners, giving a different twist to the traditional north-south

---

72. John F. Clark, "The Challenges of Political Reform in Sub-Saharan Africa: A Theoretical Overview," in *Political Reform in Francophone Africa*, eds. John F. Clark and David E. Gardinier, Boulder, CO: Westview Press, 1997, pp. 23–24.

73. See Francis Laloupo, "La Conférence Nationale du Bénin: Un Concept Nouveau de Changement de Régime Politique," *Année Africaine* (1992–93), pp. 78–114.

74. Heilbrunn, 1994, p. 454.

75. Decalo, 1990, pp. 217–18.

cleavage.[76] That imbalance was increased by an influx of former soldiers, mostly northerners, from the French colonial army. At the end of the Algerian war, France demobilized several hundred Togolese enlisted men who came home, to seek employment.[77] Hardened by years of service in the French army, these men became a clear threat to the security of such a small country as Togo almost immediately.

Dispatched to Lomé by the French government, the unskilled former soldiers, unemployable and uneasy in the south, petitioned the Olympio regime for their integration into the national army. Olympio refused, harshly branding them as mercenaries for their activities in Algeria.[78] His contempt, not only for the establishment of regular armed forces, but also for re-employing *petits nordistes* (little northerners) became apparent. Gutteridge is accurate in his description of the situation:

> Organized by a sergeant named Emmanuel Bodjollé the Togolese group became a powerful pressure group working for the expansion of Togo's minute two-company army, which had been handed over by the French in 1961, so that they themselves could be absorbed in military employment...Like one or two of the more thoughtful African politicians Olympio was not anxious to expand his defence forces, largely on the grounds of expense and his estimate of relative social priorities.[79] Olympio opposed enlarging the army for economic reasons,[80] and would rather entertain the idea of enlisting the mostly *Ewe* unemployed living in Lomé. His anti-northern, anti-military attitudes reached their climax when

---

76. Decalo, 1996, p. 48.

77. Samuel Decalo, "The Politics of Military Rule in Togo," *Geneva-Africa* 12/2 (1973b), p. 73.

78. John R. Heilbrunn, "Authority, Prosperity, and Politics in Benin and Togo," Ph.D. Dissertation, University of California, Los Angeles, 1994, p. 456.

79. Gutteridge, 1969, p. 43.

80. Olympio cited the wasteful nature of military allocations and Togo's severe budgetary constraints for his refusal of the ex-servicemen' request. See Samuel Decalo, "The Politics of Military in Togo," *Geneva-Africa* 12 (1973), p. 73.

he still rejected a counterproposal, requesting only that sixty highly qualified men be integrated into the army.[81] In the meantime, the Army commander, Major Kleber Dadjo, a *Kabiyè*, favored the expansion of the armed forces.[82] Left with no choice, the veterans staged a mutiny that turned into a tragic coup d'état.

The Military Coup of 1963

While Olympio disliked the army, probably because of its ethnic configuration, the largely *Kabiyè* army also despised him. Besides the army, the general population, including *Ewe*, resented his social policies. With a background as the financial officer of the United Africa Company (UAC) in Togo, Olympio imposed a program of fiscal austerity on the population. Through this move he hoped Togo would become economically as well as politically independent from France.[83] At an early stage of his presidency, he also alienated former advisers and friends by relying exclusively on his own opinions. His authoritarian tactics[84] also created a great deal of animosity within his close circle, as well as within the army.[85] Against the suggestions of several advisers, he persisted in his position and denied the veterans' petitions. Consequently, he became the roadblock that needed to be removed.[86]

When the rumor of a coup, or at least a mutiny, started circulating, Olympio refused to lend it any credibility. As a strong believer in a docile army, under the control of civilians, it did not occur to him that the ex-soldiers had no choice but to get rid of him.[87] What began as a mutiny quickly became a military coup. The coup began with fake telephone calls to Olympio's ministers, convening them to an ur-

---

81. Decalo, 1996, p. 6.
82. Decalo, 1990, p. 218; also Heilbrunn, 1994, p. 458.
83. Heilbrunn, *op. cit.*, p. 398.
84. Finer, 1967, p. 504.
85. Robert M. Press, *The New Africa: Dispatches from A Changing Continent*, Gainesville: University Press of Florida, 1999, p. 86.
86. See Decalo, 1973b, *op. cit.*; also Heilbrunn, 1994, p. 457.
87. Onwumechili, *op. cit.*, p. 53.

gent cabinet meeting that January 13, 1963.[88] All but the ministers of Information and Interior responded and found themselves kidnapped by the ex-servicemen who had secured weapons through their contacts in the standing army. The plotters were a group of six men, none in active military service, who operated under the leadership of Sergeants Emmanuel Bodjollé and Étienne (later Gnassingbé) Éyadéma, who assaulted Olympio's residence. Confronted by the plotters, Olympio tried to escape to the U.S. embassy. During Olympio's flight, Éyadéma shot him in cold blood.[89]

Following that tragic shooting, all former political exiles were invited back to Togo. Power was handed over to Nicolas Grunitzky, a southerner, who returned from Cotonou, Benin, as President and Antoine Meatchi, a northerner, who returned from Accra, Ghana, as Vice-President. Although the plotters wanted Meatchi to be President, French opposition to his nomination allowed Grunitzky to take the higher position. Most of the coup ringleaders, were not only integrated, but also received an immediate promotion to officer rank.[90] The new regime, very similar to Olympio's, raised some eyebrows, since the northerners thought that their time had come to be in control of Togo. The military did tolerate the new cabinet, probably knowing that it was too diverse ideologically to last. Despite the rhetoric of "national reconciliation," Grunitzky's indecisiveness exacerbated obvious factional and personal infighting. Without any significant power base of his own, Grunitzky failed to fulfill his mission as a conciliator. Ethnic, regional, ideological and personal tugs-of-war, resulted more often than not in stalemates.

The army itself was not immune from ethnic cleavages either. A long-standing disagreement between Bodjollé and Éyadéma resurfaced. The rumor of Bodjollé's attempt to tip off Olympio during the coup, was finally resolved by his removal from the army, which left Éyadéma as the *de facto* military leader. The army commander, Dadjo, although the highest-ranking officer in the army, had no real control over the forces.[91]

---

88. Decalo, 1990, p. 213.
89. Gutteridge, 1969, p. 44.
90. Heilbrunn, 1994, p. 459.
91. Decalo, 1973b, p. 77.

Grunitzky's difficulties also stemmed from the fact that he had to placate his "sponsor," the military, by accommodating their demands. With increased financial difficulties, the civil service that had suffered from a major compression of wages under Olympio's regime, began to grow restless. Despite an across-the-board increase in wages, followed by a ten percent cut in government officials' salaries, union leaders demanded better living conditions. Union grievances rapidly built up in 1965, and were exacerbated by the army's brutal dispersal of an authorized church service commemorating Olympio's death in Lomé. This act radicalized the opposition movement. More demands had already been sent to the government when, in December 1965, the executive body decided to restructure and reclassify the entire civil service for greater efficiency. This move turned out to be a mistake. Because of strained relations between the government and workers, the latter assumed that the government decision was simply a punishment for their actions. In retaliation, they called for a general strike that was averted through a combination of mutual compromises. However, these compromises only postponed the showdown, as the workers were determined to reach their goals. The government resisted any unilateral move by the unions, although Grunitzky and Meatchi disagreed on the most appropriate strategy.[92] By 1966, frustrations grew, while the friction at the top of the government increased. An obvious fight within the government to win the favor of either Grunitzky or Meatchi raged also. Both the cabinet and the top echelons of civil service were polarized behind one or the other, with each group trying to embarrass and undermine the position of the other.[93] As long as Grunitzky remained faithful to the army, he enjoyed the military support. Even after reductions of defense allocations and continued pro-south developmental policies, he was still supported by the armed forces. His *faux pas* occurred with his demotion of the Vice-President Meatchi. After that act, his usefulness to the army came to an end and a move by the military became inevitable.

---

92. Decalo, 1990, p. 216; also Heilbrunn, 1994, pp. 403–4.
93. Decalo, 1973b, p. 80.

The 1967 Military Coup

Although a 1965 referendum had confirmed the Grunitzky-Meatchi coalition, and there were preparations underway for the merger of all political parties into a one-party system, the political ambitions of both leaders sharpened. Even the army was becoming polarized to such an extent that Meatchi's friends were trying to build more support within the army. The latent crisis erupted in November 1966, while Grunitzky was in France for a medical check-up. At a cabinet meeting presided over by Acting President Meatchi, Grunitzky's loyal Minister of Interior, Fousséni Mama, informed the cabinet that his forces had discovered that the anti-Grunitzky leaflets being distributed in Lomé were Meatchi's handiwork.[94] In an unexpected move, Meatchi denied the charges and dismissed Mama, precipitating a serious cabinet crisis. Upon his rushed return to Lomé, Grunitzky reinstated his friend, Mama, to a less important post as the minister of education. Given Meatchi's support within the army, and Grunitzky's own vulnerability, he could not yet purge his rival although it fell within his constitutional prerogatives. That situation triggered massive demonstrations and open appeals by southern political leaders to march on the presidential palace. The *Ewe*, unhappy with Grunitzky's handling of the Mama-Meatchi crisis, called for the resignation of President Grunitzky, who had failed to remove his rival from his cabinet.[95]

On November 20, 1966, the situation reached its climax when elements of the armed forces took the national radio and assumed strategic positions around the capital, Lomé. However, the widely expected military coup never materialized. To the surprise of many, Éyadéma, instead, summoned the military to disperse the mobs and arrest their leaders. Through frenzied consultations with other ranking officers, Éyadéma gave Grunitzky more time to resolve the social unrest. Unfortunately, the additional time did not improve relations between Grunitzky and the largely *Ewe* mobs. Adding insult to injury, Grunitzky made several belated moves, including repudiation of the

---

94. Decalo, 1990, *op. cit.*
95. *Id.*, p. 219.

moderates in his cabinet, and the removal of Meatchi's powers, which Éyadéma interpreted as an invitation to take over.[96]

On January 13, 1967, a national holiday and the fourth anniversary of Olympio's murder, Éyadéma ordered Grunitzky's resignation and abolished all political parties and structures. He justified his acts by citing the high risks of civil war. In Decalo's views,

> The 1967 overthrow of Grunitzky in Togo [cannot] be viewed as stemming solely from the very real failings of civilian rule. Grunitzky was very much a front man for General Éyadéma who had led the veteran's coup of 1963 that resulted in the death of President Sylvannus [sic] Olympio. With the rapid erosion of the few sources of support that Grunitzky did possess, Éyadéma had little choice but personally to seize power. The alternative—allowing the formation of a government by the only cohesive ethnic force in the country, the Ewes—was foreclosed all along since a prominent plank in their platform was the arrest and trial of Éyadéma for the murder of Olympio.[97]

An eight-man *Comité de Réconciliation Nationale* (Committee for National Reconciliation) was set up under the Chairmanship of Colonel Dadjo. Despite promises of speedy elections and a new constitution, Éyadéma dissolved the new body, gathered all executive powers into his hands, and formed a government that lasted until 1990, when massive demonstrations forced political reforms through a national conference.[98]

The Military and National Conference in Togo

During his early years in office, Éyadéma surrounded himself with innovative technocrats and intellectuals, and gave them relative autonomy in their spheres of influence. Most of these technocrats were southerners who resented Éyadéma, but took some

---

96. Heilbrunn, 1994, p. 405.
97. Decalo, 1973b, p. 82.
98. See Nwajiaku, *op. cit.*; also John R. Heilbrunn, "Togo: The National Conference and Stalled Reform," in *Political Reform in Francophone Africa*, eds. Clark, John F. and David E. Gardiner, Boulder, CO: Westview Press, 1997.

credit for Togo's booming economy. Through an aggressive export-led economy and the nationalization of the phosphate industry, government revenues increased. Éyadéma's regime found no difficulties meeting both the civilian and military needs of Togo. As long as the population enjoyed a tranquil and happy life, the brutality with which Olympio was killed, and the identity of the person who pulled the trigger, were temporarily forgotten. However, all too quickly, the good times waned by the late 1970s. This did not bode well for Togo.

The early days of technocrats and intellectuals gave way to the appointment of relatives and political cronies. Mismanagement, embezzlement, and corruption marred both the economy and the political process. And, since perpetrators of these economic crimes remained unpunished because of their political connections, they continued to damage Togo's economy bringing the country to its knees as public finances plunged and debts piled up.[99] While bankruptcy threatened Togo and most citizens restricted their lifestyles, relatives and cronies of those in power continued to live beyond their means as long as they remained loyal to the system. According to Gutteridge:

> Under the Éyadéma régime Togo became increasingly indebted to France and West Germany and really ceased to have international status. The degree of indebtedness was such that many of the Ewe elite saw the situation as a triumph for French "neo-colonialism" and blamed the economic difficulties of the country on its military leaders on the grounds that economic development since 1963 has misfired.[100]

By the late 1980s, the southerners, frustrated by their social displacement (northerners were now at the helm of most state enterprises), started displaying their anger. Southerners had never fully granted legitimacy to the Éyadéma's regime, but chose to cooperate because it suited their interests at the time. Gradually, southerners started looking for ways to let Éyadéma know their feelings. Beginning with subtle re-

---

99. Decalo, 1990, p. 229.
100. Gutteridge, 1969, p. 45.

quests to return to their previous position, the southerners' demands for political and economic reforms grew louder.[101] Gradually, Olympio's memory and legacy started to haunt the *Ewe* leadership. New momentum for a change in Togo's political scene coincided with the wave of democratization and events in neighboring Benin. After several years of political blunders, economic mistakes and ideological shortsightedness, civil society forced Togo to embark on a path of renewal.[102]

The actions of the military, an integral part of Togo's old order, have disrupted the democratic process. The military found democratic reforms threatening and intervened several times in favor of Éyadéma's regime. The transitional government had to manage a large, disgruntled army, which appeared to be exclusively loyal to the *ancien régime* and its head of state.[103] The institutional connections between the state, the army and the single party, conflicted clearly with the requirements of the democratic process.

Taking their cues from Benin, the political opposition of Togo, comprised mainly of disgruntled southerners, organized a pro-democracy movement bent on changing the political system. Éyadéma, clearly, opposed fundamental changes. After several months of pressure, he became open to the idea of a national conference.[104] Unfortunately, the military leadership generally opposed any political gathering geared towards altering Togo's political scene. The history of the relations between the army and civil society in Togo, and the mistrust and hatred between northerners and southerners, largely explained the reluctance of the military to convene a national conference.

Since the birth of Togo's armed forces up to its enlargement by force, the mainly northern components of the military had always been concerned about giving too much power to the southerners. They rightly perceived the call for democracy as the *Ewe*'s way of getting even with the *Kabiyè*. Another serious concern of the military

---

101. See Heilbrunn, 1993, *op. cit.*; also Decalo, 1990, 220.

102. See Dossou, *op. cit.*; Adjovi, *op.cit.*; Nwajiaku, *op. cit.*; Robinson, 1994, *op. cit.*

103. Earl Conteh-Morgan, *Democratization in Africa: The Theory and Dynamics of Political Transitions*, Westport, CT: Praeger, 1997, p. 84.

104. Heilbrunn, 1997, p. 230.

was the brutality with which it had responded to massive demonstrations.[105] Acting almost as a private army dedicated to the interests of Éyadéma and the *Kabiyè*, agents were constantly dispatched to repress any "subversive" actions, very common in the early 1990s in Togo, Lomé specifically. While the military never hesitated to use imprisonment, torture, and intimidation to reach its goals, the violence openly displayed by Togo's armed forces had become outrageous. Far from resolving Togo's political crisis, repressing the opposition only escalated southerners' demands. By 1991, the social unrest in Lomé expressed itself as a clash between the army and civil society rather than an argument between the government and the opposition. Several high ranking elements of the army who happened to be from the south, had been "replaced" under questionable circumstances. Some died in hospital beds of suspicious illnesses, while others were sent into involuntary retirement. When Lomé erupted in turmoil in 1990, the military hierarchy saw the potential downfall of its "protector." Consequently, corporate interests demanded that necessary actions be taken to deter any opposition movement.[106]

By 1989, Éyadéma had started shifting his position. He was willing to assent to multi-party politics, "if that is the will of the people."[107] At the same time, hard-liners within the ruling *Rassemblement du Peuple Togolais* (RPT) were rejecting any idea of multipartyism. While the pressure was clearly coming from outside Togo, political and economic demands ignited from within. Civil society, and specifically students, became more vocal in their protest. In August 1990, an independent *Ligue Togolaise des Droits de l'Homme* (LDTH) was formed in direct challenge to the government *Commission Nationale des Droits de l'Homme* (CNDH), because of the impression that the CNDH was not doing enough to uncover the numerous abuses of human rights in Togo. Several political activists, including Logo Dossouvi and Doglo Agbelenko, were detained on suspicion of distribution of anti-government leaflets.[108] During their

---

105. Decalo, 1990, p. 228.
106. *Id.*, p. 228.
107. *Id.*
108. Press, *op. cit.*, pp. 88–89.

trial, violent demonstrations erupted in Lomé, resulting in four deaths.

In October 1990, a commission was established to draft a new constitution geared to ease the political situation. Although the Togolese people approved that constitution, calling for a multi-party political system, social unrest continued.[109] In January 1991, Éyadéma granted amnesty to all those who were implicated in political offenses. The sentences of criminal offenders were also reduced. Even mandatory contributions to the single party, the RPT, were abolished to indicate a desire to change the political atmosphere in Togo. A boycott of classes by university students and secondary school pupils in March 1991 evidenced the gap between the government and the population. It became clear once again that stability would not come easily. In April, further student unrest ensued, prompted by demonstrations in Lomé by pupils at the Roman Catholic mission schools, in support of their teachers' demands for wage increases. The opposition was unwilling to settle for any concession other than the convening of a national conference. In fact, several opposition movements joined their forces in the *Front des Associations pour le Renouveau* (FAR), to press for immediate political overture.[110]

Finally, Éyadéma yielded to the opposition's request, and a prominent leader of the opposition, Mr. Yaovi Agboyibor, was invited for a *tête-à-tête*. According to the results of these talks, Éyadéma agreed to amnesty for all dissidents, to the legalization of all political parties, and the organization of a national forum to discuss the country's political evolution. However, due to renewed social and labor unrest, the preparation of the conference proved extremely difficult. Any attempt by the opposition leaders to design a strategy with which to handle the conference, was disrupted by supporters of the incumbent regime. The sheer fear that the term 'national conference' might replicate events in Benin, delayed the actual opening for several days.

Initially scheduled to open in late June, the conference became a reality on July 8, 1991. In attendance were the government repre-

---

109. Heilbrunn, 1997, p. 239.
110. *Id.*, pp. 232–33.

sentatives, the newly legalized political parties, union leaders, student representatives, and religious delegates. Despite the tense atmosphere, things seemed to be on track until, similar to the Benin scenario, and confirming Éyadéma's concern, the conference declared itself 'sovereign,' suspending the 1979 constitution and dissolving the national assembly.[111] All these acts were clearly in violation of a June 12 agreement the opposition has entered into with the government.

However, at that point, the opposition felt it had nothing to lose, and took a huge gamble that turned out to be the biggest political miscalculation in Togo's history.[112] Furious over the steps 'illegally' taken by the conference, the government representatives simply walked out and boycotted the proceedings for a week. Upon their return, they presented the gathering with a caveat, stating that they may reject any or all of the conference resolutions. That preemptive strike simply demonstrated Éyadéma's determination to cling to power.

As if to prove their resolve, in defiance of the government, the delegates resolved to sequester the assets of the RPT and the *Confédération Nationale des Travailleurs du Togo* (CNTT — the Labor Union). The conference also decided to create a commission to look into the financial dealings of these organizations, together with an authority to take steps to prevent the illicit flight of capital during the national gathering. The conference delegates even imposed an exit visa on any government official traveling abroad. These clear signs of frustration and anxiety made the political situation more complex.[113]

Meanwhile, during the proceedings renewed allegations of human rights violations were relayed by the media. In an almost surrealistic environment, witnesses, among whom were agents of Éyadéma's regime, exposed instances of torture and murder in 'death camps.' Following these horrible allegations, Éyadéma, already upset for having been deprived of most if his powers, abruptly suspended the national conference. That bold act called for a bolder one on the part of

---

111. See Nwajiaku, *op. cit.*

112. Heilbrunn, 1997, pp. 236–37.

113. See Hugo Saga, "Chaillot n'est pas la Baule," *Jeune Afrique* 1613 (November 27 – December 3, 1991), pp. 4–9.

the delegates: they proclaimed a provisional government under the leadership of Joseph Koffigoh.[114]

Although in the end Éyadéma reluctantly confirmed by decree the transitional government of Koffigoh, the conference ended on August 28, 1991 without a clear sense of purpose and achievements. Unlike other African countries where a national conference brought some sense of renewal and reconciliation, the national gathering in Togo was more a distraction than anything else. In Wiseman's words, "in Togo, it would appear that, for [a] moment, those struggling against democracy have the upper hand over those struggling for democracy."[115] Decalo's assessment also reveals Éyadéma's new status since the end of the national conference in Togo:

> In Togo, General Éyadéma, in 1990 on the verge of being consigned to the dustbin of history by a resurgent national Conference in Lomé brutally clawed his way to an officially 'competitive' presidential election victory (most opposition leaders boycotted an exercise marked by intimidation, murder and terror). He then mobilized the Kabre [Kabiyè] ethnic vote in the 1994 legislative elections, transforming himself into the only viable political leader in the country, and technically a democrat to boot.[116]

Despite the apparent failure of Togo's national gathering, other African states continued to look for peaceful means of altering their faltering political and economic systems. Following the Benin's example then, several African countries, including Gabon, the Congo, Mali, and Niger, also held national conferences with varying degrees of success.[117] In their explanation of the rationale behind the emula-

---

114. Heilbrunn, 1994, p. 687.

115. John A. Wiseman, *The New Struggle for Democracy in Africa*, Brookfield, VT: Avebury, 1996, p. 69.

116. Samuel Decalo, "The Future of Participatory Democracy in Africa," *Futures* 26/9 (1994), p. 989.

117. Jean-Jacques Pérennès et Hugues Puel, "Démocratie et Développement au Sud," *Économie et Humanisme* 319 (Octobre–Novembre 1991), p. 11.

tion of the Benin case by other Francophone African nations, the editors of *West Africa* contend that:

> [The French revolutionary] precedent seems to have influenced the political movements in Benin in their campaign for a national conference, and, when they called it, in their immediate capture of sovereignty. In Francophone Africa, where there are many weak, interdependent mini-states, there is also often a knock-on effect relating to language, media, class and age networking, and other channels of communication. Political events in one are picked up in another, as has been seen in the past with both student agitations and military coups.[118]

In the end, Éyadéma yielded to the opposition's demand for a national gathering to look into Togo's economic and political problems. Both internal and external pressures forced him to agree to the national conference. But, when the compromise between the government and the opposition broke down due to the opposition's eagerness to reach its goals with or without Éyadéma's cooperation, the real intentions of the army and the government surfaced. Consequently, the military simply threatened to shut down the proceedings and took actions to intimidate the Prime Minister elected by the conference. Evidently, the military had never wanted a democratic transition in Togo, fearing it might have to answer tough questions about its past behavior. That attitude dealt a severe blow to the democratic process. Its consequences are felt to this day as democracy continues to elude Togo.

The government's economic program for 1997–99, supported by the IMF and the World Bank, was aimed at achieving sustained and diversified economic growth. By downsizing the bloated civil service, and controlling the staggering national debt, Togo might be on the right track. Éyadéma's rule and his northern and military origins continue, however, to be rejected in the south. Although the presumed final eclipse of Éyadéma anticipated by the National Conference never materialized, the pressure was definitely on for both economic and political reforms.

---

118. *West Africa,* "Moments of Truth," 12–18 August 1991, p. 1313.

Conclusion

Democratization has generated a great deal of hope on the continent, though Africa's journey toward democratic institutions has been painstakingly slow. While some countries embarked on a democratic path with hesitation, given the risks involved, others are still resisting. After a successful national conference and a few years of economic growth under president Soglo, Benin seems to have renewed with frequent strikes and social unrest since the return of Kérékou and his former "comrades." Relations between the government and civil servants have remained strained because of the lack of political will to satisfy the workers' demands. In fact, early hopes for a genuine democratic renewal are rapidly being dashed especially after the 2001 presidential elections, which, according to several observers, were marred by numerous irregularities. In Togo, both the latest presidential and legislative ballots were not only challenged by the opposition, but also denounced by some European countries whose representatives monitored the elections.[119] Subsequent political events and numerous failed attempts at reconciliation between Éyadéma's regime and its foes illustrate the importance of what is at stake. In fact, the parliament's December 2002 amendment to the constitution, allowing Éyadéma to rule for unlimited terms, will only worsen an extremely volatile situation. The crisis in Togo's democratization process is far from over, and the hardening of positions on both sides is clearly a bad omen for any speedy farewell to authoritarianism in West Africa.

Enduring democracy, Rustow contends, is most often the result, not of élite consensus or a mass civic culture, but of the difficult negotiations between contending actors with widely divergent interests and civil society institutions. The opposition in West Africa must seriously consider this proposition. Although Benin seems, so far, to be on the right track, political leaders must remain aware of the determinants of political change to consolidate the hard won democracy. Given its weak position, the Togolese opposition needs to resume ne-

---

119. BBC News, "Togo Election Fraud Alleged," June 2, 2003.

gotiations if it is ever to trigger genuine political reforms. Only through sustained dialogue can a seemingly intractable political feud between Éyadéma and the opposition be resolved.

CONCLUSION

In the last decade of the 20th century the African continent was swept by a wave of democratization, ushering in a new era in African politics. Although the early euphoria has died down due to recent disappointments with the state of democratization on the continent, it is undeniable that a new era has begun in Africa.[1] In his attempt to capture the new fight for political freedom in Africa, Robert Press summarized eloquently the fervor on the continent:

> A long-simmering discontent and anger with politics as usual boiled over in Africa at the end of the Cold War in 1989. Pervasive poverty and international and domestic pressures for democracy set the stage for change to some degree, but mostly it was the power of an idea, the idea of freedom, that changed the shape of African politics more than at any time since independence. Africans caught a fever of freedom which spread rapidly across the continent, prompting confrontations and other challenges to longtime authoritarian rulers. Ordinary people, not just political opposition leaders, stood up for democracy, often against great odds, sometimes against brutal force.[2]

Opinions on the roots of such a change were, at first, divergent. Several scholars attributed the political reforms to the existence of a vibrant civil society. However, the very fact that democratization oc-

---

1. John Wiseman, *The New Struggle for Democracy in Africa*, Brookfiel, VT: Avebury, 1996, p. 35.
2. Robert M. Press, *The New Africa: Dispatches from a Changing Continent*, Gainesville, FL: University Press of Florida, 1999, p. 3.

179

curred mainly in countries where the military has either embraced or at least tolerated it, suggests that the behavior of the armed forces is a key determinant of genuine political change in Africa.[3] Welch's view on the wave of democratization on the continent seems to connect the decline of military rule with democracy.

> The rule of the "man on the horseback" is declining, as a consequence of the global political and ideological changes... Civil-military relations are changing dramatically with the spread of the call for democracy around the world. Although armed forces remain primary political actors in most states, their direct political roles have been reduced in recent years. The result, to overstate the case, is fundamental transformation and nowhere is it more marked than in developing countries. The Third World is now witnessing the slow, difficult, but significant consolidation of civilian governments after, in many cases, several decades of military rule.[4]

In their euphoria, several analysts expected competitive democracy to bloom everywhere and supplant civilian and military oligarchies.[5] Although some analysts were skeptical,[6] most observers assumed that

---

3. Chuka Onwumechili, *African Democratization and Military Coups*, Westport, CT: Praeger, 1998, p. 73.

4. Claude E. Welch, Jr., "Changing Civil-Military Relations," in *Global Transformations and the Third World*, eds. Robert O. Slater, Barry M. Schutz and Steven R. Dorr, Boulder, CO: Lynne Rienner, 1993, p. 71.

5. See Stephen Riley, "The Democratic Transition in Africa: An End to the One-Party State?" *Conflict Studies* No. 245 (October 1991), pp. 1–36; Julius O. Ihonvbere, "The Dynamics of Change in Eastern Europe and their Implications for Africa," *Coexistence* 29/2 (1992), pp. 277–96; Colin Legum, "The Coming of Africa's Second Independence," *The Washington Quarterly* 33 (Winter 1990), pp. 129–40; John Wiseman, "Democratic Resurgence in Black Africa," *Contemporary Review* 259 (July 1991), pp. 7–13; Richard Joseph, "Africa: The Rebirth of Political Freedom," *Journal of Democracy* 2 (Fall 1991), pp. 11–24; and Martin Klein, "Back to Democracy: Presidential Address to the 1991 Annual Meeting of the African Studies Association," *African Studies Review* 35/3 (1992), pp. 1–12.

6. See Gilbert M. Khadiagala, "The Military in Africa's Democratic Transitions: Regional Dimensions," *Africa Today* 1&2 (1995), pp. 61–74; Eboe Hutchful, "Militarism and Problems of Democratic Transition," in *Democracy in Africa:*

the military would join the bandwagon of democratization and facilitate the democratic transition in Africa. Because of frequent military intervention in the region, West Africa was a litmus test for democratic renewal on the continent. More than a decade later, it is hard to credit the military with a genuine desire to withdraw from African politics. After decades at the helm, incumbent military leaders were, understandably, reluctant to return to the barracks, and therefore used delaying tactics to perpetuate their hold on power.

Africa's inheritance of weak political institutions did not allow liberal democracy to prosper in post-colonial Africa. Arbitrary boundary demarcation, resource extraction and human exploitation have not been conducive to the pursuit of the democratic ideal on the continent. As a result of the Cold War superpower rivalry and neo-colonialism, nascent African nations have failed to find appropriate political and economic models capable of delivering the expected improvement in living conditions. Although such modern institutions as parliaments and presidents were present, they were superseded by personal rule through a centralization of state power. Power and authority were simply removed from civil society and peripheral institutions of the state, and hoarded instead in the hands of a few, or often a single dominant individual, the head of State. Patronage, based on the distribution of state resources, became the main bond between governors and governed. Due to the nature of politics on the continent, competition for political power became fierce, and the military vowed to have its voice heard.

The perception of the military as the most highly organized and technically competent organ of the state and the monopoly over legitimate violence provided fertile ground for the politicization of the armed forces. From corporate demands and preferential treatment, the military's influence gradually took a clear and assertive political dimension. Before the shortcomings of civilian governments, economic mismanagement and rampant corruption, the men in uniform

---

The Hard Road Ahead, ed. Ottaway, Marina. Boulder, CO: Lynne Rienner, 1997; and Pierre Moukoko-Mbonjo, "Régimes Militaires et Transition Démocratique en Afrique: À la Recherche d'un Cadre d'Analyse Théorique," *Afrique 2000* 13 (1993), pp. 39–58.

took upon themselves to "salvage" their countries. While some military leaders (Éyadéma of Togo, Jammeh of the Gambia, Doe of Liberia, etc.) were motivated by personal ambitions, others (Kérékou of Benin, Ratsiraka of Madagascar, Sankara of Burkina Faso, etc.) gave an early impression of intervening to right years of wrongs and once finished, returning to their barracks. The allure of power and its privileges and advantages simply proved stronger than the professed intention to return to a constitutional *democratic* order. Consequently, the armed forces, although they did not fare better than the civilians they replaced, hung on to power well past their welcome.

Until the end of the Cold War and the subsequent wind of democratization, African leaders had "hijacked" the inherited modern states, adapted liberal democratic institutions to their own interests, and then "patrimonialized" the political system. Whether civilian or military, African leaders behaved as monarchs, omnipotent and unaccountable to their people. With a concentration of power at the core, opportunities for organized opposition became limited. No rival source of power could be endorsed or tolerated by incumbent regimes. In fact, opposition parties were daily harassed if not outlawed outright. The political elite no longer confined the protection of its monopoly to neutralizing challenges and competition. It also restricted rival political activity emanating from civil society, plunging civil society into a deep coma until the early 1990s. Labor unions, professional groups and other voluntary associations were constantly threatened, and their leaders often co-opted with the objective of silencing any dissent. Since the "mouth that eats does not speak,"[7] former civil society activists become benevolent government informants. Although there were a few conscientious leaders who resisted governments' inducements and paid dearly with their liberty and even life, they were a minority and their activities usually met little tangible success.

Within a centralized state, even such economic functions as production, distribution and sale of goods that belong ideally to the realms

---

7. Cited in Jean-François Bayart, *The State in Africa: the Politics of the Belly*, London: Longman, 1993, p. 188.

of civil society are the monopoly of government institutions. Because leaving these activities to free market might empower ordinary citizens, the government invents elaborate schemes to maintain economic movements under its tight control. With no regard for the laws of supply and demand, African economies operated under unorthodox principles and autocratic regimes paid the price. In the late 1980s, events from Eastern Europe and the thaw of the Cold War helped. Africans took to the street to protest sharply declining living conditions. At its inception, the movement for reforms was economic and/or social, only later did it become political. However, the call for democracy, expected to yield important political returns on the continent, did not achieve the expected results in West Africa in particular.

In the wake of democratization, there was some hope that finally the military would abandon politics to civilians, despite early signs to the contrary. Evidently, the military was not enthusiastic about the democratic process in the early days of reforms. Concerned about its performance in West Africa, the military was rather uneasy about political reforms and eager to foil any attempt to introduce a genuine democratic transition. With a few exceptions, the military by and large refused to cooperate in renewing hope in the region. After decades of ignoring similar demands, banning opposition parties, demonstrations, and strikes, military leaders realized that, this time around, a less blunt response was necessary. However, the survival instinct as well as other more substantive reasons discussed in the cases examined in the preceding chapters prevented them from participating willingly in their own removal from power.

As the cases studied in this book clearly indicate, it is quite premature to certify any complete and irreversible military disengagement from politics in West Africa. While a new political environment, both regionally and internationally, has imposed new rules and raised expectations, many West African military heads of state have managed to maintain their grip on power. Pretending to embrace democracy, they altered both their behavior and their polities, and most became "constitutional autocrats" who kept power through regular and ostentatious "free and fair" elections. Using the "incumbent's privileges" West Africa's new "military democrats" took all necessary precautions to "win" multiparty elections. Losing was simply not an option. As the cases of Mauritania, the Gambia, Togo, (and Burkina Faso and Guinea among others) demonstrate, skillful manipulation of internal and external variables allowed leaders to prolong their stay at the helm. The military continues to be a major, if benevolent, player in Benin politics, while Côte d'Ivoire finally experienced a short-lived military rule with devastating consequences.

In "democratic" Mauritania, a former military leader, Maaouya Ould Sid'Ahmed Taya has cunningly succeeded in setting up, since 1992, a political system in which the rule of law is not guaranteed despite apparent democratic institutions. Many public officials, often cronies, friends or relatives of the president's, use their positions to serve the interests of their ethnic groups. Mauritania's current political environment fits more the one described in Machiavelli's *The Prince* or Hobbes's *Leviathan*, rather than Montesquieu's *Spirit of the Laws*. There, political order and legitimacy take on a different meaning. Using long-running ethnic feuds pitting Arabs and Arabized Moors against Black Mauritanians, Ould Taya has created a repressive and fundamentally volatile atmosphere. The state is run as his private property, the basic political freedoms are denied. Increasingly, a dangerous sense of disenfranchisement among all strata of the population is setting in. Although personal rule breeds a political environment of factionalism, schisms, purges and coups, Ould Taya's skills assured him continuity since he can "win" elections amid credible but rapidly forgotten allegations of massive fraud. A shrewd diplomacy to gain the favors of the West may not be enough to prevent a predictable breakdown. Mauritania's "pseudo-democracy" was indeed severely tested during the 2003 presidential election. However, the opposition was unable to reedit one of the scenarios played out in Madagascar and Kenya in 2002. Either would have been a positive step toward genuine democratization. Now, more likely, Mauritania's 'non-democratic transition' will continue increasing the likelihood of a much more violent scenario than even Madagascar.

In The Gambia, the soldier-turned-civilian president, Yahya Jammeh, ended the longest surviving democracy in Africa only to display unmistakable authoritarian and deadly tendencies. Through ingenious moves, he managed to alter the political equation in The Gambia to suit his own personal ambitions. He came to power denouncing a corrupt and oligarchic regime whose performance left much to be desired. Far from being a messiah, Jammeh turned out to be yet another military coup stager eager to use state institutions to climb faster the societal ladder. Having taken advantage of Gambians' willingness to give him the benefit of the doubt, he showed his intentions quite early on, leaving no doubt on his clear intention to remain in power. Through clientelism, he controlled the patron-client networks and secured support from his immediate lieutenants. Although he cut the initial transition period by half mainly in response to international and domestic pressure, he stood for and "won" the 1996 elections. After an initial euphoria, military intervention in the Gambia has been accompanied by arbitrary arrests and detentions, a severe economic crisis and general political uncertainty.[8] To the astonishment of his critics and opposition, Jammeh proved to be a savvy politician. He demonstrated his willingness to go to any length to retain power. His "victory" in the 2001 presidential elections and the manner in which it was achieved stand out as a reminder of his determination and ruthlessness.

In Togo, the 'presidential-monarch,' Gnassingbé Éyadéma, remains the main obstacle on the path to democracy. A former disgruntled soldier, Éyadema came to power to strike an equilibrium between the north and the south on one hand, and between civilians and the military on the other, but also for revenge. His personal vendetta and peculiar calculations led to both the 1963 and 1967 military interventions. After his second coup, there were hopes that he meant to introduce genuine political and economic reforms in Togo. These hopes were dashed quite early when it became obvious through the reorganization of politics in Togo that Éyadéma came to stay. Using the single party as a token of "unity," he succeeded in concentrating power in his own hands. While the early years of his tenure saw a surprisingly efficient management of the economy, corruption and mismanagement gradually set in, putting the country in a precarious economic and political situation by the early 1990s. Forced like many

---

8. Ebenezer Obadare, "The Military and Democracy in the Gambia," in D. Olowu, A. Williams and K. Soremekum eds. *Governance and Democratisation in West Africa*, Dakar, Senegal: CODESRIA, 1999, p. 349.

others to embark on a democratic transition he utterly rejected, Éyadéma has since shown his fierce determination to remain in power at all costs. The recent changes to the constitution and continuous measures to disenfranchise the opposition may well guarantee his wish, to die in office, but the cost to Togo may be staggering as this only increases the risk of violence and bloodshed.

In Benin, former Marxist president, Mathieu Kérékou, is back in power after a five-year break. When he was made the leader of the "October Revolution," many thought that Kérékou was going to be a different leader, one really concerned with the well-being of his people. Besides his vehement anti-West rhetoric, his early actions strongly presaged a radical and qualitative overhaul of politics in Benin. However, as the years passed by, the movement took a turn for the worse, when Marxism-Leninism was chosen as its guiding principle. Consequently, both the politics and the economy fell in the hands of "enlightened" close associates of Kérékou's, leading the country to a dead end. But, when the winds of change reached Benin, Kérékou decided to cooperate with civilians to lead Benin to a new dawn. To his credit, the democratic transition was peaceful. It allowed the former dictator to redeem himself and to a certain extent, the military too. However, old habits die hard and the Beninese "come back kid," now back in power, continues to display his lack of political skill and dubious commitment to real democracy.

In Côte d'Ivoire, General Guéi's coup confirmed the military's continued involvement in West African politics. Clearly, president Bédié's tactless moves, and especially his obstinacy not to hear out rebellious soldiers, helped to trigger the movement. After several decades of seemingly firm civilian control over the military, Côte d'Ivoire joined the cohort of African countries where the military took power. Regardless of the locus or the causes of the coup, coming a decade into the democratization era, it has forced a rethinking of civil-military relations in Africa in general and in Côte d'Ivoire in particular. For decades, the military remained under civilian control in Côte d'Ivoire, if only nominally. This was because of Houphouet-Boigny's personal political acumen, not because the Ivoirian army was more docile than other armies in the sub-region. General Guéi's refusal to leave after losing the election only confirmed that the military in West Africa has not abandoned its claim to political power. Since 1999, subsequent real or imaginary coup attempts, and the current political instability are not reassuring to future civilian leaders as long as far-reaching reforms of the body politic are not carried out.

The analyses in this volume demonstrate that the road to democracy as well as the pace of democratization in Africa still depends, to a large extent, on the armed forces.[9] The transition from military to civilian rule in West Africa requires undoing military intervention in politics as a preliminary step in recreating democratic institutions.[10] Since independence, African armies have assumed significant roles as managers and arbiters of political conflicts and their disengagement will have to be negotiated. Achieving effective democratic civilian control of the military is the first step to establishing accountable political systems in Africa. The cases studied demonstrate that the military remains a potent political actor to be reckoned with, as it has worked, either directly or behind the scenes to defend its own interests and those of its allies.[11] Louis Martin captures well the conditions of democratic success in Africa:

> Although the success of democratic transitions in Sub-Saharan Africa will depend ultimately on institutionalization of civil control of the military (the prerequisite to the idea of the rule of law), it will depend in the short run on the manner in which former praetorians [military leaders] are dealt with...Establishing a stable relationship with the armed

---

9. See Eboe Hutchful, "Militarism and Problems of Democratic Transition," in *Democracy in Africa: The Hard Road Ahead*, ed. Ottaway, Marina. Boulder, CO: Lynne Rienner, 1997; also Samuel Decalo, *The Stable Minority: Civilian Rule in Africa, 1960–1990*. Gainesville: FAP Books, 1998.

10. See Robin Luckman, "The Military, Militarization, and Democratization in Africa: A Survey of Literature and Issues," *African Studies Review* 37/2 (September 1994), pp. 13–76; and William J. Foltz, "Democracy: Officers and Politicians," *Africa Report* 38/3 (1993), pp. 65–67.

11. Stephen Riley, "Political Adjustment or Domestic Pressure: Democratic Politics and Political Choice in Africa," *Third World Quarterly* 13/3 (1992): 539–51, p. 541.

forces and ensuring their withdrawal from politics…will require "rewarding" means of subordination.[12]

In the same vein, Huntington believes that to impose an "objective civilian control" over the military in order to render it "politically sterile and neutral," civilian leaders will have to work with the military at the initial stage of democratization.[13] Advising on the strategies for democratization in the Third World, Diamond rightly states that "where the military remains firmly in control, openly or behind the scenes, negotiating with it a plan for gradual democratization of political institution may offer the best hope for committed democrats."[14] The future of democracy in West Africa is critically dependent on the civilian control of the military because the issue of civil-military relations is central to the political and economic development of the countries of the region. Ironically, the military's disengagement is taken as a given, democratization efforts focusing largely on constitutional reform of electoral rules rather than institutionally minimizing military power.[15]

After many decades of mistrust, the military and civilian politicians will need to redesign their relationships for a smooth political transition in their country. In fact, Larry Diamond and Mark Plattner make a good case for a badly-needed new civil-military relationship in Africa:

> Sound civil-military relations are the product of longstanding national tradition and a complex set of formal and informal measures that affect the government, civil society, and the military itself. If civil-military relations are to be given an

12. Michel-Louis Martin, "Operational Weakness and Political Activism: The Military in Sub-Saharan Africa," in *To Sheathe the Sword: Civil-Military Relations in the Quest for Democracy*, eds. John P. Lovell and David E. Albright. Westport, CT: Greenwood Press, 1997, p. 96.

13. Samuel Huntington, The Soldier and the State: The Theory and Politics of Civil-Military Relations, Cambridge, MA: Belknap, 1957, pp. 84–166.

14. Larry Diamond, "Beyond Authoritarianism and Totalitarianism: Strategies for Democratization." *Washington Quarterly* 12/1 (December 1989): 141–63, p. 147.

15. Jendayi Frazer, "Conceptualizing Civil-Military Relations during Democratic Transition," *Africa Today* 1&2 (1995), p. 39.

ideal framework, it is vital that the state clearly demarcate the limits of the military's role and that both the broad public and the military feel that a role is legitimate. This requires that civilian leaders take the lead in defining the military's overall strategy and defense planning, in laying out the armed forces' roles and missions, and in regulating the military's budget, recruiting and training practices, force structure, and level of armaments.[16]

Civil control of the military is managed and maintained through the sharing of control between civilian leaders and military officers. This theory of shared responsibility, suggested by Bland, rests on two assumptions. First, the term "civil control" means that the sole legitimate source for the directions and actions of the military is derived from civilians outside the military/defense establishments. Second, civil control is a dynamic process susceptible to changing ideas, values, circumstances, issues, and personalities and to the stresses of crises and war.[17] Ideally, a professional military should hold the defense of state security as paramount and foster values of order and hierarchy internally to support that goal.[18] However, military intervention in politics has made the division between the armed forces as an institution and the military as government a critical issue in West African politics.

In a democracy, the challenge of civil-military relations is to "reconcile a military strong enough to do anything the civilians ask them to with a military subordinate enough to do only what civilian authorize them to do" and the civilian problem has centered around the question of "how to ensure that your agent is doing your will, especially when your agent has guns and so may enjoy more coercive power than you do?[19] On the other hand, the military's challenge has been to embrace the whims of society, which threaten to blunt the ca-

---

16. Larry Diamond and Marc F. Plattner, *Civil-Military and Democracy*, Baltimore, MD: John Hopkins University Press, 1996, pp. xx–xxi.

17. Douglas L. Bland, "A Unified Theory of Civil-Military Relations," *Armed Forces and Society* 26/1 (1999): 7–25, p. 10.

18. Huntington, *op. cit.*, pp. 59–79.

19. P.D. Feaver, "The Civil-Military Problematique: Huntington, Janowitz, and the Question of Civilian Control," *Armed Forces and Society*, 23/2, p. 149.

pability of the armed forces, or to risk alienation from the very people it purports to defend if it impedes social change. While popular wisdom on the topic of civilian control of the military would deny any political role to the military, as evidenced in the concept of "apolitical" armed forces, the typical African army has been so politicized that it has a stake in politics beyond that of militaries throughout the Western world. Only a redefinition of boundaries and a more astute management by civilians will, hopefully, prevent the African military from intervening continuously in the political process. This redefinition must heed the insight of long time scholars of civil-military relations in Africa. Robin Lukham,[20] for example, has long argued that we must be careful to distinguish between the kind of 'politics' we mean in reference to the military, an institution of the state and by definition a political institution. Lukham further argues that while in the context of democratic institutions, the military and the state security apparatus must remain completely outside the arena of "partisan politics," the military, duly subordinated to democratically elected authorities, will be called on to carry out what may be, at time, a 'political' role. That role is not incompatible with democratic systems with well thought out civil-military relations.

Until then, the process of democratization remains fragile, vulnerable, and susceptible to reversal by the military, on its own behalf or at the behest of unscrupulous factions of the political society. Because of the complex civil-military *problématique* in Africa, both civilian leaders and military officers need to reevaluate their relations for a brighter prospect for democracy on the continent. As Samuel Huntington has argued, the major problem of civil-military relations remains the "praetorian problem...the need to curb the political power of the military establishment and to make the armed forces into a professional body committed to providing for the external security of the country."[21] While old liberal democracies and emerging democ-

---

20. Robin Lukham, "Taming the Monster: Democratization and Demilitarization," in Eboe Hutchful and Abdoulaye Bathily, eds., *The Military and Militarism in Africa*, Dakar, CODESRIA, 1998.

21. Samuel Huntington, *The Third Wave: Democratization in the Late Twentieth Century*, Norman, OK: University of Oklahoma Press, 1991, p. 231.

racies alike must guard against that persistent 'praetorian problem,' they also need to concentrate on how to manage civil-military relations after the power of the military has been curbed.[22]

According to James Burk, the extensive empirical domain of civil-military includes:

> direct and indirect dealings that ordinary people and institutions have with the military, legislative haggling over the funding, regulation, and use of the military, and complex bargaining between civilian and military elites to define and implement national security policy. Moreover, each of these relations varies in form and consequence depending on whether they are found in strong democratic or weak authoritarian states, in economically developed or impoverished states, in states at war or states at peace.[23]

As the cases demonstrate, the nature of contemporary politics and the monopoly of violence by the military allow incumbent military leaders to manipulate the political system and in most cases, retain power. Following the normative belief that civilian political control over the military is preferable to military confiscation of the state, democratization, at least at its early stage, should seek how civilian control over the military is established and maintained. Instead of being thought of as a struggle for power between irreconcilable adversaries, civil-military relations should be conceived of as exchanges between "friendly adversaries,"[24] in order to avoid African democratization ending up as a mere fleeting vogue. While democracy has a new chance on the continent, African leaders, both political and military, need to reach the *modus vivendi* capable of creating, expanding, and sustaining democracies in Africa.

---

22. Douglas L. Bland, "A Unified Theory of Civil-Military Relations," *Armed Forces and Society* 26/1 (1999), p. 13.

23. James Burk, "Theories of Democratic Civil-Military Relations," *Armed Forces and Society* 29/1 (Fall 2002), p. 7.

24. Sam C. Sarkesian, "Military Professionalism and Civil-Military Relations in West Africa," *International Political Science Review* 2/3 (1981), p. 291.

Not surprisingly, the "new wave" of democratization has yet to produce any undisputed consolidated democracy. The expectation that the salience of African military intrusions into politics would be on the decline as moves towards democratic transition and economic liberalization intensified never materialized. Rather, there seems to be a revival of the "cult of the military," incumbent military leaders using constitutional means to strengthen their position. Whenever the military has tasted the forbidden political fruit, it has usually been a Sisyphean task persuading it to return to and (more importantly) stay in the barracks.[25] Proponents of the military's withdrawal from politics and of a complete end to authoritarian rule in Africa in general and in West Africa in particular might be disappointed because we may not have heard the last of military intervention in African politics. One of the safest predictions about West African politics is to forecast a continued strong influence and, at worse, frequent forays of the armed forces into the political system. In spite of legitimacy deficit, the military will, unfortunately, continue to remain a force to be reckoned with in the political arena.

---

25. Obadare, *op. cit.*, p. 356.

Epilogue

One of the difficulties in analyzing and chronicling the evolution of the democratization processes in West Africa is that events often overtake the analysis and even the most cautious prognostications. Since our case studies were completed, the conclusions drawn, and predictions made, in at least three of the countries examined, major developments have occurred. Indeed, in West Africa as a whole, the Liberian crisis took a hopeful turn in August 2003 with the agreement that led to the exile of President Charles Taylor, which opened the increased possibility of a final solution to a major source of destabilization in the region. In still another hopeful inching toward the end of authoritarianism, in May, the regional colossus, Nigeria, held bitterly contested elections which, nevertheless, renewed President Olusegun Obasanjo's mandate. The coup attempt in Mauritania, the increasingly doubtful prospects for durable peace and democratic renewal in Cote d'Ivoire, and the "reelection" of President Éyadema in Togo made it necessary to add a brief update to the original study.

The bloody coup attempt that occurred in Mauritania on June 8 and 9, 2003 illustrated tragically the nexus we have posited and discussed in the introduction. It reminded us of what the outcome of a political standstill or too slow a farewell to autocratic politics can be. We had concluded that Mauritania's recent evolution and the resulting political impasse had increased the vulnerability of Ould Taya's regime to the putschist proneness of the numerous Arab nationalist groups inside the military. Sure enough, in June, a group of Arab-Berber officers tried to overthrow the regime. For 36 hours, there was in fact a power vacuum as the putschists took control of the major symbols of power and forced Ould Taya and most of the dignitaries of the regime to take refuge in foreign Embassies. It was by far, the bloodiest and costliest coup in Mauritania's history. The coup highlighted the vulnerability of the regime and debunked one of its most prized assets: the arduously crafted and projected impression of stability and invulnerability. This considerably weakened Ould Taya.

Because the constraints of the November 7, 2003 elections, Ould Taya, opted for a calculated minimization of the events and their impact, and resisted his instincts to severely punish the perpetrators (most of whom belong to tribes from the East of the country) and their supporters. His misfortune seemed to have been capitalized on by his nemesis, the former head of state, Ould Heydalla who declared his candidacy for the elections. While Ould Heydalla's candidacy seemed to have gathered momentum as many political actors saw it as the only hope left for a peaceful transfer of power, it would have been an astonishing development if he won the elections. Ould Taya retained power as expected, and was compelled to attempt to recapture the prestige lost because of the coup and did it through repression rather than through a reevaluation of the exercise of power, and power-sharing. His reelection did not help the democratic process, particularly as the election was perceived to have been rigged given Ould Heydalla's growing popularity, including within the military. It actually plunged Mauritania in a violent crisis of unpredictable consequences. On the other hand, had Ould Heydalla prevailed, of course, a totally new situation would have obtained and Mauritania would definitely have broken the democratization process gridlock. He had promised to abandon power after one term only after ushering in a genuine democracy by reforming the Constitution, the political institutions, particularly limiting the presidential powers and terms in office. The coup plotters who escaped formed an armed group, the "Knights of Change," and vowed to bring down Ould Taya through violent means. Two of their leaders were captured and their trial is impending. Mauritania's future is now even bleaker.

In Ivory Coast, with the active involvement of France, the Marcoussis, Accra and Lomé agreements ended the state of belligerence, the rebels renounced calls for President Gbagbo's resignation, and the process of solving the crisis was jump started.[1] These agreements, starting with a government of national reconciliation, the disarmament of armed groups and the creation of conditions conducive to open, free, and fair elections in 2005 at the end of Gbagbo's term, created conditions for the beginning of national reconciliation. The rebel groups now sit in the government headed by Seydou Diarra since March 13, 2003. On July 4th, the conflict was formally declared over, and an amnesty law was enacted on August 6. This reinforced the impression that, for now, Cote d'Ivoire seems to have escaped the same severe breakdown Liberia or Sierra Leone experienced. However, for several reasons, the situation remains precarious indeed, and while thankfully serious fighting has not occurred since January, 2003, genuine peace has yet to take hold.[2] First, as the process of a negotiated solution to the conflict proceeded, both sides continued efforts to procure armaments and mercenaries. Even the joint statement of the July 4 FANCI and the *Forces Nouvelles* (the coalesced rebel groups) ratifying the end of hostilities called on the political leadership to stop rearmament. While the top brass of the FANCI displays a conciliatory attitude, the extent to which this is widely shared is uncertain as the real sense of humiliation and resentment (expressed on various occasions) may yet resurface.[3] Furthermore, President Gbagbo himself,

---

1. After numerous failed attempts by West African leaders to end the conflict, on January 15, 2003, at the initiative of France, a meeting between the Ivoirian armed factions, political parties, and government took place in Marcoussis in the suburbs of Paris. The meeting concluded with an agreement to bring about national reconciliation and end the *de facto* partition of the country by enacting far-reaching reforms in various contentious areas. It was followed by two agreements in Accra and Lomé to hammer out litigious issues that surfaced with the implementation of the Marcoussis accord. The Accra agreement addresses the delicate issue of the Security Council membership and the appointment of the ministers of Defense and the Interior.

2. This is one of the conclusions of the latest (August 2003) report of the UN secretary general on the situation in Cote d'Ivoire. See, "Cote d'Ivoire: UN Says Security Improves, but Obstacles to Lasting Peace Remain," IRIN, http://www.irinnews.org/report.asp?ReportID=35996&SelectRegion=West_Africa &SelectCountry=COTE_D_IVOIRE, accessed 8/24/2003.

3. See claudio Gramizzi, "La Crise Ivoirienne: De la Tentative de Coup d'Etat au Gouvernement de Reconciliation Nationale," Bruxelles, GRIP, 2002.

stripped of most of his executive powers, while insisting on reconciliation, has cultivated an ambiguous attitude regarding the Marcoussis, Accra, and Lomé process when aspects of the agreements do not suit him. The *Forces Nouvelles*, while more flexible than previously, still insist on the implementation of the entirety of the agreements, including the appointment of people they approve of to the politically and strategically important functions of Minister of Defense and Minister of the Interior. When the rebels claimed these positions, Gbagbo allegedly initially agreed to this at the Paris meeting, but the FANCI who were not represented at that meeting vetoed the decision. The parties remain stalemated on this crucial issue and it remains to be seen if the momentum for peace and reconciliation brokered by France and the ECOWAS will, in the end, overcome this obstacle and the residual mutual mistrust between the parties. Finally, Prime Minister Diarra's government is still faced with the task of implementing the numerous reforms agreed to in the Paris and Accra deals while preparing the 2005 elections in which Mr. Alassane Dramane Ouattara is likely to participate for the first time. These are likely to be contentious elections and, whatever the outcome, could very well constitute yet another severe test the precarious peace may not be able to pass easily. Already in late August 2003, the Prime Minister admitted that the peace process is confronting difficulties due to the continued vacancy of crucial security positions on the government of national reconciliation and alluded to continued militia activities in the country. Shortly thereafter, one of the emblematic figures of the rebellion, Ibrabim Coulibaly (a.k.a IB) was arrested in Paris for allegedly attempting to recruit mercenaries to stage another coup and/or assassinate President Gbagbo. Cote d'Ivoire may not yet have come back irreversibly from the brink, which can only delay its democratic transformation. Sure enough, with the bombing of rebel positions by Government fighter jets and helicopters, the ceasefire broke down. The killing of French peacekeepers and France's retaliatory destruction of the Ivoirian air force complicated the situation further and led to widespread violence followed by frantic efforts to restore peace.

In Benin, living standards have been steadily declining and it will take more than coalitions and regular government reshuffling to tackle the severe economic problems facing the country. Early hopes for genuine democratic renewal could be rapidly waning. In the 2001 presidential elections denounced by the opposition as fraudulent, Kérékou won an additional five years in power. Much to the opposition's dismay, the December 2002 municipal and March 2003 legislative elections gave a clear majority to President Kérékou and his supporters. Such a monopoly over the politics of Benin makes many observers nervous, especially because of the recent resurgence of his autocratic tendencies. Ominously, some within government circles are now advocating an amendment to the constitution to allow Kérékou to stand in 2006. With little influence of the opposition, democracy in Benin, long touted as exemplary in the sub-region, is at risk of becoming a hollow and deceptive make-believe. However, the civility of the ongoing debate, as well as Kérékou's constructive attitude during the national conference, suggest that all may not be lost.

Meanwhile, Togo continues its descent into chaos and uncertainty. The opposition cried foul in the 1998 presidential elections even though the main opposition leader, Gilchrist Olympio, was allowed to participate. It accused Éyadéma and his ruling party, Rally of the Togolese People (RTP), of massive fraud and vote rigging. Even the observers from the Economic Community of West African States (ECOWAS), the African Union and the Entente Council witnessed many irregularities. After the subsequent parliamentary victory of Éyadéma's party, with no opposition candidates in competition, a political crisis ensued and Togo's path towards democracy remained doubtful. A breakthrough came on 29 July 1999, when parties signed the framework agreement (*Accord Cadre de Lomé*), agreeing to respect the constitution and to come together to prepare early legislative elections. A joint follow-up committee was set up to create the conditions for a more relaxed political climate and to draw up a new electoral code, promulgated on April 5, 2000.

To appease both the opposition and the international community, Éyadéma promised not to run again in 2003, and was in fact constitutionally prevented from running. In 2002, the Constitution was amended by "his" parliament, removing the term-limit, and allowing Éyadéma another "win" in the June 2003 presidential elections from which Olympio was banned. The European Union declined to send observers to monitor the June poll, noting that it was unlikely to be free and fair.[4] Since then, both reconciliation between the government and the opposition, and democratization have been at a standstill. After their failure to choose a consensual candidate to challenge the incumbent President in the June 2003 elections, the traditional Togolese opposition parties are likely to pay dearly for their persistent political squabbling.

The absence of progress in talks between Togo's opposition and presidential bloc has led to the European Union's withdrawal of funding for the facilitation of dialogue between the two sides and has heightened fears of an ever worsening political climate. For more than a decade facilitators from the EU, France, Germany and La *Francophonie* (the community of French-speaking nations), had tried in vain to broker a sustainable peace in Togo. Éyadéma has continued to shrug off criticism of his country's lack of democracy and allegations of widespread human rights abuses to carve out a most ironic role as a regional peacemaker, notably between Ivory Coast rebels and the Gbagbo government. In sum, the democratization process appears clearly out of steam in Togo, and both the EU's decision and Éyadéma's "victory" are clearly bad omens for a decisive farewell to authoritarianism.

In The Gambia, growing economic hardship fueled by mounting inflation and a declining national currency has once more exposed President Jammeh's vulnerability. The opposition parties stand to benefit from this popular dissatisfaction over the regime's poor economic performance but only if they form a united front in the 2006 presidential election. However, the recent passage of the Media Commission Bill by an APRC dominated national assembly to muzzle the press is likely to dull both domestic and international opposition, and in so doing, consolidate Jammeh's grip on power. Yet insistence on good governance as a precondition for Western aid could, as did the repeal of Decree 89, nudge the regime in a more democratic direction.

The recent developments in the case studies and indeed in West Africa as a whole suggest that the democratization process still pre-

---

4. "TOGO: Eyadema wins 57% majority in presidential election," *IRIN*, Lomé, 5 June 2003.

sents a decidedly mixed picture, which only mirrors both the immense hopes of many and the vexing deferring of genuine democracy in too many countries in the sub-region.

BIBLIOGRAPHY

Adjaho, R. *La Faillite du Contrôle des Finances Publiques au Bénin (1960–1990)*. Cotonou: Éditions du Flamboyant, 1992.

Adjovi, S. *De la Dictature à la Démocratie sans les Armes*. Paris: Éditions CP 99, 1993.

Africa Research Bulletin (Political and social series), June 1973.

Africa Research Bulletin August 1991 and November 1996.

Aka, P. "The Military and Democratization in Africa." *Journal of Third World Studies* 16 (1999): 71–86.

Allen, C. "'Goodbye to All That': The Short and Sad Story of Socialism in Benin." *Journal of Communist Studies* 8, 2 (1989): 63–81.

Amin, S. *Neo-Colonialism in West Africa*. New York, NY: Monthly Review Press, 1973.

Ammi-Oz, M. "La formation des Cadres Militaires Africains Lors de la Mise sur Pied des Armées Africaines." *Revue Française d'Études Politiques Africaines* 133 (1977): 84–99.

Amnesty International. *Amnesty International Report*. New York, NY: Amnesty International Publications, 1997.

———. *"Mauritania, a Future Free from slavery?"* London: Amnesty International, 2002.

Ayitteh, G. *Africa Betrayed*. New York, NY: St. Martin's Press, 1992.

Bales, K. *Disposable people: New Slavery in the Global Economy*. Berkeley, CA: University of California Press, 1999.

Banégas, R. "Retour sur une Transition Modèle: Les Dynamiques du Dedans et du Dehors de la Démocratisation Béninoise." In J-P. Daloz et P. Quantin, dirs. *Transitions Démocratiques Africaines: Dynamiques et Contraintes (1990–1994)*. Paris: Khartala, 1997.

Bangoura, D. *Les Armées Africaines, 1960–1990.* Paris: Centre des Hautes Études sur l'Afrique et l'Asie Modernes, 1992.

Bayart, J-F. *The State in Africa: the Politics of the Belly.* London, UK: Longman, 1993.

Baynham, S. ed. *Military Power and Politics in Black Africa.* London, UK: Croom Helm, 1986.

Bland, D.L. "A Unified Theory of Civil-Military Relations." *Armed Forces and Society* 26, 1 (1999): 7–25.

Bourgi, A. "Entre Militaires." *Jeune-Afrique/L'Inteligent* 2066–2067 (15–28 August 2000): 34–39.

———. "J'ai Vu l'Histoire Basculer," *Jeune-Afrique/L'Intelligent* 2078 (7–13 November 2000): 20–28.

Bratton, M. and N. van de Walle, "Popular Protest and Political Reform in Africa." *Comparative Politics* 24, 4 (July 1992): 419–42.

Burk, J. "Theories of Democratic Civil-Military Relations," *Armed Forces and Society* 29, 1 (Fall 2002): 7–29.

Bustin, E. *The Limits of French Intervention in Africa: A Study in Applied Neo-Colonialism.* Boston, MA: African Studies Center, 1982.

Chaigneau, P. *La Politique Militaire de la France en Afrique.* Paris: Centre des Hautes Études sur l'Afrique et l'Asie Modernes, 1984.

"Cher Robert," *Jeune-Afrique/l'Intelligent* 2075 (17–23 October 2000): 22–23.

Chipman, J. *French Power in Africa.* Cambridge, UK: Basil Blackwell Ltd., 1989.

Clark, J.F. "The Challenges of Political Reform in Sub-Saharan Africa: A Theoretical Overview." In J.F. Clark and D.E. Gardinier, eds. *Political Reform in Francophone Africa.* Boulder, Colo.: Westview Press, 1997.

Clarke, W.S. "The National Conference Phenomenon and the Management of Political Conflict in Sub-Saharan Africa." In H. Glickman, ed. *Ethnic Conflict and Democratization in Africa.* Atlanta, GA: ASA Press, 1995.

Committee on Foreign Hearing before the Subcommittee on Human Rights and International Organizations and on Africa, 19 June 1991, Washington, DC: US Government Printing Office.

Conteh-Morgan, E. *Democratization in Africa: The Theory and Dynamics of Political Transitions.* Westport, CT: Praeger, 1997.

Crocker, C. *The Military Transfer of Power in Africa: A comparative Study of Change in the British and French System of Order,* Baltimore, A Ph.D. Dissertation, The Johns Hopkins University Department of Political Science, 1969.

Crook, R.C. "Côte d'Ivoire: Multi-party Democracy and Political Change." In J. Wiseman, ed. *Democracy and Political Change in Sub-Saharan Africa.* New York, NY: Routledge, 1994.

Da Costa, P. "Democracy in Doubt," *Africa Report* 37, 3 (May–June 1992):

Decalo, S. "Regionalism, Politics and the Military in Dahomey." *Journal of Developing Areas* 7, 3 (April 1973a): 449–77.

———. "The Politics of Military Rule in Togo." *Geneva-Africa* 12/2 (1973b): 62–96.

———. "The Military Takeovers in Africa." *International Problems* (September 1974): 80–90.

———. "Modalities of Civil-Military Stability in Africa." *Journal of Modern African Studies* 27, 4 (1989): 547–578.

———. *Coups and Army Rule in Africa,* 2nd ed. New Haven, CT: Yale University Press, 1990.

———. "The Process, Prospect and Constraints of Democratization in Africa." *African Affairs* 91, 362 (1992): 7–35.

———. "The Future of Participatory Democracy in Africa." *Futures* 26/9 (1994): 987–992.

———. *Historical Dictionary of Benin,* 3rd ed. Lanham, MD: Scarecrow Press, Inc., 1995.

———. *Historical Dictionary of Togo,* 3rd ed. Lanham, MD: Scarecrow Press, Inc., 1996.

———. *The Stable Minority: Civilian Rule in Africa, 1960–1990.* Gainesville: FAP Books, 1998.

de la Grange, A. "L'Afrique Doit se Gendarmer Seule." *Le Figaro* (Octobre 1997): 4C.

Derrick, J. "No Way Ouattara." *West Africa* (31 July–7 August 2000): 20–21.

Diamond, L. "Beyond Authoritarianism and Totalitarianism: Strategies for Democratization." *Washington Quarterly* 12, 1 (December 1989): 141–163.

————. "Toward democratic Consolidation." *Journal of Democracy* 5 (July 1994): 4–17.

————. "Is the Third Wave Over?" *Journal of Democracy* 7, 3 (1996): 20–37.

Diamond, L. and M.F. Plattner, *Civil-Military Relations and Democracy*. Baltimore, MD: John Hopkins University Press, 1996.

————. eds. *Democratization in Africa*. Baltimore, MD: The Johns Hopkins University Press, 1999.

Domergue-Cloarec, D. *La France et l'Afrique Après les Indépendances*. Paris, SEDES, 1994.

Dumont, R. *False Start in Africa*. New York, NY: Praeger, 1969.

Euromonitor, *The World Economic Factbook 1999/2000*. Chippenham, UK: Euromonitor, 2000.

Faes, G. and E. Fall, "Le Vrai-Faux Coup d'État du Général Guei." *Jeune-Afrique* 1817 (2–8 Novembre 1995): 16–19.

Fall, E. "*Sénégal-Mauritanie: Le Dossier du Conflit, Les enjeux de l'après Barrage*." *Jeune Afrique* 1491 (2 August 1989): 39–44.

Fatton, Jr., R. "Democracy and Civil Society in Africa." *Mediterranean Quarterly* 2, 4 (1991): 83–95.

Faure, Y. "Cote d'Ivoire: Analyzing the Crisis," in D.C. O'Brien, J. Dunn, and R. Rathbone, eds. *Contemporary West African States*. Cambridge, UK: Cambridge University Press, 1990.

Faure, Y. and J.F. Medard, *État et Bourgeoisie en Côte d'Ivoire*. Paris: Khartala 1982.

Feaver, P.D. "The Civil-Military Problematique: Huntington, Janowitz, and the Question of Civilian Control." *Armed Forces and Society* 23, 2 (1996): 149–78.

First, R. *The Barrel of a Gun: Political Power and the Coup d'état.* London: Allen Lane, 1970.

Fleischman, J. "Ethnic cleansing." *Africa Report* 39 (Jan–Feb. 1994):

Foltz, W.J. "Democracy: Officers and Politicians." *Africa Report* 38, 3 (1993): 65–67.

Fondation Friedrich Naumann, ed. *Les Actes de la Conférence Nationale.* Cotonou: Éditions ONEPI, 1994.

Frazer, J. "Conceptualizing Civil-Military Relations during Democratic Transition." *Africa Today* 42, 1&2 (1995): 39–48.

French, H. "The End of an Era." *Africa Report*, 39, 2 (1994):

———. "No More Paternalism but Public Executions." *New York Times* (15 May 1995): A4.

Front Arabo-Africain du Salut, *"Lettre Ouverte au President."* (Pamphlet). Paris, October 26, 1996.

Fukuyama, F. "The End of History." *The National Interest* 16 (1989): 3–4.

Gaillard, Ph. *Foccart Parle: Entretiens avec Phillipe Gaillard*, Vol. 1. Paris: Fayard/Jeune Afrique, 1995.

Gbado, B. *En Marche vers la Liberté: Préludes du Renouveau Démocratique au Bénin.* Cotonou: SYNES, 1991.

Glèlè, A.M. *Naissance d'un État Noir (L'Évolution Politique et Constitutionnelle du Dahomey, de la Colonisation à nos Jours.* Paris: Librairie Générale de Droit et de la Jurisprudence, 1969.

———. *Le Danxome: Du Pouvoir Aja à la Nation Fon.* Paris: Paillart, 1974.

Godin, F. *Bénin 1972–1982: La Logique de l'État Africain.* Paris: L'Harmattan, 1986.

Goldsworthy, D. "Armies and Politics in Civilian Regimes." In S. Baynham, ed. *Military Power and Politics in Black Africa.* London, Croom Helm, 1986.

Gregory, S. "The French Military in Africa: Past and Present." *African Affairs* 99, 396 (July 2000): 435–48.

Gutteridge, W. *The Military in African Politics.* London, UK: Methuen & Co. Ltd, 1964.

————. *Military Regimes in Africa.* London, UK: Methuen & Co. Ltd, 1975.

Gyimah-Boadi, E. "Civil Society in Africa." *Journal of Democracy* 7, 2 (April 1996): 118–32.

Hayner, P. "Fifteen Truth Commissions—1974 to 1994: A Comparative Study." *Human Rights Quarterly*, Vol.16, 4 (1994): 597–655.

Heilbrunn, J.R. "Social Origins of National Conferences in Benin and Togo." *Journal of Modern African Studies* 31, 2 (1993): 277–99.

Houngnikpo, M.C. "Democratization in Africa: A comparative Study of Benin and Togo." *Journal of Political and Military Sociology* 28, 2 (2000): 210–229.

Huband, M. "Silencing the Opposition." *Africa Report* 37, 3 (1992): 55–57.

Hughes, A. ed. *The Gambia: Studies in Society and Politics.* Birmingham: Centre of West African Studies, African Studies Series 3, 1991.

Hughes, A. "'Democratisation' under the Military in The Gambia: 1994–2000." *Journal of Commonwealth and Comparative Politics* 38, 3 (2000): 17–41.

Human Rights Watch "Mauritania's Campaign of Terror: State Sponsored Repression of Black African." New York, NY: Human Rights Watch/Africa, 1994.

Huntington, S. The Soldier and the State: The Theory and Politics of Civil-Military Relations, Cambridge, MA: Belknap, 1957.

————. *The Third Wave: Democratization in the Late Twentieth Century*, Norman, OK: University of Oklahoma Press, 1991.

Hutchful, E. "Militarism and Problems of Democratic Transition." In M. Ottaway, ed. *Democracy in Africa: The Hard Road Ahead.* Boulder, Colo.: Lynne Rienner, 1997.

Ihonvbere, J.O. "The Dynamics of Change in Eastern Europe and their Implications for Africa." *Coexistence* 29, 2 (1992): 277–96.

Imperato, P.J. "Downfall," *Africa Report*, 36, 4 (July–August 1991):

International Institute for Strategic Studies, *The Military Balance1999/2000*. London, UK: International Institute for Strategic Studies, 2000.

Jackson, R. "The Predictability of African Coups d'État." *American Political Science Review* 72, 4 (1978): 1262–75.

———. "Explaining African Coups d'État." *American Political Science Review* 80, 1 (1986): 225–32.

Jackson, R. and C. Rosenberg, *Personal Rule in Black Africa: Prince, Autocrat, Prophet, Tyrant*. Berkeley, CA: University of California Press, 1982.

Joseph, R. "Africa: The Rebirth of Political Freedom." *Journal of Democracy* 2, 4 (Fall 1991): 11–24.

———. "Africa, 1990–1997: From Abertura to Democracy." *Journal of Democracy* 9, 2 (1998): 3–17.

Karl, T. and Ph. C. Schmitter, "Comparing Neo-Democracies: Origins, Trajectories and Outcomes." In L.E. Amijo, ed. *Conversations on Democratization and Economic Reforms*, (Working Paper on the Southern California Seminar). Los Angeles, CA: Center for International Studies School of International Relations University of Southern California, 1996.

Kassy, F. "L'Adieu aux Armes." *Jeune Afrique* 1885 (19–25 February 1997).

Khadiagala, G.M. "The Military in Africa's Democratic Transitions: Regional Dimensions." *Africa Today* 1&2 (1995): 61–74.

Klein, M. "Back to Democracy: Presidential Address to the 1991 Annual Meeting of the African Studies Association." *African Studies Review* 35, 3 (1992): 1–12.

Kpatindé, F. "L'Éléphant Malade." *Jeune-Afrique/l'Intelligent* 2061 (11–17July 2000): 8–11.

———. "Les Jeux Sont Faits." *Jeune-Afrique/L'Intelligent* 2074 (10–16 October 2000): 16–18.

———. "Guei-Gbagbo: Les Secrets d'une Rencontre." *Jeune-Afrique/L'Intelligent* 2080 (21–27 November 2000): 18–21.

Laloupo, F. "La Conférence Nationale du Bénin: Un Concept Nouveau de Changement de Régime Politique." *Année Africaine* (1992–93): 78–114.

Legum, C. "The Coming of Africa's Second Independence." *The Washington Quarterly* 33 (Winter 1990): 129–40.

Limam, Z. "La Guerre des Chefs." *Jeune Afrique/L'Intelligent* 2060 (4–10 July 2000): 8–10.

Linz, J.J. and Alfred Stepan. "Toward Consolidated Democracies." *Journal of Democracy* 7, 2 (1996): 14–33.

Lombard, J. *Dahomey: Sa Géographie, Son Histoire, Son Ethnographie*. Dakar, Sénégal: IFAN, 1958.

Lowenthal, A. "Foreword." In G. O'Donnell, and Ph.C. Schmitter, eds. *Transition from Authoritarian Rule: Tentative Conclusions About Uncertain Democracies*. Baltimore, MD: The John Hopkins University Press, 1986.

Luckham, R.A. "French Militarism in Africa," *Review of African Political Economy* 24 (1982): 55–84.

———. "The Military, Militarization, and Democratization in Africa: A Survey of Literature and Issues." *African Studies Review* 37, 2 (September 1994): 13–76.

———. "Taming the Monster: Democratization and Demilitarization." In E. Hutchful, and A. Bathily, eds. *The Military and Militarism in Africa*. Dakar, Senegal: CODESRIA, 1998.

Magnusson, B. "Testing Democracy in Benin: Experiments in Institutional Reform." In R. Joseph, ed. *State, Conflict, and Democracy in Africa*. Boulder, Colo.: Lynne Rienner Publishers, 1999.

Mahmud, S. "The State of Human Rights in Africa in the 1990." *Human Rights Quarterly* 15, 3 (1993): 485–98.

Marchesin, Ph. *Tribes, Ethnies et Pouvoir en Mauritanie*. Paris: Khartala, 1992.

Martin, J-L. *Le Soldat Africain et le Politique: Essai sur le Militarisme et l'État Prétorien au Sud du Sahara*. Toulouse: Presses de l'Institut d'Études Politiques, 1990.

Martin, M-L. "Operational Weakness and Political Activism: The Military in Sub-Saharan Africa." In J.P. Lovell and D.E. Albright, eds. *To Sheathe the Sword: Civil-Military Relations in the Quest for Democracy*. Westport, CT: Greenwood Press, 1997.

Massou, A. "Abidjan en État de Choc." *Jeune-Afrique/L'Intelligent* 2097 (7–13, 2000): 32–33.

Mbaku, J.M "Democratization and the Crisis of Policy Reform in Developing Countries." In M.S. Kimenyi and J. M. Mbaku, eds. *Institutions and Collective Choice in Developing Countries: Applications of the Theory of Public Choice.* Aldershot, UK: Ashgate Publishing Company, 1999.

———. "Bureaucratic Corruption in Africa." In J.M. Mbaku, ed. *Corruption and the Crisis of Institutional Reform in Africa.* Lewiston: The Edwin Mellen Press, 1998.

———. " Making the State Relevant to African Societies." In J.M. Mbaku, ed. *Preparing Africa for the Twenty-First Century: Strategies for Peaceful Existence and Sustainable Development* Brookfield, VT: Ashgate Publishing Company, 1999.

Mey, M.O. "Structural Adjustment Programs and Democratization in Africa: The Case of Mauritania." In J.M. Mbaku and J.O. Ivhonbere, eds. *Multiparty Democracy and Political Change: Constraints to Democratization in Africa.* Brookfield, VT: Ashgate Publishing Company, 1996.

———. *Global Restructuring and Peripheral States: The Carrot and the Stick in Mauritania.* Lanham, MD: Littlefield Adams Books, 1992.

Mkandawire, T. "Economic Policy-making and the Consolidation of Democratic Institution in Africa." In K. Havnevik and B. Van Arkadie, eds. *Domination or Dialogue? Experiences and Prospects for African Development Cooperation.* Uppsula: Scandinavian Institute of African Studies, 1996.

Moukoko-Mbonjo, P. "Régimes Militaires et Transition Démocratique en Afrique: À la Recherche d'un Cadre d'Analyse Théorique." *Afrique 2000* 13 (1993): 39–58.

N'Diaye, B. "Ivory Coast's Civilian Control Strategies 1961–1998: A Critical Assessment." *Journal of Political and Military Sociology* 28, 2 (2000): 246–270.

———. *The Challenge of Institutionalizing Civilian Control.* Lanham, MD: Lexington Books, 2001.

―――. "The effect of Mauritania's 'Human Rights Deficit' on the Democratization Process: The Case Against to 'Forgive and Forget.'" *Journal of African Policy Studies* (forthcoming, 2004).

Nordlinger, E.A. "Soldiers in Mufti: The Impact of Military Rule upon Economic and Social Change in Non-Western States." *American Political Science Review* 64, 4 (1970): 1138–48.

―――. *Soldiers in Politics: Military Coups and Governments.* Englewood, N.J.: Prentice Hall, 1976.

Nwajiaku, K. "The National Conferences in Benin and Togo Revisited." *Journal of Modern African Studies* 32, 3 (1994): 429–47.

Nyang'Oro, J. "Critical Notes on Political Liberalization in Africa." *Journal of Asian and African Studies* 31, 1&2 (1996): 117–18.

Nzouankeu, J-M. "The Role of the National Conference in the Transition to Democracy: The Cases of Benin and Mali." *Issue: A Journal of Opinion* 21, 1&2 (1993): 44–50.

Obadare, E. "The Military and Democracy in the Gambia." In D. Olowu, A. Williams and K. Soremekum, eds. *Governance and Democratisation in West Africa.* Dakar, Senegal: CODESRIA, 1999.

Odetola, O. *Military Regimes and Development: A Comparative Analysis in African Societies.* London, U.K.: George Allen & Unwin, 1982.

Odinga, O. *Not Yet Uhuru,* New York: Hill and Wang, 1967.

O'Donnell, G. and Ph. Schmitter, "Introduction to the Latin American Cases." In G. O'Donnell, Ph. Schmitter and L. Whitehead, eds. *Transitions from Authoritarian Rule: Prospects for Democracy.* Baltimore, MD: Johns Hopkins University Press, 1986.

Omaar, R. "Arrests and Executions." *West Africa* (8–14 July 1991).

Omaar, R. and J. Fleischman. "Arab Vs. African." *Africa Report* 36, 4 (July–August 1999): 35–38.

Omunizua, C. "Hovering on the Brink." *West Africa* (2–8 October 2000): 20–21.

―――. "Chaos in Abidjan." *West Africa* (30 October – 5 November 2000): 9–12.

Onworki, I. "A question of Race." *West Africa* 3719 (24–30 October 1988).

Onwumechili, C. *African Democratization and Military Coups.* Westport, CT: Praeger, 1998.

Park, Th. K. et al. *Conflict over Land and the Crisis of Nationalism in Mauritania.* Madison, WI: Land Tenure Center University of Wisconsin-Madison, 1991.

Pazzanita, A. "Mauritania's Foreign Policy: The Search for Protection." *Journal of Modern African Studies* 30, 2 (1992): 288–300.

———. "The Origin and Evolution of Mauritania's Second Republic." *Journal of Modern African Studies* 34, 4 (1996): 575–96.

Pérennès, J-J et H. Puel, "Démocratie et Développement au Sud." *Économie et Humanisme* 319 (Octobre–Novembre 1991): 11–19.

"Power Struggle Is Simmering in Ivory Coast." *New York Times* (9 December 1993): A3, 3

Press, R.M. *The New Africa: Dispatches from A Changing Continent.* Gainesville, FL: University Press of Florida, 1999.

Robinson, P.T. "The National Conference Phenomenon in Francophone Africa." *Comparative Studies in Society and History* 36/3 (1994): 575–610.

Riley, S. "The Democratic Transition in Africa: An End to the State?" *Conflict Studies* 245 (October 1991): 1–36.

———. "Political Adjustment or Domestic Pressure: Democratic Politics and Political Choice in Africa." *Third World Quarterly* 13, 3 (1992): 539–51.

Ronen, D. *Dahomey: Between Tradition and Modernity.* Ithaca, NY: Cornell University Press, 1975.

———. "People's Republic of Benin: The Military, Marxist Ideology, and the Politics of Ethnicity." In J. Harbeson, ed. *The Military in African Politics.* New York, NY: Praeger Publishers, 1987.

Saga, H. "Chaillot n'est pas la Baule." *Jeune Afrique* 1613 (November 27 – December 3, 1991): 4–9.

Saine, A. "The Coup d'etat in The Gambia, 1994: The End of the First Republic." *Armed Forces and Society* 23(1996): 97–111.

———. "The 1996/1997 Presidential and National Assembly Elections in The Gambia." *Electoral Studies* 16(1997): 554–59.

———. "The Military's Managed Transition to "Civilian" Rule in The Gambia." *Journal of Political and Military Sociology* 26 (Winter 1998): 157–68.

———. "The Military and Human Rights in The Gambia: 1994–1999." *Journal of Third World Studies* 19, 2 (Fall 2002): 167–87.

———. "The Foreign Policy of The Gambia since the Coup." *Journal of Commonwealth and Comparative Politics* 38, 2 (July 2000): 73–88.

———. "The Soldier-Turn-Presidential Candidate: A Comparison of Flawed Democratic Transitions in Ghana and Gambia." *Journal of Political and Military Sociology* 28, 2 (Winter 2000): 191–209.

———. "Post-Coup politics in The Gambia." *Journal of Democracy* 13, 4 (October 2000): 167–72.

Sarkesian, S.C. "Military Professionalism and Civil-Military Relations in West Africa." *International Political Science Review* 2, 3 (1981): 283–97.

Sigel, E. "Ivory Coast: Booming Economy, Political Calm." *Africa Report* 15 (1970): 18–21.

Soudan, F. *Le Marabout et Le Colonel: La Mauritanie de Ould Daddah à Ould Taya*. Paris: JAlivres, 1992.

———. "Que Veut Guei?" *Jeune-Afrique/L'Intelligent* 2097 (20 March 2001): 24–25.

———. "L'Homme qui Veut Sauver la Côte d'Ivoire," *Jeune-Afrique/L'Intelligent* 2001 (11–17 September 2001): 30–33.

———. "Maaouiya Ould Taya: 'Le Senegal nous Veut du Mal.'" *Jeune Afrique* 1513 (January 1): 34–37.

"Strange Case of Two Generals." *West Africa* (26 March – 1 April 2001): 18–19.

"Ten Years in French Speaking Africa." *Africa Digest* 27, 5 (1970): 85–89.

Terray, E. "Les Révolutions Congolaise et Dahoméenne de 1963: Essai d'Interprétation." *Revue Française de Science Politique* 14, 5 (1964): 917–943.

Teya, P.K. *Le Roi Est Nu.* Paris: L'Harmattan, 1985.

Toungara, J.M. "Generational Tensions in the Parti Démocratique de Côte d'Ivoire." *African Studies Review* 38, 2 (1995): 11–38.

UNDP, *UN Human Development Report 1996.* Washington, D.C.: United Nations Development Program, 1996.

U.S. Department of State, *Country Report on Human Rights Practices for 1992: Mauritania.* Washington, D.C. US Government Printing Office (February 1992): 162–70.

Villalon, L.A. "The African State at the End of the Twentieth Century: Parameters of the Critical Juncture." In L.A. Villalón and Ph.A. Huxtable, eds. *The African State at a Critical Juncture: Between Disintegration and Reconfiguration.* Boulder, Colo.: Lynne Rienner Publishers, 2000.

Welch, Jr, C.E. "Soldier and State in Africa." *Journal of Modern African Studies* 5, 3 (1967): 305–22.

———. *Civilian Control of the Military: Theory and Cases from Developing Countries.* Albany, NY: State University of New York Press, 1976.

———. "Côte d'Ivoire: Personal Rule and Civilian Control." In C.E. Welch, Jr., ed. *No Farewell to Arms?* Boulder, Colo.: Westview, 1987.

———. "Changing Civil-Military Relations." In R.O. Slater, B.M. Schutz and S.R. Dorr, eds. *Global Transformations and the Third World.* Boulder, Colo.: Lynne Rienner, 1993.

Wells, A. "The Coup d'État in Theory and Practice: Independent Black Africa in the 1960s." *American Journal of Sociology* 79, 4 (1974): 871–87.

Westebbe, R. "Structural Adjustment, Rent-Seeking, Liberalization in Benin." In J.A. Widner, ed. *Economic Change and Political Liberalization in Sub-Saharan Africa.* Baltimore, MD: Johns Hopkins University Press, 1994.

Whiteman, K. The Gallic Paradox. *Africa Report*, 36, 1 (1990): 17–19.

William, H. "The Crisis of Succession." *Africa Report*, 33, 3 (1988): 53–55.

Wiseman, J. "Democratic Resurgence in Black Africa." *Contemporary Review* 259 (July 1991): 7–13.

———. "Military Rule in the Gambia: An Interim Assessment." *Third World Quarterly* 17 (1996): 917–40.

———. *The New Struggle for Democracy in Africa*. Brookfield, VT: Avebury, 1996.

Wiseman, J & E. Vidler, "The July 1994 Coup d'état in The Gambia: The End of an Era?" *The Roundtable*, 333(1995).

World Bank Report *African Development Indicators 1994–1995*. Washington, D.C., The World Bank, 1995.

Yeebo, Z. *The State of Fear in Paradise: The Military Coup in The Gambia*. London: Africa Research & Information Bureau, 1995.

Young, C. "The Third Wave of Democratization in Africa: Ambiguities and Contradictions." In R. Joseph, ed. *State, Conflict, and Democracy in Africa*. Boulder, Colo.: Lynne Rienner, 1999.

Zakaria, F. "The Rise of Illiberal Democracy." *Foreign Affairs* 76, 6 (1997): 22–43.

Zolberg, A. *One Party Government in the Ivory Coast*. Princeton, NJ: Princeton University Press, 1969.

Index